Through Our Eyes

Through Our Eyes

AFRICAN AMERICAN MEN'S EXPERIENCES OF RACE, GENDER, AND VIOLENCE

GAIL GARFIELD

RUTGERS UNIVERSITY PRESS
New Brunswick, New Jersey, and London

LIBRARY OF CONGRESS CATALOGING-IN-PUBLICATION DATA

Garfield, Gail, 1964–
    Through our eyes : African American men's experiences of race, gender,
and violence / Gail Garfield.
        p.   cm.
    Includes bibliographical references and index.
    ISBN 978-0-8135-4742-8 (hbk. : alk. paper)
    ISBN 978-0-8135-4743-5 (pbk. : alk. paper)
    1. African American men.   2. Racism—United States.   3. Violence—
United States.   4. Identity (Psychology)   5. Stereotypes (Social psychology)
I. Title.
    E185.86.G36   2010
    305.38'896073—dc22   2009030960

A British Cataloging-in-Publication record for this book is available
from the British Library.

Visit our Web site: http://rutgerspress.rutgers.edu

Manufactured in the United States of America

*I dedicate this book to the loving memory of my mother,
Rosa Lee Miller, and to my beloved brothers Raynell, Charles,
and especially Leroy, whose sadness forced me to forgive
so that I could love him more freely.*

Contents

Acknowledgments

There are times when a simple thank you seems an inadequate response to the gifts that others have so generously bestowed upon me. This is one of those times. But it is my sincerest hope that all who have contributed to this book will accept my warmest and deepest gratitude.

Foremost, I am thankful to the men who allowed me to share some of their life pleasures as well as intimate pain in their journey to become the men that they are now. Without their willingness to give freely of themselves this book would not have been possible.

Next, I thank those extraordinary people, who in their busy schedules so willingly made space for me by agreeing to read drafts, offering critical insights, and pointing me in the right direction throughout the writing of this book. To Barbara Katz-Rothman, Michelle Fine, Sandra Morales-DeLeon, Oliver Williams, Beth Richie, Valli Kanuha, Patricia Yancy Martin, Steve Woods, James Remple, and especially Alford Young, I say thank you. For lending a critical ear and allowing me to ramble on and on as I tried to put the complicated pieces of the men's lives together in my own head, I thank members of the sociology faculty at John Jay College of Criminal Justice of the City University of New York. Particularly, I thank Douglass Thompkins, Janice Johnson-Dias, Rosemary Barberet, Anthony Lemelle, David Brotherton (department chair), and my cherished research assistant Matasha Harris. And, I also received and took note of the encouragement from the larger John Jay community so I thank Provost Jane Bowers and David Kennedy, director of the Center for Crime Prevention and Control, for their support and distinguished historian Blanche Wiesen Cook for her enormous insights on why Eleanor Roosevelt did what she did.

I am profoundly grateful to Adi Hovav, senior editor at Rutgers University Press, and the Press staff, who recognized the importance of the men's stories and guided me through the process of publishing *Through Our Eyes*.

To my sisters Janice Holland and Priscilla Simon and my dear friends Linda-Goode Bryant and Dana-Ain Davis, who helped to keep me strong during very difficult times, thanks. And, finally, I say to Keith Jackson, thank you so much for holding my hand when I desperately needed a hand to hold.

PROLOGUE

"WHEN WE THINK about the violence that we commit against ourselves in different forms and the violence against other people that we commit, we must forgive ourselves for what we do to other people, but we need to forgive ourselves for what we do to ourselves. That's something that we often don't have the opportunity to do. We often don't realize that it's something we even should do.

As black men, we get so caught up in these processes of manhood and masculinity in a white male-controlled environment. We allow other people to define who we are. We just need to recognize our history in this country going back to slavery in the western world and bring all of that forward and look at our examples. The way we treat each other, the way we treat ourselves in terms of the expectations that we have of ourselves or our failure to follow through: why do we fail to step up and just be the man we need to be? We need to come to terms with who we are.

I have an understanding of where I was, to give me an understanding of where I am, and what I have the potential of doing. That's not simple rhetoric; it's not just words stringed together coming out of my mouth. That's my reality. I got to understand where I am from. I am the product of all the stuff that happened growing up: I watched my mother being battered and knocked in the head; all the instances of racism; my interaction with women in my life and their families; and all of that is important. It produced me. Going to the joint is a product of that, and I have to understand that. And it forced me to reflect on what made me the man that I am now.

It means being forced in a situation where you have time. You go to prison, you go to jail, and you are forced into a little cell, and it's hard not to see yourself. You lay on that bed, and you look at the ceiling. But so many of us lay on the bed, and we shut the world out and refuse to see; they are not ready to see. It's painful. Wherever you are, when that opportunity arises have the courage to look at yourself and all the ugliness and all the pain that comes with that ugliness. It's not so much the pain that happened to you. But more so what you did to other people and what you did to yourself. Take the opportunity to reflect and have the courage to acknowledge that I wasn't a good father, that I wasn't a good husband, that I wasn't a good son, and that I wasn't a good community member. . . . Have the courage to acknowledge all of that and then look at it and say, that's what it was, and this is what I am going to do about it.

That was me. I reflected. I acknowledged. I stepped up. I took the bull by the horns. I made things happen. Today, I can say that there isn't much that I can ask for. I'm not asking not to be a black man. Then everything would be perfect because then I would have the privileged position assigned to a white man. But I don't want to be a white man. I am a black man. I like being a black man. But I know that it brings with it the fact that I could die tomorrow because I am a black man in America: which means I still walk down the street and at any moment a cop can throw me up against the wall, an altercation can occur, and I end up with a bullet in my head. That's my reality, the reality that I live with everyday."

—Matt, 53 years old, recorded in interview with author, 1997

Through Our Eyes

Introduction

"I Am a Man"

THROUGH OUR EYES is a continuation of my search to understand the importance of violence in the lived experiences of African American women, men, and children. The physical, personal, and social violence that enter their lives comes from some place. My search is to identify those locations, their impacts, and the implications they hold for understanding not only how African Americans experience violence but also how they see themselves as a result of their experiences. Having examined the experiences of black women, I now cast a critical gaze on the lives of African American men.

This book parallels research I did with nine African American women. The theoretical framework, findings, and conclusions of that study appear in *Knowing What We Know: African American Women's Experiences of Violence and Violation*. As I did in my first book, through life history interviews I once again explore the confluences of meaning that shape the experiences of eight black men over the course of their lives.

Through Our Eyes is also based on the premise that relations of power frame meaning. Those relations include race, gender, and violence that are created by historical processes where meaning is developed, contested, and changed through social interaction. I argue that a dual reference is formed for understanding what happens in black men's interactions: Structural arrangements that place social constraints on their needs and aspirations create one reference point, whereby meaning emerges from what is done, by whom, and for what purpose; the ways in which black men interpret their own experiences create the other reference, whereby meaning arises from what they feel, think, and do as they interact within and against social conditions and practices. With these references in mind, I provide a context for understanding what happens in African American men's lives when agency and social constraints are in conflict. Herein lays the uniqueness of this book: the men's riveting first-person accounts present how they see themselves as they engage the constant tensions, dilemmas, and contradictions created by the different meanings given to their experiences.

There is a sociopolitical symmetry in the historical context that shapes both black women's and men's experiences in America. But the structural constraints that emerge from that history position their experiences differently: depending on a given social and cultural setting, they experience race, gender, and violence quite differently. I believe that those differences are significant and must be acknowledged as well as understood in their own right. In considering the importance of how those differences are experienced, this book does not offer a comparative analysis between the experiences of black women and men. Race, gender, and violence experienced in the daily lives of African American men create their own stories.

A critical part of the stories the men tell is about what happens when their reality becomes inseparable from racial and gender images, and the accompanying narratives shape what it means to be black-and-male in America. Their stories allow us to see in vivid detail how violence can become integral to that meaning. Distorted images of African American men and the myths that surround them are creations of imagination. In the cultural and social imagining of white America, black men and violence are inexplicably linked. In this context, although gender dynamics are present, most salient in black men's particular experiences is the critical link between race and violence. Today, as in the past, African American men are ever-confronted with an imposing image—the violent-black-male. This disfiguring image is accompanied by an equally disfiguring narrative that marginalizes the value of their lives and calls into question their humanity, for they are socially and cultural positioned in our society as inferior beings. This imposing image and the accompanying narrative provide an important reference for what the men feel, think, and do as they interact within and against racial constraints that are informed by an entrenched stereotype and a deeply held myth about who they are as both individuals and collectively a group.

The prominence of gender and its link to violence are by no means inconsequential to the shaping of African American men's experiences. To the contrary, in their racialized experiences, violence becomes essential to the social and cultural construction of masculinity, of defining manhood, and of what it means to be a man in American society. All men, to some degree, are socialized into violence: that socialization is largely predicated upon either an idealized dominance or the projection of power or both, in ways that link their development of a sense of manhood to violence. Depending on the form it takes and the setting in which it occurs, violence gives meaning to black men's gender identity. That meaning shapes the tensions, dilemmas, and contradictions they experience as they assert their sense of masculinity. Gender relations, like race relations, are also critical to understanding what the men feel, think, and do as they interact within and against social constraints that exclude or marginalize their needs and aspirations as black men.

Violence insinuates itself early on, and too often for many African American men it continues to have a significant presence throughout their entire lives. It evolves from uneven structural arrangements. A dual reference is provided for exploring the impact and implications of violence in their lives. In this book, a broad understanding of violence is essential: violence refers to social conditions and cultural practices that threaten, jeopardize, and compromise African American men's sense of being. The dimensions of that violence are injurious to the physical, personal, and social self. From this perspective, I not only examine what is done, by whom, and with what purpose, but I also look at what black men feel, think, and do when their sense of personhood is infringed upon or breached.

Therefore race, gender, and violence are not presented in this book as separate or discrete aspects of African American men's lives. Nor are they presented as separate and discrete aspects of power relations; rather, these aspects intersect. They converge in important ways to give meaning to the men's experiences. I believe that meaning informs how they see themselves and as a result shapes how they interact in the world. Through the men's compelling life histories, this book dares readers to look beneath the stereotypic images formed through racial lens and challenge preconceived notions about who they are as men, as informed by established gender expectations and standards of manhood. Instead, *Through Our Eyes* focuses on the physical, personal, and social dimensions of the men's lives—revealed in experiences as children, young men, and mature adults—as it asks readers to consider the enormous complexities of their lives and the humanity that lies therein. For only then will we begin to see the importance of their struggles, both within and against images and narratives of their lives, and began to understand how the men see the world and why they think and act as they do within it.

"I Am a Man"

In 1968, hundreds of black sanitation workers went on strike against the city of Memphis, Tennessee. They were protesting both the conditions under which they were forced to work and the $1.04 they received for their hourly wage. During the strike, they wore signs around their necks that simply said "I Am a Man." The meaning was neither obscure nor ambiguous. With dignity and determination, the garbage workers offered a clear, unified, and defiant message to both themselves and the white power structure of the city. No longer would their manhood be compromised, labor undermined, and justice denied.

Like other protests of the civil rights era, community leaders sent out a call to action in support of the strikers. Noted black men as diverse as union leader Roy Wilkins, civil rights activist Bayard Rustin, baseball great Jackie Robinson, and entertainer Harry Belafonte were only a few of the thousands who joined in solidarity with the striking workers. But Dr. Martin Luther King's presence cast a national spotlight on the sanitation workers' plight. During a mass rally at the Mason Temple on April 3, 1968, Dr. King gave his last speech, in which he said: "We are determined to be men." Following his prophetic "I've been to the Mountaintop" speech, the next day Dr. King was slain by an assassin's bullet on the balcony of the Lorraine Hotel.

One can point to the brutal killing of Martin Luther King and the momentous strike of the Memphis sanitation workers as important turning points that would mark a major political shift in the struggle for racial, gender, and social justice in America. That shift gradually altered what it means to be black, male, and self-determined in the context of racial and gender oppression. That shift, however, must not be confused with a break from the past. Nor should it be confused with thinking that racial and gender oppression no longer holds sway over African American men's lives, as we have entered a new millennium. To the contrary, the past and present—like continuity and change—must be seen as converging, intersecting, and overlapping, for they are both part of the same historical processes shaping what it means to be black-and-male in America, at any given moment in time and place.

In the past, black men were largely seen by white society as socially indistinguishable from one another. In other words, black men lacked individual identities worth acknowledging. In America, it did not matter if they were slaves or freemen, politicians or sharecroppers, old or new Negroes, religious or agnostics, and lawyers or criminals. Nor did it matter if they were married or unmarried, fathers or childless, men loving women or loving other men. Their common experiences of what it means to be black-and-male in the face of racial and gender oppression made it painfully clear that they were all in the same boat, regardless of significant individual differences.

Racial and gender oppression creates exclusionary and marginalizing social conditions and cultural practices that denied black men not only individuality but also humanity, regardless of enormous physical, personal, and social differences that exist among them. In the past, the struggle for racial, gender, and social justice often required that black men suppress or sacrifice important individual differences to facilitate a unity of purpose, where common needs and aspirations were extolled above all else. Even amidst their diversity, when the call to action in support of the Memphis garbage workers' strike went out, many black men again set aside their physical, personal, and social differences to answer that call. Out of political necessity, this, in turn, allowed them to embrace a racial and gender essentialism that gave a common understanding to what it means in the face of oppression to be black-and-male in America.

As in the past, contemporary racial and gender oppression is created by social conditions and cultural practices that deny the value of African American men's lives. Time and structural alterations shift the patterns and practices of racial and gender oppression and consequently reconfigure the circumstances under which black men live their daily lives. Today, the blatant exclusionary or marginalizing practices of the past are not as obvious and straightforward; increasingly the social and cultural rigidity of racial and gender oppression is more blurred. As a result, what it means to be black-and-male in contemporary American society is no longer predicated on a racial and gender essentialism but upon a meaning that has become increasingly diffused.

Yet a shift in structural arrangements does not necessarily change the fundamental structures of power relations that are critical to maintaining oppression. Even with a transformative shift, alterations to racial and gender arrangements do not inevitability lead to progressive change that embraces and allows for the possibilities of human flourishing. Rather, such alterations may simply rearticulate social and cultural constraints that adjust to the realities demanded by an ever-changing world.

The struggles for civil rights were instrumental to shifting the patterns and practices that allowed for racial and gender oppression in our society. But along with progressive trends that changed racial and gender relations in America, regressive tendencies remained, and changing circumstances importantly sustained power relations. Just beneath the surface of progress, readily emerges another reality that points to the structural continuity of exclusionary and marginalizing practices; influenced by race and gender relations, these practices continue to shape not only the life courses of African American men but also their life chances. A closer look at how black males are socially positioned in our society today—as children, young adults, and mature men—reveals some broader social trends shaping their reality. Currently, the nearly 17 million black males represent 48 percent of the African American population in the United States, but they constitute only a little more than 6 percent of the total population in the United States.

Despite that reality, black male children are disproportionately placed in foster care, juvenile detention, and special educational programs (Scott & Davis 2006, Richardson 2003, Morrison & Epps 2002, Sampson & Laub 1993, Kunjufu 2005, Eitle 2002). Young black males, with a 50 percent dropout rate, are leaving high school in obscenely large numbers (Orfield, Wald, & Swanson, The Civil Rights Project at Harvard University, 2004). Moreover, little attention or explanation is given to the alarming rate of firearm-related suicides that snatch the life away from many young black males and rank it the third leading cause of their deaths (Joe & Kaplan 2002). Conventional wisdom may point to individual responsibility to explain these broad patterns that are shaping the realities of too many black male children. These trends, however, suggest that something more is happening in their lives beyond what they may feel, think, and do as individuals. Something systemic constrains their needs and aspirations and discounts their human potential and denies the opportunity to flourish. Although the disvaluing of black male life begins early, for many black boys this trend persists well into adulthood.

Homicide continues to be a leading cause of death for adult black males in America, especially for those between eighteen and thirty-four years of age, and they also experience high death rates due to HIV/AIDS. In addition, black males are more likely to have inadequate health insurance coverage and more likely to use hospital emergency rooms as the usual source for medical care (Henry J. Kaiser Family Foundation, 2007). Nearly 40 percent of black men are not working, which reduces employment-based insurance coverage disproportionately. Another important implication of high unemployment— correlated to staggering high school dropout rate—is incarceration: a black male in his late twenties is more likely to be in jail than working or going to school (U.S. Joint Economic Committee of Congress, 2007). Nowhere is the stark reality of many black men's lives more poignant than in their involvement with the criminal justice system. Black males constitute 30 percent of all people arrested, 41 percent of those jailed, and an astounding 49 percent of those who are imprisoned. As a result of their incarceration, 13 percent of all black men are disenfranchised; they are denied a fundamental right of citizenship because they cannot vote following a felony conviction (Human Rights Watch, 2000).

Older African American men, those born and raised during racial segregation, face a shorter life expectancy in comparison to other Americans (Warner & Hayward, 2006). They have higher death rates for heart disease and certain cancers, including prostate, lung, and colon. They are also more likely to be admitted into hospital for diabetes complications, hypertension, and angina (Henry J. Kaiser Family Foundation, 2007). Many currently experience the long-term effects that low levels of education, inadequate housing, and marginal employment have had on their lives. Many older black men, either entering retirement or already retired, face growing old in poverty. The poverty rate for older black men is 22 percent. Because of underemployment or work histories in menial jobs, older black men are less secure financially, and the lack of adequate pensions and other retirement benefits may require that some continue to work past the average age of retirement (Jackson, Chatters & Taylor, 1993).

These broad socioeconomic trends have staked a claim to many black men's reality—as children and as adults—and the implications speak to a systematic disvaluing of their lives. Notable about these trends is their existence side-by-side with trends suggesting that structures of racial and gender oppression are no longer critical barriers, especially in the pursuit of individual needs and aspirations. From the seeds planted by the civil rights movement, today one can easily point to reconfigured patterns of employment, housing, education, and popular culture that affirm the presence of racial and gender integration. Nowhere is this affirmation more evident than in the existence of a fairly large and flourishing black middle class. From this progress, one may reasonably conclude that race and gender oppression no longer hold sway over black male life. The enormous social, political, and economic currency that many individual African American men have obtained may lead one to falsely conclude that we now live in a "post-race" and "post-gender" society, where such identities are increasingly irrelevant. To assume that we exist in a "color-blind" and "gender-neutral" society—amid change and progress—provides a distorted understanding of the realities of what it means to be black-and-male in America.

The actualizing of needs and aspirations may imply that achievement rests solely on individual desire and effort, and this, in turn, allows for better integration into the dominant white society, regardless of social circumstances and cultural practices. In *White-Washing Race*, Brown and others vehemently dispute this contention, but the debate continues (Brown, Carnoy, Currie et al., 2003). Regardless, there are African American men whose lives do appear to transcend or debunk socioeconomic trends that limit the capacity of other black men to realize their human potential, especially when achievement and income are linked. Anthony J. Lemelle notes that "implied in this reasoning is the belief that middle-class incomes result in white middle-class role behavior" (Lemelle, 1995, p. 18). Consequently, many black men who have achieved a degree of economic wherewithal have blended, seemingly, into the ambiguity of multiculturalism as they reap the benefits of the civil rights struggles while minimizing its importance to their lives.

Yet the power of racial and gender structural relations creates its own narrative for black men's lives, regardless of what they may feel, think, and do. For some black men, this has created an interesting schism in their reality. Kevin Powell, for instance, came to realize that in this narrative "the scenes have changed, but the scenes remain, inexplicably the same," as he eagerly stepped into the pretence of a multicultural world based on individual merit. He counted himself among those "who believed the Civil Rights Movement was about changing policies of legal desegregation, freeing African Americans to exercise their birthright of free movement in this social order without the fear of attack or retribution. In other words, to realize, without legal restraint, the full experience of human freedom" (Powell, 2003, p. 32). As he pursued his needs and aspirations while gaining increased acceptance, recognition, and compensation for his individual accomplishments, Powell realized that in the "transmitting of the civil rights narrative the script was flipped":

> The hardheaded fight against segregation was swapped for the warm symbolism of integration. Over time, this symbolic integration has found its goal in the triumph of the myth of multiculturalism. But even though the colors of the rainbow can all chill together . . . they are not all sharing *in the power*. So what's the point of multiculturalism if it is reduced to folks eating each other's foods, marrying each other, having multiracial children, and proclaiming myopically that interracial relationships, be they friendships or loveships, will rid the country of its historically paralyzing racial quagmire? Or *is* that the point? (Powell, 2003, p. 32)

Although the signs of exclusion and marginalization are blurred, Powell believes that "psyche" scars of the past remain and that the "wriggle worm of White supremacy, White entitlement, White power is still there" as well. The flipping of the script, he learns, is based on rearticulated race and gender relations: the social conditions and cultural practices of exclusion and marginalization changed, but the implications and impact for black male life remain all too familiar. Powell encountered barriers limiting his ability to pursue his chosen profession, and those barriers were deeply rooted in oppressive race and gender relations.

Unlike Powell, some men have never had illusions about the resiliency of oppressive race and gender relations in shaping what it means to be black-and-male in America. Yet, even so, they continue to cling to the false belief that African American men are still in the same boat today and possess the same unity of purpose as in the past, regardless of individual differences. In this belief, critics often grant race a priority over the relevancy of gender and sexuality in shaping black men's reality. But Harlon L. Dalton points out:

> Black people should be honest about the fact that we are not all in the same boat when it comes to dealing with racial abuse. Some of us are shielded from it most of the time; others face it on a daily basis. Most of us live somewhere between those extremes. Even in situations where we do occupy the same boat, we differ greatly in our capacity to protect ourselves if and when it begins to take on water. Some of us are outfitted with life preservers, flares, and maybe even an inflatable raft, whereas others have no choice but to cling to the deck. (Dalton, 1999, p. 120)

As seen in the past, embracing racial essentialism requires that black men suppress or sacrifice important differences, particularly those regarding gender and sexuality.

Nevertheless, the continued belief in an essential unity based on race was instrumental to the call for The Million Man March held in Washington, D.C., in 1995. This March, organized by the Nation of Islam's leader Minister Louis Farrakhan, was a historic and unprecedented gathering of African American men. From its name to the organizing principles and the dynamics of the actual March itself the complexities of race and gender relations—as articulated to the larger white society but particularly to the black community—were on full display. With a focus on "atonement and reconciliation," Minister Farrakhan asked hundreds of thousands of black men participating in the March to take individual responsibility for their lives. Or, as Robert F. Reid-Pharr notes, African American men "were once again advised that self-help is the best medicine" for curing their ills. Reid-Pharr attended the March and commented:

> The black man was instructed to return home and start providing for kith and kin, to stop making excuses about the scarcity of legitimate, well-paying jobs, and to access his inner manhood, that great and mysterious wellspring of masculinity hidden deep within his psyche, waiting to be harnessed to the project of a beautiful black tomorrow. This all-powerful masculinity was offered as the solution to, and compensation for, the stark curtailments of resources and opportunities that confront African American men in this country. (Pharr, 1996, pp. 36–37)

In this context, the critical observation by former slave and abolitionist Fredrick Douglass continues to resonate: "Power concedes nothing without demand. It never has and never will. Show me the exact amount of wrong and injustices that are visited upon a person and I will show you the exact amount of words endured by these people." Standing on the National Mall—appearing to confront U.S. political and economic might—speaker after speaker at the March demand no explicit action from the U.S. government on behalf of African American men. Participants of the March, however, endured many, many words.

Black men were exhorted to assume responsibility for their own individual lives and livelihoods by taking steps to address their moral and personal failings. As they stood on the National Mall, they pledged to be better "men." Presumably they would exercise—henceforth—free will over their decisions and actions. They would assert agency. African American men can and do exercise agency in their individual decisions and actions; their feelings, thoughts, and actions, however, occur within and against the context of social and cultural constraints that intrude upon their physical, personal, and social beings.

I argue that agency is not a free-floating phenomenon that rests solely on the sea of individual intent and is exerted simply at will. Rather, agency exists within and against the context of social circumstances and cultural practices that are created by structural constraints. Assuming individual responsibility for one's physical, personal, and social life is not a strategy, in and of itself, that moves African American men—either individually or collectively—beyond the rigid boundaries of racial and gender oppression. Assuming individual responsibility is by no means an emancipatory strategy. Black men's oppression is not derived solely from "bad attitudes, wrong choices, or by their own frailties and addictions." Of course these qualities do exist and can prove extremely destructive in black men's lives. But they do not exist in a vacuum that somehow occurs outside the boundaries of social and cultural constraints. Instead, these qualities reveal themselves, most often in response to social and cultural constraints.

Therefore, an emphasis on "atonement and reconciliation" in the absence of political demands and actions is conceptually problematic. Even more troubling was the exclusionary and marginalizing tendency of The Million Man March itself. Considerable debates raged within the black community regarding the intent of the March and who could—or could not—participate. Central to those debates was a critical question: what does it mean to be black-and-male in America?

Clearly, from the organizers' standpoint, the March's meaning did not include black women. Reid-Pharr argues that acknowledging the importance of black masculinity was "predicated on the absence of black women." The context of patriarchal manhood framed the March's rhetoric, whereby black men were asked to assume their rightful places as heads of families and leaders of black communities. The most anticipated speaker of the March, the honorable Minister Louis Farrakhan, articulated black men's roles and responsibilities and proclaimed his vision of what it means to be "real men." Reid-Pharr observed:

> Louis Farrakhan put himself forward as the emblem, the ideal type, if you will, of a newly emergent black masculinity. He appeared as a shining exemplar of a renewed Black man, striking the posture of the stern—if gentle—father, savior, patriarch, messiah. He scorned our enemies while asking us only to look inward, to find the evil within and cast it out. If we did so, he prophesied, if only we could learn to humble ourselves, we would surely see a new dawn of cleanliness and order, the Black Millennium. He stood, then, as a sort of Emersonian representative man, embodying a masculinity so pure that simply by gazing upon it one could extinguish the fires of ambiguity and uncertainty that rage in the hearts of black men across America. (Reid-Pharr, 1996, pp. 44–45)

To assert their "God-given patriarchal role," to assert black manhood, Minister Farrakhan said to this audience of hundreds of thousands:

> Black man, you don't have to bash White people, all we gotta do is go back home and turn our communities into productive places. All we

gotta do is go back home and make our communities a decent and safe place to live. And if we start dotting the Black community with businesses, opening up factories, challenging ourselves to be better than we are, White folk, instead of driving by, using the "N" word, they'll say, look, look at them. Oh, my God. They're marvelous. They're wonderful. We can't say they're inferior anymore. But, every time we drive by and shoot, every time we carjack, every time we use foul, filthy language, every time we produce culturally degenerate films and tapes, putting a string in our women's backside and parading them before the world, every time we do things like this we are feeding the degenerate mind of white supremacy and I want to stop feeding that mind and let that mind die a natural death. (CNN Transcript, 2007)

Louis Farrakhan's message was neither a call for racial, gender, and social justice nor a call for fundamental change in the structures of power relations that enforce racial and gender oppression in this country. In many ways his message actually affirmed the legitimacy of those structures. Luke Charles Harris argued that "Farrakhan's rhetoric implies that many problems within the Black community are exacerbated by Black men's abdication of their 'patriarchal responsibilities' as 'heads of households and leaders of the community' and the solution is for Black men to live up to these God-given patriarchal roles" (Harris, 1999, p. 60). While asking black men to assert patriarchal manhood—assert power, control, and dominance over their families and communities—Minister Farrakhan's solutions to the problems facing black men would, in fact, strengthen, rather than disassemble or even alter existing structures of racial and gender oppression.

With the express intent of encouraging black men to be "men," by assuming their proper manly role as defined within a patriarchal structure, it was fairly easy for March organizers to justify black women's exclusion, even though political backlash resulted from that decision. The role of black gay men in the March, however, could not be as easily dismissed, by either gay men or March organizers.

Obvious tensions, dilemmas, and especially contradictions loomed over the March regarding black male participation. Racial and gender essentialism, borne out of political necessity, no longer provided a common understanding for what it means to be black-and-male, particularly for many black gay men. It was ironic that essentialism did provide a point of reference for which a common understanding could be assumed, regardless of sexual orientation or preference. Amidst differences, there appeared to be a mutual understanding for the need of black male unity, a concept that allowed many black gay men to embrace a desire for racial solidarity, as advanced by march organizers. Aware of the implicit contradiction, many black gay men were torn over the decision to either attend or forgo the March, especially given March organizers' open rejection of the sexuality of black gay men and active marginalization of their presence.

Discussing the black gay male discourse surrounding the March, Darren Lenard Hutchinson observes that some believed they should participate, "despite the homophobia of its organizers and the heterosexist tone of its purpose—because 'sexuality' is separate from the issue of black male solidarity that March organizers claimed as their goal." Meanwhile others argued that "participation will constitute acquiescence to the homophobic ideology underlying the politics of the March." In assessing the differing views, Hutchinson concludes:

> Both sides of the debate furthered the important project of increasing black gay visibility and of creating a more multidimensional construction of black identity, neither side was "right" or "wrong" for its decision on whether to march. A decision to avoid the March to protest its heterosexist and sexist themes is no less political than a decision to join the March and make the political statement that black gays exist and are an integral part of the black community. The former action places black political organizers on notice of the disunity that results from narrow, homophobic, and sexists political agendas, while the latter action makes black gay identity visible. Both of these messages are critical elements in the ongoing project of reshaping black identity. (Hutchinson, 1999, pp. 35–40)

Many black gay men were unwilling to suppress or sacrifice their sexual identity. With a deep sense of racial unity, excluding both lesbian and straight black women, some black gay men, however, stood side-by-side with their black heterosexual brethren and listened as Minister Farrakhan extolled the virtues of individual responsibility within a defense of patriarchal manhood. The Million Man March was staged in the laudable tradition of past civil rights protests, but, unlike the past, the intent of this March was not a call for racial, gender, and social justice. No political demands or determined actions, beyond those of individual responsibility, surfaced. Consequently, given the limited vision of the Million Man March, the question that Martin Luther King posed in 1967, a year prior to his assassination, was still relevant: "Where do we go from here?"

Dr. King's response to that question was also framed within the context of black male unity and responsibility. His answer differed: King's unity emphasized responsibility within the context of racial and social justice, rather than responsibility solely within the individual. Within the context of political demands and actions, Martin Luther King exhorted a nation to accept the role and responsibility of the individual as intricately linked to a process of social and cultural change. Dr. King's response was male-focused. But the civil rights movement was the most important precursor to the liberation movements of both women and gays. I suspect that his response would have been broader, influenced and strengthened by the needs and aspirations as articulated by those movements, had they existed at the time, or at least I hope that this would have been the case.

Nevertheless, in providing answers to the question, "where do we go from here?" the tone, tenor, and context of Dr. King's message recognized the specific responsibility to challenge structures of oppression:

> First, we must massively assert our dignity and worth. We must stand up amid a system that still oppresses us and develop an unassailable and majestic sense of values. . . . We must no longer be ashamed of being black. The job of arousing manhood with a people that have been taught for so many centuries that they are nobody is not easy. . . . The Negro must boldly throw off the manacles of self-abnegation and say to himself and to the world, "I am somebody. I am a person. I am a man with dignity and honor. I have a rich and noble history, however painful and exploited that history has been. . . ." This self-affirmation is the black man's need, made compelling by the white man's crimes against him . . . As we talk about "where do we go from here?" we must honestly face the fact that the movement must address itself to the question of restructuring the whole of American society. . . . Now, when I say questioning the whole society, it means ultimately coming to see that the problem of racism, the problem of economic exploitation, and the problem of war are all tied together. These are the triple evils that are interrelated. . . . Your whole structure must be changed. A nation that will keep people in slavery for 244 years will "thingify" them and make them things. And therefore, they will exploit them and poor people, generally, economically. And a nation that will exploit economically will have to have foreign investments and everything else, and it will have to use its military might to protect them. (King, 1967)

Dr. King's words and actions embraced an understanding that individual responsibility was inseparable from that of collective responsibility in changing social conditions and cultural practices that structures oppression in American society.

Clearly the question of "where do we go from here" continues to resonate and have meaning for black men and women, regardless of their sexual orientation or preference. African American men have a critical role to play in shaping the contemporary response to this question. But that response must be purged of both the ideological underpinnings and practices that shape exclusion and marginalization. Individual responsibility, accompanied by collective demands and actions transforming the structural foundation of the conditions and practices that denies human flourishing, is the call. This call to action seeks to undermine the hierarchy of needs and aspirations created by rigid race, gender, sexuality, class, and other important social distinctions, within both the black community and the larger society. No longer must we allow exclusionary and marginalizing tendencies to reaffirm the privileged position of black heterosexual masculinity in the black community, even though many heterosexual and homosexual black men and women daily contest that privilege while simultaneously remaining disvalued within the larger white society.

This book offers my response to the question, "Where do we go from here?" In detail, I present the lives of eight African American men who are searching for what Athena D. Mutua calls "progressive black masculinities." As Mutua suggests, this particular form of masculinity is a work in progress, an on-going project that none of the men themselves have fully obtained but toward which their current individual lives are struggling. "Progressive black masculinities" are grounded in an understanding that the "innovative performances of the masculine self eschew dominance and are engaged in the struggle to transform social structures of domination." Furthermore, as Mutua tells us, "the structures of domination that limit and subordinate black men are not limited to racism alone but include other structures such as gendered racism, sexism, class, heterosexism, and so on." Consequently, "in struggling to transform these structures, progressive masculinities seek to liberate not only themselves but also others" (Mutua, 2006, p. xxii).

The men of this book do not interpret or describe their lives within the context of "progressive black masculinities," but their words and actions imply that they are traveling along a path toward this aim. Their struggles to realize a "progressive black masculinity" signify a work in progress. The project is incomplete, for the men continuously struggle within and against the regressive tendencies of hegemonic racial ideologies and conventional ideas about masculinity that shaped both their childhoods and their adult lives. Their search for identity encompassed enormous struggles within and against structures of race and gender oppression, where a sense of self was created and recreated as a result of ever-changing social circumstances and cultural practices. Therefore, a "true" progressive black masculinity may in fact be beyond their grasp, for they continue to face an imposing history that defines what it means to be black-and male in America, regardless of what they feel, think, and do.

In spite of a broader social history, in which their images and narratives seem preordained, the men's on-going challenge, however, is to define for themselves what it means to be black-and-male in the context of their own particular lives if they are to realize their full humanity. In essence, each man must shape his own personal history, and they proceeded to do just that by actively engaging the cultural and social landscapes of their particular lives. The journey is ever transformative, but the journey is filled with tensions, dilemmas, and contradictions. Because of this, often the very rawness of their experiences make us uncomfortable, for the men make decisions and pursue actions both within and against their self-defined needs and aspirations. But what they feel, think, and do in the course of living their lives allow us to see a transformative process at work, where change and continuity coexists. Sometimes, the steps in their journey are extremely slow, arduous, and painful to witness. Even so, the men pursue their lives and are constantly engaging in a process of becoming, as they make steps toward developing a progressive black masculine social and cultural stance. As the reader will see, the process of becoming is deeply rooted in history—not a static record, but a dynamic chronicle that encompasses both unremitting devaluation and human flourishing.

THE AFRICANLIKE PERSONA

To position the men's experiences of this book, it is important to recognize that their individual and collective lives are socially linked to the historical legacy of slavery. Historically, whites justified the cultural, political, and economic institution of slavery by creating an image of blackness that positioned blacks into their "proper" role in society. Toni Morrison calls this image an "Africanlike" persona. For her, this image does not "suggest the varieties and complexities of African people and their descendants who have inhabited this country"; this image instead speaks to a "denotative and connotative blackness that African people have come to signify." As Morrison aptly concludes, this "Africanlike" persona functions as "a way of talking about and a way of policing matters of class, sexual license, and repression, formations and exercises of power, and meditations on ethics and accountability" (Morrison, 1992, pp. 6–10).

Among the many indelible historical images emerging from the "Africanlike" signification is one of the violent-black-male. Two dimensions of this image are recognizable in a contemporary representation: the criminal-black-male and the angry-black-male. These images are purposeful because stereotypes are social markers that play "a key role in communication, instruction and the general transmission of culture" (Pieterse, 1992, pp. 10–11). The social rhetoric accompanying these particular images characterizes black men's moral character as less than human and their behavior as animal-like. Although fabrications, these images and the implied messages have real effects nonetheless.

Today images, such as the criminal-black-male and angry-black-male, and the defining narrative erases African American men's individuality, marginalizes their experiences, simplifies their reality, and excludes their human potential. The ways by which these demonizing images operate in American society offer an important context for understanding the social and cultural realities of black men's lives. Their actions, within and against the realities imposed by these images, provide an equally important context. Throughout their experiences, the men of this book insist on retaining a sense of their own human worth, even as they attempt to reduce the value of their lives, and their actions reflect this insistency. As readers will see, the tensions, dilemmas, and contradictions of their individual and collective lives often make this a difficult task to negotiate, especially as they engage the seeming omnipresence of the socially constructed personas of the criminal-black-male and angry-black-male.

Criminal-black-male

The violent-black-male image and one of its contemporary derivations, the criminal-black-male, were formed during slavery. Lemelle explains that nothing was natural about American plantation slavery; he describes it as a well-organized system where the effects produced "an orgy of human degradation, indecency, and debauchery" (Lemelle, 1995, p. 26). In this system, the mere presence of blackness represented a gross transgression against whiteness: a transgression that crossed social and cultural restrictions formed either through custom or law. What did this mean for the day-to-day reality of black male life? Under slavery black men were "forced to steal food and clothing to survive, forced to lie in order to cultivate reading and writing skills, forced to deceive in order to associate with the master class" (Lemelle, 1995, p. 26). As chattel slaves, these and other acts were constitutionally prohibited because enslaved blacks were considered three-fifths human with no legal standing.

Principles of human rights or the sacred value of human life did not apply to black men. Whether enslaved or free, they "were forced to accept illegal actions almost as a way of life," whereupon "virtually every normal human aspiration was in fact unlawful" (Bryne, 1994, p. 33) Christopher Booker argues that simply attempting to satisfy the most basic of human needs established a legacy that came to define the black male presence in America today. Their mere presence was criminalized. To satisfy "basic physiological, social, spiritual, and psychological needs was deemed to be criminal by the authorities, who egregiously meted out violence to enforce their rule." For this immediate discussion, I set aside the egregious violence rendered by white authorities; it is imperative to note Booker's main point: he views the period of slavery as "the first phase of the criminalization of the black male, a key formative phase of the black presence in the United States" (Booker, 2000, p. 39).

Transgressions by blacks and the punishments rendered for violation are deeply woven into "the foundation of U.S. society." Forcefully brought to America in shackles, the legacy engendered by the social construction of the criminal-black-male persona continues to resonate. This image and the message it conveys are thus realized today by countless numbers of African American men, who daily engage some aspect of our justice system as criminal offenders. For too many black men the image, narrative, and reality of the criminal-black-male meet behind the steel doors of concrete jail cells and razor-wired prison walls across this country. This was indeed the case for Matt, Richard, and Jamie, three of the men I interviewed.

Matt was incarcerated for seventeen years, ten months, and seven days. He faced two life-sentences for killing two white men during an armed robbery. Richard, who had been incarcerated several times before, served a sentence of fifteen years to life for killing a young black man and shooting four others during a dispute over drug money. And Jamie served twenty years for killing a black drug dealer during a botched robbery attempt. Their experiences could easily be reduced to that of the criminal-black-male stereotype, and a typical narrative might render their lives worthless. Yet, to do so would deny the complexity of Matt's, Richard's, and Jamie's experiences as they sought to give value to their own lives in extreme circumstances that negate their very humanity. Their realities do not represent the experiences of all African American men. The majority of black men, the majority of the men I interviewed, have never endured long-term incarceration for a felony murder offense; they have never had to endure forceful confinement, where they are trapped in a steel cage like animals.

This is not to suggest that some of the other men I interviewed did not encounter social constraints imposed by the state. To the contrary, growing up in a northern city, as a young man, Thomas was stopped by the police on many occasions while driving and spent nights in the local jail as a result, while John grew up in a southern town and experienced the brutality of police violence during civil rights protests. All of the men, in their response to either family members' or friends' experiences, at one time or another engaged some aspect of the criminal justice system. These and other experiences—whether direct or indirect—assumed an important presence in the men's lives and left an impression on the ways they viewed what it means to be black-and-male in America.

Angry-black-male

Another image holds broader consequences for African American men's lives, one that is difficult for many black men to avoid. That image is revealed in the angry-black-male persona, which is also a contemporary of the more historic violent-black-male stereotype.

The angry-black-male stereotype is rooted in a particular social construction of reality—the subordination of black manhood; patriarchal manhood and hegemonic masculinity marginalize and often exclude African American men's claim to manhood. The historical subordination of black masculinity emerges from complicated race, gender, and class dynamics. As noted earlier by Booker, those dynamics require us to examine the significance of white male violence and its importance in shaping what it means to be black-and-male in American society.

In documenting the cultural history of gender and race relations in the United States, Gail Bederman contends that, during slavery, manhood was linked to whiteness, and, in turn, whiteness was linked to social power (Bederman, 1995). In other words, manly power was confirmed through white racial supremacy. In the ideology and practices of the slavery discourse, James Messerschmidt notes that "the master-slave relation constructed a masculine power hierarchy in which the 'white master' was the representative of hegemonic masculinity" (Messerschmidt, 1997, p. 17). At the top of this social hierarchy were propertied white males, and Patricia Hill Collins argues that they maintained privileged position through violence. In describing the development, nature, and—more important—the maintenance of this hierarchal system, she claims that "chattel slavery marked the emergence of a hegemonic White masculinity rooted in a dual relationship of the White gentleman/White lady . . . and in a racialized master/slave relationship." But Collins suggests that the use of violence:

> Laid the foundation for forms of masculinity that installed propertied White men at the top of the social hierarchy, Black men at the bottom, and landless working class White men somewhere in between. The ability of White men to whip and kill Black men at will and force them to witness violence against their female partners and children served not just as a tool of racial control, but violence also became deeply embedded in the very definition of masculinity. Because enslaved African men were denied the patriarchal power that came with family and property, they claimed other markers of masculinity, namely, sexual prowess and brute strength, . . . Black men were permitted dimensions of masculinity that most benefited Whites. (Collins, 2004, p. 58)

In a system such as slavery that was predicated on white male power, control, and dominance over others, the privileges derived from "patriarchal manhood" could not be realized by black men. Or, as Edward Blyden bluntly states, "the Negro can never attain in this country . . . true manhood" (Blyden, 1971, p. 12). Yet bell hooks points out, black men still "wanted to be recognized as 'men,' as patriarchs, by other men, including white men" (hooks, 2004, p. 7). And, even though denied access to white male privileges,

Booker contends that black men still accepted the dominant "values, standards, and behaviors" of hegemonic masculinity. But to what effect and at what cost?

In the imagining of white America, black men's inferiority could only result in anger. Born, presumably, of jealousy and envy, the angry-black-male persona is an expected character trait for African American men. This imagining of black male anger is not far removed from the reality of many black men's lives: for in the face of persistent poverty and a lack of meaningful employment opportunities, many are unable to fulfill the primary responsibility of patriarchal manhood. As Booker suggests, "the ability to earn a decent living . . . is seen as critical to the fulfillment of a man's responsibilities to his family and loved ones" (Booker, 2000, pp. ix–x). In other words, at the very least "real men" assume responsibility for the material well-being of the ones they love. In accepting this limited definition of manhood, bell hooks maintains that many black males "spend their lives feeling like a failure, feeling as though their self-esteem is assaulted and assailed on all sides, because they cannot acquire the means to fulfill this role" (hooks, 2004a, pp. 85–86). As a result, many black men are indeed angry.

African American men, however, are not the only ones to accept the legitimacy of patriarchal manhood and hegemonic masculinity, while denied meaningful access to privileged resources. In addition, many men, of all races, are angry. They are angry because, as Patricia Hill Collins points out, they uncritically accept ideas about gender that privilege the "masculinity of propertied, heterosexual white men as natural, normal, and beyond reproach. In this fashion, elite white men control the very definitions of masculinity:" they determine the standards by which to evaluate not only their own masculine identities, but also those of all other men, including African American men (Collins, 2004, p. 186). Most men in our society, not included in this select or "elite" group of white men, "are effectively othered and kept/put in their place."

Yet they are judged by patriarchal and hegemonic standards nonetheless, whereupon subordinated and marginalized masculinities are appraised and valued by how closely they replicate dominant social norms. One resource readily available to the majority of men, regardless of race and class differences, allows them to assert their manliness within acceptable standards—violence. In this context, anger becomes useful to the social and cultural reproduction of patriarchal manhood and hegemonic masculinity itself. Male anger is *sometimes* performed through violence.

In the absence of other resources, many men rely heavily upon violence for achieving manhood privileges. Messerschmidt believes that men use any resource at their disposal to communicate masculinity, and "violence serves as a suitable resource for constructing masculinity" (Messerschmidt, 1997, p. 12).

For some, violence is an authentic expression of manhood expected as a rite of passage for boys to become men. In other words, masculine authenticity is affirmed through violence: that is, violence becomes one of the simplest ways of doing masculinity, of expressing manhood "rights," and of asserting male power, control, and dominance over others—especially over lesser men and weaker women and children. bell hooks contends that all men know this: "As a consequence all men . . . must demonstrate at some point in their lives that they are capable of being violent" (hooks, 2004a, p. 49).

Black men are no exception. They are not somehow exempted from this social process of knowing that has come to shape their socialization into manhood culture. Within and against social and cultural constraints, black men too draw upon the resources available to construct their own particular version of manhood, and for some anger and its engendered violence are part of that construction as they uncritically seek the power, privileges, and legitimacy of masculinity.

But what of the angry-black-male persona? Where does it fit within the overall context of what it means to be black-and-male in American society? I believe this image signifies a gender allegiance with white patriarchal manhood and hegemonic masculinity; some degree of violence is expected in the on-going social and cultural construction of becoming a man, regardless of race.

Yet the accompanied narrative of this image reinforces a critical racial difference between white and black men. Occupying the bottom rung of the masculine hierarchy, black masculinity is marginalized and in many ways excluded. As a result, African American men are rendered as less than human, a fundamental difference that affirms the animal-like qualities of black men. They are seen as immune to feelings of pain, fear, remorse, and compassion, especially in the context of their experiences of violence, although pain, fear, remorse, and compassion are considered quintessential qualities that separate human beings from other animals; these qualities allow for asserting one's humanity. But they are not manly qualities that are revered in the dominant and highly stylized discourse of patriarchal manhood and hegemonic masculinity.

African American men face a false dilemma that has very real implications for their lives. Within and against cultural and social constraints, they must decide whether they will claim their humanity and define for themselves what it means to be a man. Making this claim within dominant normative constraints often calls into question their "true" manhood. Conversely, they must claim their masculinity as defined within established standards as they seek manhood privileges. Yet, they are inhibited from making such a claim and seeking such privileges, for they are black. It is difficult for them to position themselves solidly in one way or another within the context of racial discrimination and gender oppression where—ironically—both carry rejection. The reality that challenges black male life, reveals this dilemma as it enters their experiences so early, so uninvited, and so relentlessly. For some, anger and the accompanying violence shape their ways of doing masculinity. This dilemma is clearly reflected in the experiences of the men I interviewed.

John grew up in a conventional household where his father was the head of the family. Following his mother's death, at the age of six, John's father became a strict "disciplinarian" as well as a "functioning alcoholic," who beat him almost daily. His father would "hit him with anything he could get his hands on." Becoming almost immune to physical pain, but not to the anger it engendered, John adopts the persona of a tough boy, an acceptable image for a boy to mask his feelings. He engaged in constant fights with neighborhood children as a way to mitigate the pain and frustration of his childhood. While Bobby, a middle child, grew up in an all-female household, where his mother forbid him from hitting his sisters, even if they hit him, which his oldest sister did with pleasure. Under her guidance, his mother also told him that "the next time you come into the house crying over being beat-up I'm going to beat you up. You better use whatever you have to defend yourself" against the neighborhood boys. At an early age, Bobby took his anger out on the football gridiron, where his violence and aggression were not only accepted, but valorized to the extent that his prowess and proficiency enabled him to become a celebrated high school athlete.

Sometimes the anger and violence the men experience were deeply personal and uninvited. Daniel's parents separated. On New Year's Eve, they attempted to reconcile. While taking a drive to talk things over, Daniel's father shot his mother five times and then threw her from the car. Upon hearing of the shooting, Daniel went in search of his father to kill him. He found him lying in a pool of blood in their home, with a gun shot wound to the head. Daniel took his anger, walked out of the house, and did not tell a soul that his father was dead on the kitchen floor. And Richard, as a seven-year-old child, watched as his mother stab a neighbor in the heart with an ice pick, for which she served ten years in prison. In her absence and his family's deepening poverty, at the age of thirteen Richard took to the streets carrying only his anger, pain, fear, and self-destruction with him.

The anger and violence the men experienced was physical, personal, and socially unrelenting. Each man, from childhood to adulthood, followed his own particular path in seeking to meet the social expectations for hegemonic manhood or rejecting its obligations altogether. Whether they attempted to conform to type or rebel against it, their actions occurred within and against social constraints that intruded upon their sense of human worth. This intrusion into their lives constructed a race and gender dynamic that was not only historically rooted but also socially unavoidable; anger and violence played a critical role. As both individuals and as a group, the men experienced the effects of Jim Crow segregation and school desegregation, the civil rights and Black Power movements, and the Vietnam War. But education, fatherhood, marriage, work, along with male alliance, spirituality, and of course sexuality were also important parts of their construction of manhood, for which structural constraints intruded and shaped each particular experience of what it means to be black-and-male in America.

HISTORICAL PROCESSES

Through life history interviews, *Through Our Eyes* seeks to understand the meaning that is given to the men's experiences, as they engage their cultural and social world. Toward this end, this book explores the significance of race, gender, and violence in shaping their experiences by posing the following questions:

1. How has violence shaped their physical, personal, and social experiences, from childhood through adult maturity?
2. How have they interpreted and what meaning did they give to the different dimensions of those experiences, over time?
3. In what ways have those interpretations and that meaning changed or remained the same?
4. How have those interpretations and that meaning influenced their views of self, over the course of their lives?

In seeking answers, this book focuses on the ways the men's experiences are created and recreated through their interactions with their social and cultural environments and what happens as a result. It draws on the theoretical perspective that reality is constructed through the knowledge gained from social and cultural interactions (Berger & Luckmann, 1966). In other words, actions have meaning. As a heuristic approach, this perspective allows me to recognize that the men's interactions occur within and against broad historical processes. These processes, in turn, shape the social conditions and cultural practices under which they live and by which meaning is given to the specific ways they experience race, gender, and violence. Or, as Teresa De Lauretis suggests, the men's experiences are created by their "subjective engagement in the practices, discourses, and institutions that lend significance to the events of the world" (De Lauretis, 1984).

Simply stated, through the process of living, the men engage the conditions and practices of everyday life. Their interactions construct meaning about the world, and that meaning holds important consequences for how they see themselves as African American men. From this perspective several important underlying assumptions guide the development of this book.

African American men come to know their experiences through the different cultural and social locations they occupy in society (Mendieta, 2003).

Positionality gives texture and shape to black men's lived experiences. This refers to not just the different roles and statuses they acquire, such as husbands, fathers, and workers, although this is implied. Rather, it importantly refers to the position they occupy under different cultural and social arrangements that are created by historical circumstances. Among the more significant influences positioning black men's interactions are race, gender, and violence. These influences have histories, and black men's interactions do not occur in isolation or outside of that history. Instead, their interactions are forged within and against social conditions and cultural practices formed by that history.

The ways African American men are positioned in their interactions reflect relations of power (Foucault, 1980).

Relations of power are seen as the "politics of everyday life" where social conditions and cultural practices create inequality that produces disparities in opportunities. This inequality constrains on black men's human needs and aspirations. The dimensions of power that they encounter circulate through hierarchical social relations, but power also circulates through physical and personal relations as well. These relations of power intersect (Crenshaw, 1994). As a result, physical, personal, and social relations reflect how black men engage their everyday environments as well as reflect the different dimensions of their sense of personhood.

Uneven relations of power create conflict between agency and that of social and cultural constraints.

The historical influences of race, gender, and violence are critical markers of difference. That difference is created and mediated through uneven relations of power: the unevenness of power that black men experience through their social and cultural interactions constrains their needs and aspirations. However, those constraints are not absolute; for within and against constraints, black men assert agency, which here refers to what they feel, think, and do, especially in those interactions that threaten, jeopardize, and compromise their sense of personhood. Even as they assert agency, black men are neither totally helpless nor fully autonomous. They are neither passive victims, which implies "the one-way exercise of power, harm without strength," nor are they solely agents exercising free will over their lives in the absence of constraints, which suggest "freedom from victimization"

(Mahoney, 1994). Rather, both dimensions are present as black men engage their social and cultural world.

When agency and social and cultural constraints are in conflict, sometimes violence occurs. African American men experience violence as a violation to their physical, personal, and social sense of personhood. These dimensions are reflected in the degrees of disrespect or moral indignation they experience.

Social philosopher Axel Honneth's analysis of the relationship between "disrespect and human integrity" is useful to an understanding of how violation evolves, circulates, and changes in black men's experiences of violence. As such, the nature of "disrespect and human integrity" is also useful for understanding how African American men interpret and what meaning they give to their experiences of violence: interpretation and meaning have implications for how they see themselves. Basic to Honneth's argument is that we implicitly owe our integrity to the respect we receive from others. He argues that "individuals who see themselves as victims of moral maltreatment" assign meaning to such treatment that reveals the degree of insult and disvalue, which are related forms of disrespect (Honneth, 1995). Honneth contends the significance of this disrespect:

> Characterizes a form of behavior which does not represent an injustice solely because it constrains the subjects in their freedom from action or does them harm. Rather, such behavior is injurious because it impairs these persons in their positive understanding of self—an understanding acquired by intersubjective means. There could be no meaningful use whatsoever of the concepts of "disrespect" or "insult" were it not for the implicit reference to a subject's claim to be granted recognition by others. (Honneth, 1995, p. 249)

In considering how disrespect affects human worth, Honneth has identified three areas that are injurious to the physical, personal, and social self. The first type of disrespect pertains to physical integrity, where the body is injured. For him, physical maltreatment represents disrespect whenever the body is controlled against one's will; regardless of the intent, humiliation and shame occur. It is not the "raw pain experienced by the body"; rather, the "coupling of this pain with the feeling of being defenseless" has a "destructive impact on an individual's practical relationship to self" (Honneth, 1995, p. 250).

The second area of disrespect is personal and affects a person's "normative understanding of self." Honneth positions this form of disrespect in the context of structural exclusion "from the possession of certain rights" as a member within a given community or society. This kind of disrespect is "typified by the denial of rights or by social ostracism, thus it lies not solely in the comparative restriction of personal autonomy, but in the combination of these restrictions with the feeling that the subject lacks the status of a full-fledged partner in interaction who possesses equal moral rights" (Honneth, 1995, p. 250).

And, the last area is a social disrespect that entails "negative consequences for the social value of individuals or groups." Social disrespect, denigrating "individual or collective lifestyles," is signified by "the degree of social acceptance." The downgrading of "forms of life and convictions as being inferior or deficient" robs individual and groups of "every opportunity to accord social value to their abilities." This "devaluation" is depriving of social recognition, depriving of worth and esteem (Honneth, 1995, pp. 251–252).

These theoretical assumptions provide depth to an understanding of how African American men interpret and give meaning to their particular experiences. They allow me to recognize the importance of their sense of violation in the context of violence while bridging the gaps between the local events that occur in their lives and the larger social and cultural context in which those events are constructed. The degree of disrespect engendered becomes a significant marker for understanding how the men interpret and what meaning they give to their lived experiences. In detail, this book focuses on three overlapping areas that threaten, jeopardize, and compromise African American men's sense of personhood: violations to the physical self that demeans the integrity of the body; violations to the personal self that disregards individual human worth; and violations to the social self that systematically devalue the individual as reflected in a collective or group experience. Whether occurring together or separately, these dimensions of violation in the context of their experiences of violence can and do evolve from black men's direct interactions: interactions they witness or interactions that occur through their instigation or own volition. All of these interactions constitute their lived experiences.

INTERSECTING HISTORIES

Through Our Eyes is about history. It is about the social and cultural history imposed on what it means to be black-and-male in American society. But, more important, it is about the individual history the men make as they struggle to give meaning to their identity as black men. Therefore, life history, as a research method, is a useful device for capturing what happens at critical phases in the men's lives and how both continuity is maintained and change evolves as they engage social conditions and cultural practices shaping the events of the world.

In saying this, I recognize that I, as a black woman and social researcher, also play a role in that history. I entered the men's lives; I assumed a responsibility in framing and retelling their individual and collective histories. I am thus obligated to frame and tell with the same sense of dignity and integrity

their stories demand. Yet, amidst my professional responsibility and obligation, my interactions with the men posed significant intellectual, political, and
personal challenges.

What is intellectually attractive to me about life history interviews is
that the method allows individuals to interpret their own stories. The meaning given is noted in the feelings, thoughts, and actions provided. In other
words, the men told me what they wanted me to know on their own terms.
I was ever mindful of their experiences. My challenge was to note not only
those experiences that they own but also those experiences that they disown
and even those experiences that assumed ownership over them. I assumed
accuracy and accepted the veracity of their interpretations as provided.

Intellectually, I knew that I must try to set aside moral judgment, even
though judgment could never be completely suspended. This notion of
judgment introduced a political challenge: after working, thinking, and writing about violence against women for more than twenty years, my views on
violence are well-formed. In detail, the men reflected on the "good, bad, ugly
and indifferent" parts of their lives. For some, their description of the use of
physical violence in particular proved to be a daunting and difficult task for
me in my role as a listener. I was both passive in listening to the details of their
encounters and aggressive in seeking to understand why they thought and
acted as they did. Personally, in that understanding, I was forced to reflect on
my own vulnerability as a black woman; they simultaneously considered their
own vulnerability as expressed by their pain, fear, and remorse as black men
telling their stories.

Initially some of the men were reluctant to share the intimacies and
details of their life histories. As they started to reflect on their lives, however,
they concluded that the "good, bad, ugly and indifferent" parts of their stories
were well worth sharing. Their desire to tell their stories gradually overshad-
owed any reluctance, for most of the men had simply never given voice or
told their side of the story before. As an African American woman, I was not
indifferent because we share similar racial references and experiences that
allowed for mutual trust. Again, that trust was rooted in the belief that
I would bring a similar sense of dignity and integrity to their particular stories,
as had been given to me.

The eight African American men whom I interviewed were not
randomly selected. I did not recruit from male-centered programs or organizations, which could influence how they referenced their experiences.
Rather, I recruited the men through informal networks. Although they were
recruited from two large cities most of the men were neither born nor raised
in those areas but migrated as adults. Initially, I recruited fifteen men. For
various self-defined reasons, only ten men actually completed the interview-
ing process, and data on two men proved insufficient and unusable. My study

did not actively recruit black men who fell within any predefined sociode-mographic category. Moreover, it did not exclude participation based on sociodemographic considerations.

There were only two selection criteria for participation. First, the men had to be at least forty years old. This particular population was selected because I believed that men of this age group are best able to offer reflective knowl-edge on their life experiences. Second, they must be willing participants—that is, willing to commit to a fifteen-hour interview schedule, where interviews were conducted for five, three-hour sessions, and tape recorded. Confidentiality was assured, and ethical research standards were adhered to as participation was strictly voluntary. To maintain that confidentiality and to ensure anonymity, all names, geographical locations, and any other markers of identity that appear in this book are fictitious.

An overall profile of the men reveals both similarities and differences among them. They ranged from forty-eight to sixty-five years of age. They were born and raised in three geographical areas: the Southeast, Northeast, and the Midwest and grew-up in small towns and urban centers.

All of the men identified themselves as heterosexual. At some point in their lives, six of the men were married. Currently, five of the men are mar-ried, two have been divorced and remarried, two are in relationships of three years or longer, and one is separated from his wife. Only one of the men did not have children, while the others had twenty-two children among them.

All of the men, at some point in their lives, attended college, and several attended vocational programs or received certification training along the way. One attended college for a year. Another has an associate degree. Two have bachelor of arts degrees. Two have master of arts degrees. And two have Ph.D.s. Their current professions include small business owner, therapist/counselor, college professor, community organizer, personal fitness instruc-tor, social worker, and building and/or housing manager. Financially, the men described their economic status in a variety of way that ranged from lower, middle, to upper middle class.

They identified their racial and cultural background as black and/or African American. Five of the men described themselves as dark brown skinned, while one identified as brown, and two identified themselves as light brown in skin complexion. Five of the men described their religious and spiritual orientation as Christian. Three indicated that they did not have a religious affiliation or affinity.

Only two of the men served in the U.S. military, and one received a dis-honorable discharge, but during their military service neither was placed in combat situations. All of the men, at some point in their lives, engaged in physical fights and altercations with others, either during childhood or as adults. Four of the men were never arrested for a crime. Of the four who were arrested at some point in their lives, one was never convicted of a crime, while three were convicted and sentenced to long periods of imprisonment for serious felony offensives.

PERSONAL HISTORIES

The men interviewed are a part of the baby boomer generation. They were born during the 1940s and 1950s, at a time when race, gender, and violence shaped as well as demarcated social and cultural relationships not only in America but also around the world. Through the men's eyes, through their interpretations and experiences, this book looks at how the world unfolds in the aftermath of World War II. It follows the men's on-going search to understand what it means to be black-and-male in America. Through their interpretations and lived experiences of childhood to that of adulthood, this book is divided into five chapters.

Chapter 1, "Little Men," provides a careful look at the men's early cultural and social development as boys growing up in their particular families against the backdrop of the postwar years. During that period, most of the men's fathers were returning veterans, either of World War II or the Korean War. Their fathers' presence or lack thereof played critical roles in shaping their sons' gender development and in constructing what it means to be a boy in the particular context of their lives. They all embraced no dominant or specific gender identity and role. Rather a multiplicity of identities ranged in posture from Tough Boys, to Manish Boys, to Weak Boys; physical, personal, and social violence was insinuated into their experiences. Each of those identities at difference times and in different ways imposed its own particular cultural and social meaning on their experiences. We see within and against that meaning how they gradually began to construct their own gender awareness of what it means to be a boy in a particular family and the interacting community.

Chapter 2, "The Souls of Black Boys," introduces the significance of race in shaping the men's developing identity as black boys at a time when the international community, led by the United States, affirmed the dignity and worth of all human beings. When, as boys, they venture beyond the familiarity of their home environment, early on they encountered cultural and social exclusion and marginalization based on race. In those encounters they experienced the Temptation of Hate, the Temptation of Despair, and the Temptation of Doubt, for which physical, personal, and especially social violence played critical roles in their lives. How they experienced those temptations provided a foundation for their gradual understanding of what it means to be a racialized self that lacks cultural and social worth, as in the embodiment of black boys. However, within and against that imposed meaning, we see how they are determined to know and give value, in whatever ways they can, to their own sense of self-worth.

Many of the gendered and racialized lessons the men learned as a result of their boyhood experiences traveled with them into "Manhood," chapter 3. Shadowed by the Cold War incursion into cultural and social life, the men come of age. As young men they sought freedom, self-determination, and independence: they wanted to exercise power, control, and dominance over their own lives. Their decisions and actions, however, brought them face-to-face with cultural and social expectations and rules of conformity for manhood. Faced with tensions, dilemmas, and contradictions, to varying degrees they acquiesced, manipulated, or resisted those expectations and rules. But more often they all participated somewhere in the vortex of adherence and avoidance as they pursued education, joined the military, joined street gangs, robbed for a living, played football, and became militants in asserting a black masculine stance; in all violence became increasingly instrumental to those endeavors. We see the consequences of what happened as a result of their decisions and actions to accept or avoid established expectations and rules of cultural and social conformity.

In chapter 4, "Imprisoned Manhood," I take a closer look at the consequences of Richard, Jamie, and Matt's nonconformist decisions and actions. Each served long-term prison sentences during a period when, belatedly the United States joined the international community as a signatory to the United Nation's International Covenant on Civil and Political Rights, which included provisions on the fundamental rights of prisoners. Richard's, Jamie's, and Matt's decisions and actions aggressively played into the well-worn stereotype of the criminal-black-male. In the pursuit of deviant behavior predicated on the workings of violence, each embraced the realities of Guns and Things, Murder and Things, and finally Prison and Things. By embracing those realities, they compromised their sense of humanity and were removed from society. Within and against their imprisonment, with critical reflection grounded in education, we gradually see a powerful transformation in the human spirit, whereby they learned to value the lives of others as they valued their own.

In chapter 5, "Manhood Rearticulated," the other men with considerable modifications, largely adhered to established expectations and rules of conformity. Each, in his own way reshaped those expectations and rules by asserting The Will to Learn, Learning to Love, Learning to Nurture, Learning to Go On, and Learning to Start Over. In that reshaping they minimized the possibilities or intentionally eschewed violence, especially in their personal lives. This, however, was at a time when the new conservative right put forth a bold and aggressive manhood stance, as symbolized by Ronald Reagan; this stance asserted power, control, and dominance in rearticulating U.S. foreign and domestic policy agenda. Similar to the experiences of Richard, Jamie, and Matt, gradually we see how the other men, even when their humanity is compromised, struggle to maintain a sense of self-worth.

In my conclusion, I offer an overall critique of the importance of race, gender, and violence in shaping the men's experiences over the course of their lives, in the current post-race, post-gender, and post-nonsense debate. At a critical moment in history when the first African American man, Barack Hussein Obama, is elected President of the United States.

AUTHOR'S NOTE ON THE TEXT
Introducing the Men

The following biographical sketches are designed to introduce the reader to the eight African American men whose narratives formed the basis for this study. Their names, references to others, and geographical locations have been changed to protect confidentiality and anonymity.

John

John, born in 1944, was the oldest of the interviewees. He was also the only man raised in the rural South under Jim Crow segregation. John's mother died when he was six years old, and his alcoholic father not only emotionally and financially denied him, even though they lived under the same roof, but also physically abused him. As a small child, John was forced to fend for himself, and he was quite industrious in doing so. When he was sixteen, he left home. While working a series of menial jobs, he decided to attend a local historically black college, where tuition was minimal. There he became active in the civil rights movement. Following his graduation from college he moved to New York City at the insistence of his brother. Again working a series of menial jobs, John finally got a low-level management position at a movie theater that allowed him to eventually build a successful professional career. In the meantime, he developed a family life that included two wives and four children, all of whom were girls. A single father, he raised his daughters, as he continued to embrace the importance of work, spirituality, and his African heritage in shaping the meaning of his life.

Richard

Richard was born in 1957, where he and his two sisters lived with their single mother in the housing projects. His mother worked as a domestic worker for a white family, but she also received welfare. Additionally, to make ends meet, his family held rent parties where people would pay to attend. One night following a party, Richard's mother stabbed a neighborhood in the heart with an ice pick, and killed him. She was convicted of murder, and Richard was forced at the age of seven to largely fend for himself and his sisters. That fateful night and the violence it engendered led Richard down a destructive path where he committed murder. Through his long prison experience, Richard gradually regained a sense of his own humanity. To give meaning to his life, Richard works tirelessly as a counselor, primarily with African American men, in his attempts to help them find meaning in their lives.

Thomas

Thomas was born in 1946, and for eleven years grew up as an only child in a racially diverse urban community in Chicago with his mother. Later they were joined by his step-father and brothers. During childhood, Thomas attended predominantly white public schools. Through his school experience he learned what it meant to be a black boy in white society. But through his interactions with black men, particularly in his church and at a youth center, he learned what it meant to be a black boy in the community of African American men. Following high school, Thomas attended a church-based community college in California and, as a leader of the black student union, eagerly participated in the black power movement of the period. Through that activism, Thomas found his passion for black politics. Homesick, he dropped out of college and returned to Chicago because all he wanted to do with his life was work in the black community. For forty years he did just that, as a single black man, who never married or had children.

Jamie

Jamie, born in 1963, was the youngest of the interviewees. As an only child of a single mother, he grew up in the housing projects of Minneapolis. His mother placed a priority on education, and he was a bright child who excelled academically. By the time he reached high school, there was a dramatic change in Jamie's behavior. Because of the excitement and particularly the danger of living in the projects, he joined a local street gang, where in his own words he became "buck wild." Jamie's behavior took him down a destructive path, where he eventually committed murder. At twenty years of age, he was convicted to a sentence of twenty-five years to life in a maximum security prison. Initially, Jamie readily embraced prison culture as a way of simply surviving. But in his maturity, basic survival was not enough; he wanted something more and took advantage of the limited opportunities that were available. Through aggressively pursuing education, he began to transform his life. In that transformation, on a daily basis Jamie reminded himself of the life he had taken. This is a transformation in process, where he is "constantly working to make myself better."

Matt

Matt, born in 1959, grew up in a family that was constantly on the move. His parents were in business together. As an event promoter, Matt described his father as a "hustler and player," and his mother as a singer. As a young child, Matt and his sisters moved from city to city with their parents as they promoted their business. Finally, his mother decided to leave Matt's father, and she took with her the children. She struggled to make ends meet as a single mother, and Matt saw himself as the man of this all female family, until his mother married George, a wounded army veteran, whom Matt hated because he fashioned himself as a "hustler and player." His mother sent him to live with his uncles in Chicago, where Matt was introduced to and became a member of Folk Nation, a street gang. Returning to live with his mother in Baltimore, he dropped out of high school at seventeen years of age and joined the army. After completing basic training, where he excelled, Matt was stationed at an army based in California. There, with time on his hands, he interacted with the local "hustlers and players" and became a pimp. Leaving the army and California, he returned to Baltimore, where he became a robber. On one fateful night, Matt and his gang killed a white patron and wounded another at a restaurant, for which Matt received two life sentences in prison. After seventeen years, ten months, and ten days he was released. Walking away from prison, Matt carried with him a sense of empowerment built around education that he now shares with others as a college professor.

Daniel

Daniel was born in 1951, in the South. When his father returned from the army his family moved to the Midwest where he grew up. Especially close to his mother, Daniel saw his father as distant and formal, but both of his parents prioritized education. Daniel excelled as a student/athlete. His father demanded control over the family, and he used violence against Daniel and his mother to maintain it. There was a series of separations and reunions between his parents, but the last attempt to reunite resulted in his mother struggling to survive gunshot wounds and his father lying dead on the kitchen floor. From that trauma, Daniel moved on with his life where he became an engineer and later a highly successful businessman, but through it all he had difficulties in "connecting" with others, particularly women, outside of his immediate family. With his mother's help, at the age of forty Daniel got married, and through his relationship with his wife and young son he has learned a new meaning for manhood.

Bobby

Bobby was born in 1960 and grew up in an all-female household with his mother and two sisters. He described his mother as "distant, cold, and mean"; his older sister by eleven months was a "bully, mean, and a pain in the behind"; and his younger sister was a "sweetheart." Growing up in public housing, because he was small in statute, Bobby was constantly bullied and beaten by the other children in the projects. This continued until his mother took the family to live with her parents. There he was determined to change the way that he looked and started lifting weights. As he got "bigger and stronger" he found his passion, football. It became a consuming interest that dominated his life, and he excelled as a star high school player. But his football future abruptly ended when he injured his knee, an injury that had a lasting effect as Bobby struggled to redefine his life.

Robert

Robert was born in 1954, as the youngest of nine children in a large blended family. He was doted upon and made to feel special, but that sense of specialness did not extend to his interactions in public school. There, because of a reading disability, he felt less competent than the other children. Later, because of the constant bullying, he felt fearful. After finding a knife in his belongings, Robert's mother decided to enroll him in parochial school, where his grades improved and he began to excel in sports. When he entered his dream college, Robert saw himself as a student/athlete and eagerly pursued both. In college he quickly learned that there was an advantage to being a recognized athlete on campus, especially with girls. Robert had a serious relationship with a white woman. She became pregnant, but her decision to have an abortion placed a strain on their relationship, which ended. From this devastating experience, Robert turned his attention to his studies. As the first member of his family to earn a college degree, it reaffirmed to him that he was indeed college material and pursued graduate education as a result, where he eventually received a Ph.D. His studies and volunteer work introduced him to the issue of men and violence, an introduction that shaped his research and clinical experience as a college professor and later his experience as a husband and father.

CHAPTER 1

Little Men

WAR

During the 1940s, the profundity of race, gender, and violence occupied a worldwide stage as man's inhumanity to man was once again on full display. The world was in the grips of the Greatest War: The contested terrain was no less than global domination, for ideas of racial superiority and hegemonic manhood were vested in the strength of nation-states to employ ruthless and murderous violence. As the United States sought to defend the virtues of democracy over totalitarianism by winning the war against fascism and a new world order, Americans were summoned to wage an international battle for equality of opportunity, freedom, and justice.

From the beginning of unrest in post–World War I Europe, blacks in the United States followed closely and noted the rise of fascism, especially in Germany. During the 1936 Olympic Games, Hitler quickly left the Olympic Stadium to avoid shaking Jesse Owens's hand after he won four gold medals in track events. And the superiority of Aryan manhood took another symbolic blow in 1938, when Joe Louis knocked out German Max Schmeling to regain the world heavyweight boxing title. Beyond symbolism, blacks understood all too well what was at stake. Fascism was spreading by invasion and occupation throughout Europe and Asia, and the strategic importance of Africa could hold the key to international dominance. In 1941, the Japanese attack on the U.S. naval base at Pearl Harbor engaged the United States fully in the Second World War, and blacks eagerly threw their support behind the global struggle for equality, freedom, and justice. Blacks, however, first had to wage that struggle against Jim Crow segregation and discrimination at home.

Immediately, blacks found their support of the war effort marginalized and largely excluded. Entrenched and persistent racial segregation barred blacks from taking full advantage of employment opportunities—except for the most menial of jobs—in both the industries that manufactured war materials and the armed forces. Responding to this blatant racism, A. Philip Randolph, president of the first black labor union, the Brotherhood of Sleeping Car Porters, and Bayard Rustin, a political activist and founding member of the Congress of Racial Equality (CORE), issued a call for blacks to March on Washington, D.C. Randolph argued vehemently that democracy in America was an utter failure. He pointed out that blacks were "flogged by Jim Crow and lynching; disfranchised by poll taxes and white primaries; suffocated by 'goodwill and a white God;' and impoverished by 'charity,' when all they wanted was equality—social, political, religious, and economic equality" (Anderson, 2003, pp. 8–9). Under the slogan "We Are Americans Too," Randolph delivered a keynote address at a conference held by the March organizers:

> There must be no dual standards of justice, no dual rights, privileges, duties or responsibilities of citizenship. No dual forms of freedom . . . Our goals include the abolition of discrimination, segregation, and Jim Crow in the Government, the Army, Navy, Air Corps, U.S. Marine, Coast Guard, Women's Auxiliary Army Corps and the Waves, and defense industries . . . We want the full works of citizenship with no reservations. We will accept nothing less. (Randolph, 1941)

In the face of growing black anger, resentment, and frustration President Roosevelt acknowledged the political difficulties and hypocrisy of maintaining America's rigid system of racial oppression at home while challenging racial bigotry and injustice aboard. In his attempts to also appease southern white legislators, whose support he needed in Congress to fund the war effort, Roosevelt walked a carefully constructed tightrope as he addressed "the Negro dilemma." To minimize the obvious hypocrisy, Roosevelt appeared to have capitulated to the demands of March organizers, who threatened to bring 100,000 blacks to the "White House lawn." Reluctantly, Roosevelt signed Executive Order 8802, which declared: "There shall be no discrimination in the employment of workers in defense industries and in Government, because of race, creed, color, or national origin." This was the first presidential directive on race since Reconstruction, and it established the Fair Employment Practice Committee (FEPC) to monitor discriminatory practices within all national defense work. This directive, however, offered limited enforcement powers. Racism in both the war industries and the U.S. military persisted, for this antidiscrimination directive did not extend to the armed forces, which remained largely racially segregated for most of World War II.

THE AFTERMATH OF WAR

In the aftermath of the Second World War, more than 50 million people lay dead, white male hegemonic power was realigned in the world, and the struggle for "equality of opportunity, freedom, and justice" by black Americans gained new urgency. The men of this book inherited this history, as their lives began to take shape in the postwar years of the 1940s and 1950s.

Within and against this social history, these men as children gradually began to carve out space for their personal histories to emerge. But they initially occupied the environments in which they were born—the family. In those family environments their lives gradually formed, and essential to their development was an understanding of what it meant to be a boy, to have a gendered identity, especially in each particular household. Often, such meaning was accompanied by violence.

The social and cultural context of the men's early childhood lives varied, as their parents made the transition from the immediacy of the war to the postwar years. During the war, many black fathers served in the military, and for those who were married, during their absence wives provided financial support for the family, often as domestic workers. Following the war, their parents—as either individuals or married couples—migrated from various parts of the South to different areas of the industrial Northeast and Midwest. They searched for nonrestrictive job opportunities and a better quality of life. Settling into new ways of daily life, they welcomed change in the postwar climate that allowed them to envision greater possibilities for themselves. But they also recognized a continuity with the past that staked a claim to the possibilities they envisioned, thereby limiting real opportunities. In this climate filled with increased hopes and dreams, the recasting of old social and cultural constraints limited "equality of opportunity, freedom and justice." Into this world of both possibilities and limitations parents gave what guidance they had to give to their sons.

Like all children, this new generation of boys was susceptible to their parents' wills. They were neither "good" nor "bad" mothers or fathers. Instead, their parents made good and bad decisions within the context of their own lives; these decisions, thus, shaped their personal adequacies and inadequacies as parents. In other words, they were simply human: each possessed strengths, weaknesses, and contradictions deeply rooted in the social and cultural realities of their lives. At times their parents were loving, sacrificing, and indulging; at other times, they were cruel, selfish, and unforgiving toward their sons' growing needs and aspirations. The men as children stepped into their parents lived realities. Those realities, in turn, reflect the different circumstances in which each of the men would grow up.

Significant differences in family structure and economic condition among the men's early experiences contextualize each of their childhoods. Within and against social and cultural expectations that were predicated on patriarchal norms of the 1940s and 1950s, some of the men as children grew up in conventional two-parent households. Others grew up in single-parent households. Some were raised under the watchful eyes of close family members, but several, forced by circumstances, largely raised themselves. At certain points in their early lives, a combination of some, or even all, of these different structures of family involvement readily played roles in their childhood experiences. Despite the particular structure, the material conditions under which the family functioned exerted a tremendous impact on their survival. While growing up, most of the men found the necessities readily available: food, clothing, and shelter were more than adequate to meet their basic material needs. Some men, however, experienced the ravages of deep poverty: food, clothing, and shelter were scarce commodities as they moved through childhood.

Differences in family structure and economic condition are critical to position each of the men's individual childhood experiences. Although important, those socio-demographic differences provide only a partial reference for understanding what happened in the men's early lives. To fully appreciate the complexities of their experiences, we must recognize the common grounds in their early lives. Simply stated, they were all boys growing up in black families. Their racial identity in the context of everyday family dynamics, albeit important, for now is of lesser concern to their early childhood development. Within the family their gender identity became the more salient feature that influenced how they began to see themselves—as boys. Gender identity embodies meaning rooted in social and cultural expectations of masculinity: those expectations linked the boys' individual differences to a collective reality. Within and against the meaning given, they struggled to develop a sense of their own self-worth as they engaged the particular dilemmas, tensions, and contradictions of their parents' personal lives.

Their awareness of what it means to be a boy gradually developed over time. But what role did violence play in shaping their early gender identity in their family interactions? How did they come to see themselves, as a result of those dynamics? And, vulnerable to both broad and particular cultural and social influences shaping that identity, who took their hand and guided them through the uncertain and sometimes treacherous terrain of boyhood? With a social, cultural, and personal history awaiting their arrival, the men as children stepped into the world. This chapter follows some of men's early childhood experiences as each began to gradually understand the meaning of their lives as boys growing up in their particular family, during the aftermath of World War II in the 1940s and 1950s.

TOUGH BOYS

Born in 1942, John was the only man interviewed who grew up in the rural South. He was born in Albany, Georgia, while his father was serving in the army and stationed in Africa. John's mother was forty-two years old when he, the youngest of her six children, was born to his family of a brother and four sisters who were already teenagers or young adults. During his early childhood, John does not remember his father but recalls a close and loving relationship with his mother, who called him "my little lamb." His mother spent little time with either him or his siblings, for the family depended on her income during this period. She worked as a domestic worker, a maid, where she "cooked and cleaned house" for a white family. Although his mother was not a live-in maid, John said that "she didn't have days off, she worked seven days a week." He remembers that she "would go to work before sunrise and would take the bus early in the morning." On her way to work, she dropped off John at his grandmother's house, where he stayed until one of his siblings picked him up after school. John's mother relied on his older brother, but especially his sisters to take care of the household while she worked. They lived in a three-room house: "a living room, which was the bedroom where we slept, a bedroom which was my mother and father's room, and a kitchen and a bathroom." As John said, "we had a very clean house even though we were all on top of each other." The children were responsible for keeping the house clean and orderly. John's chore was to pol-ish the furniture, and he "polished the legs of the dinner table and the bottom parts of the chairs every Saturday."

In John's family, "Saturday was spent on cleaning, and Sunday was spent going to church." Like several of men interviewed, attending Sunday church services was an expected part of their family life, and, for most, it was not an option. From this early introduction, the church and the accompanying spir-ituality played a major role in the men's adult lives as well. As John said:

We started in the morning going to Sunday school which was like 9:00 a.m., and we would come back home and then go to the 11:00 a.m. service. The 11:00 a.m. service went to 1:00 p.m. We would come back home, and then we had to go to evening service and after that we went to BIPU, which was a young people's organization at the church. The whole day was spent in church. The whole community did this. It wasn't that we went to church and nobody else did. Everybody in the commu-nity went to church. We went to a Baptist Church.

The family's financial dependence on their mother's income changed when his father returned from the army. Until John was five years old he had no memory of his father. But he does, however, remember the exact day his father came home. Waiting with his mother at the bus station, John recalls most vividly that he was dressed in a little army uniform his mother had made especially for him.

John's father had been a private in the army, and as an infantryman spent most of his time in Guinea: "He was in Africa, and he brought back pictures of him being in Guinea with some of the natives in Africa. But he never talked about his experiences because he got injured. He had shrapnel in his body from a hand grenade. He used to dream about it; he had bad, really bad nightmares. He used to wake up screaming at night. But he never talked about what happened."

Upon his homecoming, John's father immediately assumed his role as head of the family and resumed the expected financial responsibility. He went to work at a local lumber mill as a crane operator, where he moved large piles of wood from one place to another or placed them directly on trucks. His father "would go to work and stay all day. There was no union or anything, so he just worked from morning to night."

Meanwhile, John's mother quit her job, and the family relied on his father's income for support. The war had taken a serious toll on his father, and John's mother soon realized the uncertainty in being financially dependent on her husband. John's father had started drinking a lot, primarily on the weekends. He drank "moonshine, and stayed out all night on the weekend, but would come home early Monday morning so he could go to work." His mother knew that he was a functioning alcoholic so she made adjustments. John said: "I used to have to go on payday with my sister to pick up my father's pay before he got it. We would have to go to the shop; they would give us his pay, and we would bring it back to my mother."

As the youngest, John really had no concerns because he felt loved and protected, especially by his mother. She made him feel special; she doted on him. But major changes started to occur in their relationship. His mother's health began to rapidly decline. She developed a serious heart condition—"she had a hole in her heart"—and became bedridden. John entertained her and tried to make her laugh: "I used to tell my mother jokes, and I remember how loud she used to laugh. Some of those jokes had cuss words in them. She used to say 'you can tell me a joke but you better not cuss when you tell it.'" In addition to telling childish jokes, John also did what he could to ease her pain. He said: "my mother used to say that I had 'healing hands.' She used to always love for me to rub or scratch her back because she just couldn't do it. And I would always do it." John adored his mother, and his experience strongly suggests that she shared his love and devotion. Her illness made him extremely fearful, and even as a small child he fully recognized the uncertainty of what could happen to him if she died:

> I would wake up in the middle of the night because I would hear her moaning and for me that was really scary because I used to always wonder if my mother died what was I going to do. I knew that she was sick. I knew that she was in pain, but I was just afraid that she was going to die. I was afraid of being alone. I knew that my father didn't care for me. I just knew that if my mother died I was going to be alone, and eventually that's what happened.

When John was six, his mother died. Soon thereafter, his relationship with his father took an ominous turn. Shortly after his mother's death, his father began to drink more and started to beat John.

> My father would physically hurt me. My father would hit me with any-thing he could get his hands on, for no other reason than him being drunk. That's what the whippings were about. He hit me with sticks, razor straps, anything for any reasons. He left marks and burns on me. Nobody said anything. He didn't beat my sisters and brother. I think he beat me because maybe I was so close to my mother; or maybe because the other children were bigger and would rebel or wouldn't accept it. I didn't rebel, how do you? I was young, and there was no rebelling against him. I was taught that you had to honor your parents. He used to beat me, it seem, everyday. He drank everyday, he would beat me every-day. It was at the point where he didn't listen to anybody. He didn't listen to his mother, who was my grandmother. He had power over me. And when he felt like displaying his power, he did.

For some unknown reason, John's father seemed to resent him, a feeling that, even as an adult, John has never understood and finds impossible to explain. This resentment is evidenced by and revealed in John's interaction with his father. Later, as we will see, his father's resentment turns into what John describes and his experience suggests are physical and psychological "child abuse."

How would John cope with his mother's death and father's violent behavior? He retreated into silence. With a sense of being desperately alone, he goes about the business of becoming a boy. His growing and unexpressed anger toward his father guides him, as he gradually learns that being physi-cally abusive and violent are norms of masculinity, lessons that shape for him the meaning of being a boy. Childhood violence—especially fighting other boys—becomes an integral part of that meaning. John adopts a tough boy persona. His demeanor communicates to others a sense of emotional detach-ment, particularly in situations that threaten his self-worth and safety. Such a tough boy persona enables John to become more self-reliant. Although this persona masks John's feelings of fear, pain, and loneliness, it does shape his perception of self: he sees himself as immune to the violence of others yet capable of rendering violence himself. John's self-perception is meaningful, for it is crucial to his survival: he must prove to himself that, against the odds, he can survive largely on his own, especially while living under his father's roof. It is a difficult test because John must survive absent not only emotional attachment from his father but also basic material comforts such as food and clothing.

John is not the only man interviewed whose father became extremely abusive toward him early in childhood. That violence had a profound impact not only in shaping childhood experiences but also in perceiving themselves. For example, Daniel's deeply troubled relationship with his father was similarly defined by violence.

Daniel was born in 1951, in the rural South: Atwood, Alabama. His mother, having dropped out of high school, was only sixteen years old when Daniel was born, and eighteen when his younger brother arrived. As the oldest child, Daniel describes his early relationship with his mother as a "classic nurturing relationship. It was great. I loved her a lot and felt loved by her." But this affection did not extend to his father, with whom he had limited contact at the time. When Daniel was born, his mother and father were not married, and, during the early years of his life, Daniel's father served in the army and stationed in Germany.

Daniel recalls his early years living among a "community of women" who made him feel special. He remembers "all these young women who were my mother friends," and his "other mothers, their sisters and daughters," always doted on him. His first real memories of significant people in his life are those of his "amazing grandmother and grandfather," whom he called Madear and granddaddy Frank. Until about the age of four, Daniel, his younger brother, and his mother lived with his maternal grandparents in a two-bedroom house.

Of his large extended family, Madear and granddaddy Frank had the largest presence in his life. He describes his grandmother as having a "big personality" and also having "a pistol on the dresser because she didn't take any mess." Madear, a domestic worker, "cleaned people's homes and cooked." He describes granddaddy Frank as a "gentle giant who didn't talk a lot." His grandfather worked as a handyman on a local farm. At this point Daniel begins to notice white people; specifically he began to notice his grandparents' demeanor in the presence of whites. Although his grandparents loomed large in his early life, as a child Daniel simply could not understand why they became small people when they were around whites:

> My grandfather was really a gentle and quiet man, but he was different around these white people that he worked with. My childhood recollection was about size. How big someone feels to you. That's what I had a sense of. When my grandfather was around white folks he seemed smaller. And my grandmother was confident. But when we would go downtown in Atwood and she would interact with white people, she was somehow not as strong. There was this difference. But I didn't know what that difference was that made them somehow shrink around white folks. But there was definitely a difference.

That difference in public demeanor did not extend, however, to the privacy of their home, where Daniel recalls that his grandparents, especially Madear, took up a lot of space. So much space that, it appeared to him, little "space" was left for his mother to occupy. He speculated that his mother may have appeared small because his grandparents saw and treated her as a child. Not only were they displeased that at sixteen and unmarried she started having children, but, to complicate the matter even more, they, especially Madear, did not like her grandchildren's father. After completing high school, Daniel's father joined the army and left this young mother largely dependent on her parents to help raise two small boys. Madear's attitude was obvious to Daniel, even at an early age: Madear "never liked my father and she was clear about that. She didn't want them to be together. She said my 'father was an asshole.' She would say as much to him and to anyone who would listen."

Around the age of four, a major change occurred in Daniel's life. His mother became pregnant with her third son by his father. Soon, thereafter, for reasons unknown to Daniel, the immediate family leaves the South and moves to Indianapolis to stay with his father's brother. Daniel's mother and his brothers lived with his aunt and uncle for almost a year. Then, his father "gets out of the military and we get our own place." Immediately, his father assumed financial responsibility for the family. Daniel remembers that his father always "had a job. It was always something with cars and mechanical things. He was definitely talented with cars, building, and driving them. Even as a young child I remember him really enjoying driving fast."

Daniel describes his father as "distant and formal." His father did not want his mother to "work outside of the home." Instead, her job was to stay at home and care for the three small boys. As the oldest, Daniel was expected to help his mother, abide by rules his parents had established, and do the usual childhood chores (making sure toys were put away after playing, watching out for his younger brothers, and helping in the kitchen). Moreover, there were also clear rules about being respectful to adults: "I never called anyone by their first name. If adults were around, I wasn't supposed to be in the conversation, but go in my room and play."

As the man of the house, Daniel's demanding father exerted his control over the family. During this period, Daniel's life and memories of his father began to crystallize. His father's rigid nature, attitude, and behavior introduced "real stress" into family life. Upon reflection, however, Daniel believes that the reason for all the rules—the codes of conduct that he was to follow—"was not to create issues or problems for my father. That's what the rules were for." When Daniel broke the rules, usually his father administered punishment. For major violations, corporal punishment (beatings) was the usual method of discipline; his father used his hands to hit Daniel either "on the butt or back of the head." Even though Daniel received "spanking" from his mother, being hit by his father had a very different feel and effect on him.

At this point in Daniel's young life he started to become "very aware of violence," an awareness highly influenced by his experience; in turn, his experiences began to shape his perception of self. In response to his father's violence, Daniel adopted a defiant stance. No matter the severity of the punishment rendered, intuitively, Daniel refused to cry. As he said, "I was committed to not crying. I did have a sense of myself as the center of this universe, and I believed at that moment there was something special about me that I wouldn't let him take from me. I was tough."

Even though Daniel saw himself as tough, he used this emotional mask to minimize pain, fear, and vulnerability. As a child, he was more than capable of being physically and psychologically wounded. He was neither impervious to physical pain nor unaffected by the verbal abuse—"shaming, belittling, and emotional abuse"—that accompanied the beatings he received from his father. Yet, his increased awareness of violence was not based solely on the corporal punishment and/or verbal abuse he received from his father; it was also influenced by the physical violence and the verbal abuse—fighting and arguing—occurring between his mother and father, at the time. Daniel said:

> At five and six, I don't know exactly why at this point, maybe it is just really clear, but I'm very aware of the violence between them. I saw my mother get hit and lots of arguing. And my earliest real feeling was anger at my father. So I told my uncle. I said David (an interesting side note is that I never called my father anything but his first name) beat up mama and that is wrong. That's a problem. Can you do something? What I remember even then was my uncle's anxiousness about it. The first time I brought it up he was really quiet. He didn't have much to say, and it was very disappointing: which is interesting, because in my child brain, I was thinking if someone beat up my little brother, then I would have to do something. I understood my role with my little brother; this is obviously your role too.

As a little boy, Daniel knew all too well that he was too small to either stop or confront his father's violent behavior. The adult males around him, particularly his uncle on whom he depended, did nothing as well. Thus, in this environment of adult complicity and tolerance, his father's violence dominated the family dynamics. In other words, violence in Daniel's household became so normalized that Daniel could not avoid the important messages. Through his father's behavior, he gradually learned the lessons of patriarchal manhood: men assert their will over women and children, and violence can be an important resource for so doing.

As he went about the daily routine of learning and adopting the patriarchal expectations and behaviors of boyhood, beneath the surface, Daniel's increasing anger and resentment toward his father's violent behavior slowly simmers. That violence eventually defined their relationship. Although this is a meaningful realization, it is even more noteworthy that in Daniel's growing awareness he did not come to value that violence; in fact, in his adult life, he consciously tried to distance himself from violence. But as a child, the violence continued to exert a defining presence in his young life.

In both Daniel's and John's early experiences, their fathers modeled a manhood stance whereby dominance and control over women and children through violence was the norm in their families, although that sense of male power was largely restricted to their own households. Their sons noted those lessons, and even in their immaturity they could reasonably surmise from their fathers' behavior that being a man had something to do with being violent. Their tough boy persona did not shield them from the reality this imposed. Similar to John's experience with his father, the physical and psychological violence in Daniel's life as he grew older gradually became worse in both its frequency and magnitude. Violence became a norm that structured the boys' troublesome relationships with their fathers, but there was a critical and fateful difference. Throughout Daniel's youth that violence set in motion a destructive chain of events that ultimately turned deadly during his adolescence.

MAN-ISH BOYS

Richard was born in 1955 and grew up in Newark, New Jersey. His parents migrated from Jackson, South Carolina: "They weren't married before they came. I believe they got married as a result of my mother being pregnant with my older sister." Richard lived with his mother and older and younger sisters in public housing, the projects. When they first moved north his father was in the army, where he fought in combat missions during both World War II and the Korean War. Even after his father was discharged from the army, Richard did not spend "quality time" with him:

> I can't say that I really knew my dad as far as who he was and what made him tick. We didn't spend a lot of quality time together. He was a very amusing person who spoke several languages. But my dad during that time didn't spend a lot of time at home. From what I understand he was quite a ladies man and he had a serious drinking problem. I don't know exactly what his issues were at the time, and I didn't understand the effects the war had on him.

This limited interaction with his father led to an emotional estrangement between father and son. When he was about five years old, that distance became permanent because Richard's parents separated. Even so, as the middle child and the only boy in the family at the time, his mother made him feel special. Richard adored his mother and describes her as "very loving, quiet, nurturing, and a calm woman." He said, "I always wanted all of my mother's attention. I guess all kids do, but I would manipulate to get the most attention from her."

After his father left, the family started to have severe financial problems. Although his father contributed sporadically to the household, to make financial ends meet his mother took a job as a domestic worker for a white family in New York City. She "went to work five days a week and what she did was cook and clean." While his mother worked, Richard and his two sisters were left under the watchful eyes of the "matriarch of our family," his maternal grandmother, who lived nearby. He described his grandmother as "a very stern woman, but she showed loved": "She made sure everyone in the family was really taken care of. Something wasn't going right, call grandma. She would make the final decision on everything. She was a lot of fun. If she told you to do something it would be in your best interest to do it."

When Richard's "father stopped making contributions to the household," his grandmother "chipped in and helped us along." But grandmother's financial contributions were not enough to help sustain the family. In addition to working as a maid, his mother decided to go on welfare. As Richard said, "the job and then welfare was how we were able to barely get by and sustain ourselves." Being on welfare was an intrusive ordeal, to which his family had to adjust to receive benefits and maintain eligibility. Richard described what happened during this period:

> Back then if you were on welfare and if you had appliances or anything like that it would show that you didn't need welfare. Because you were living beyond that status of whatever they had in place. I remember the case worker, who was always a white woman, would come over and mama would let us know most of the time. We would take the television and take the food and hide it over to Mrs. Darlene's house. The caseworker would inspect the house. Check out the rooms and see what's in the closet. She would ask my mother questions: "you sure there's no man living here?" Any items that may have looked new, "where did you get this from? How can you afford it?" My mother was fine. She was beyond being humble. "Yes ma'am, no ma'am," just playing the game until the woman leaves. And then we would go and get our stuff from Mrs. Darlene.

Even as the family struggled to get by on welfare and the meager earnings his mother made from working as a maid, as a child, Richard enjoyed his family life. He knew that they were poor, but this did not stop the family from having fun. He said his "mother used to do things that felt really special." Sometimes the family went to the movies:

> We used to always go and see the King Kong movies. She would fry chicken and put it in her pocketbook. Basically we were pretty poor at that time. I just figured everybody's mom did that, and if they didn't, shame on them. We would be in the movie theatre, and people had pop-corn, and we had chicken. That was really cool. Sometimes she would even get Kool-Aid in. I don't know how, but we would just sit there and enjoy the movie. Sometimes they had matinee where we would see two or three movies for one price.

At other times, Richard's mother would take the family on a day outing into Manhattan:

> We would go on discovery time. Let's go discover. We would walk to Central Park. We would go there and feed the pigeons. She would point out different kinds of trees to us and the lake. She would make everything an adventure. We would go to Harlem, and she would tell us about history. We had fish and chips at the Muslim restaurant. I remember meeting Gordon Parks there when I was about five years old, but I didn't have a clue who he was. I remember her taking us to Staten Island on a couple of occasions. We would ride the ferry, a big ship, and we would pretend it was taking us around the world.

For Richard, these outings with his mother and sisters were indeed special occasions. Yet, abruptly, they ended.

Money was an ever-pressing need for the family. Both his mother and his grandmother were quite resourceful in figuring out how to make financial ends meet. They started to have "rent parties," where they would charge people to attend to help defray household expenses. For Richard, these par-ties were "always about we're going to make some money: we're going to sell some food, sell some drinks, and play some cards. It was always about trying to make some extra money."

One night his mother's youngest sister, who was sixteen and lived with her mother (Richard's grandmother), attended the rent party. At that party, "there was this older guy, a married man, that lived across the hall from us and she was over there." After the party was over, Richard's grandmother sent his mother to get her sister. But his mother and the guy got into "a big argu-ment." Richard described what happened next:

> My mother was telling him this is my little sister: that she's too young for him. That she shouldn't be over here, and you shouldn't be messing with

her. My grandmother tried to calm things down. She (grandmother) went to her house and my aunt Marie stayed with us. Later on that morning, probably about 3:00 a.m., the guy from across the hall was banging on the door and calling my mother crazy names. He banged so loud, he woke the whole house up. So my mother opens the door. She said, "Leroy go home, you're drunk." He reached through the door, grabbed my mother by the throat and started choking her. She told us (Richard and his two sisters) go into the bedroom room and we did. You could see this guy's hands through the door. Our kitchen was right here and this is the front door right here. And there's a drawer that she kept knives and forks in. This guy is choking her. My mother reached in the drawer, and all I heard him say was I will be back. I don't know what exactly happened, but I found out later she stabbed him. She grabbed the first thing she could put her hand on, which was an ice pick, and she stabbed him in the chest with it. He went home. About two hours after that the police came knocking. They came in and said "the man next door came over here and somebody stabbed him. He's dead." So my mother said you (Richard and his two sisters) all go in the bedroom. And my aunt Marie screamed, "You killed him!"

At the age of seven, Richard's mother killed the neighbor, and the police arrested her on murder charges. This incident and the intervening circumstances surrounding it irreparably changed the trajectory of Richard's life. As an adult, he continues to have vivid memories of and reflects on what happened that fateful night. As a child, however, Richard only knew "that a real bad thing had happened." He lacked the maturity or the words "to really express myself the way I wanted to about what happened." He felt a profound sense of "loneliness for my mother." Confused and afraid by what was happening, desperation and isolation begin to grip Richard's young life. That desperation and isolation, in turn, began to manifest itself into feelings of "anger and hatred"; therefore, during this early period in his life, Richard "stopped trusting people at all."

The only boy in the family at the time, Richard was extremely protective of his sisters, even though he wanted to run away following his mother's arrest. From somewhere, he had acquired the belief that it was his responsibility as the boy in the family to take care of his sisters, during this period of family crisis. Richard assumed the role of a little man: thus, he "needed to do something to get us out of this situation. I felt like I had to do some adult things for us to survive. I had to take responsibility. I felt no one could tell me anything at that time. I got to do what I got to do." Shielded by distrust and armed with anger and hatred, lacking guidance, at the age of seven, Richard set about doing what he needed to do to simply survive.

Until this point, Richard had been a little boy. But violence and its destructive nature insinuate themselves into his early life and strip him of his childhood. Violence produced an indelible presence in his life: It transformed who he was becoming and how he viewed himself, not only as a child but also through adolescence and adult life. Forced by circumstances beyond his control, as a boy of seven, Richard becomes a little man. As a child he lacks maturity and is ill-equipped for the responsibility he wants to assume. Consequently, he draws upon the only resource readily available for expressing his little man persona—violence. Richard is not the only man interviewed who became deeply scarred by early violence as he struggled to understand what it meant to be a boy in the family. The absence of a father's influence largely shaped that meaning for Richard. He was left to his own devices to figure it out: distrust, anger, and violence became important parts of the meaning he developed.

Similarly, other men had fathers who were largely absent for much of their childhood. Consequently, like Richard, they sought other models in whom they could readily observe the meaning of masculinity. For some boys, those role models may not have been traditional in the context of patriarchal and hegemonic masculine norms, but the lessons they learned nonetheless provided alternative routes to the more conventional paths of achieving an effective manhood stance. Such models provided an influential presence in the men's young lives. Although non-normative in these models of doing masculinity violence provide critical links in the varied approaches to establishing manly presence.

Matt is introduced at an early age to and later seduced by a different model of masculinity. Born in Milwaukee, Wisconsin, in 1955, he described his family as "nontraditional." His father, a sergeant first class in the army, fought in Africa and Europe during World War II; as a result of combat related injuries he was discharged from the army as a disabled war veteran. Matt's father was fifteen years older than his mother. His parents grew up in the same community. Years later, after returning from the war, his father began to notice Matt's mother with interest. They were married, and his parents started a business as "event promoters"; his father promoted entertainment acts for local venues, and his mother sang rhythm and blues. Their business venture required extensive travel around the country, and they took their young children on the road with them while they managed, pursued, and promoted entertainment opportunities.

In terms of personality and behavior, Matt describes his father as a "hustler and player." This description implies a self-presentation rooted in a lifestyle that apparently opposes patriarchal demands and expectations and relies instead on both legal and illegal risk-taking behaviors to assert greater control over life and livelihood. At some point, Matt's mother tired of the uncertainty and the relentless gamesmanship required to maintain the family's lifestyle. On reflection, Matt thinks that she "got burned out from all of that hanging out with my father. She had had her fill with singing. She wanted a different life." So his mother left "my father, and instead of going back to Milwaukee she moved to Baltimore" and took the children with her. Following that move, Matt does not recall exactly when his mother went to college, but she did, even though "she didn't really complete her bachelor degree." She acquired "skills" through which she was able to get a job at a hospital as a medical secretary. Although she worked full-time, as the sole provider of the family, it was still difficult for Matt's mother to make financial ends meet, and the family moved constantly from one neighborhood to another.

Early on, Matt remembers the family living "basically in a studio apartment: I remember us being in the bedroom looking at television as kids and mama would be on the couch sleeping." Even as his mother struggled financially Matt, nonetheless, describes this period in his young life as "a good time for us. It was peaceful. As kids everything we needed, we got. Mama had a job, a pretty good job for a single black woman at that time, and she could pay her bills, and we all had clothes. I recognized that we did a lot better and were a lot better off than a lot of people around us, that was clear." During this period, Matt was around six years of age. As the only boy in the family at the time, he felt protective of his mother and sisters and began to see himself as a little man in the family:

> My relationship with all my sisters was good. We used to fight like sisters and brothers do, but growing up I was always the big brother. At that point, yeah I was definitely protective of her and my sisters to the degree that I understood what that meant. You know, I don't know where I got that from. But I was protective, yes, yes very protective. I felt like a man, if that makes sense. I mean, I felt like a male child. I felt like a little man. I don't ever remember feeling like a little boy—definitely male-ish— I felt masculine. You know, within the environment it's me and my sisters and my mother, so I felt like I was the man of the house, and there were certain things that I was supposed to do.

Taking on what he viewed as manly responsibilities, in the absence of maturity, shaped how Matt interacted with not only his family but also outsiders. Matt's parents got divorced when he was around seven, and about that time "a lot of stuff starts to happen."

One significant thing that occurred was that "this guy comes by to see my mother, and it was George." Matt said: "I remember the first time I met him. It was at the apartment. What stands out about that meeting is that I didn't like him. It's because as a young man you're not my father—you're just this guy." George had come over to the house to pick Matt's mother up so they could go and visit one of his relatives in the hospital. Matt wanted to go with them, but his mother said "no." And George asked, "Why won't you let the boy go?" Matt did not view George's question as supportive; rather, he "was offended by him suggesting that I should do something that mama said I shouldn't do."

This seemingly minor incident set the tone for Matt's contentious relationship and future interaction with George. Shortly after their introduction, George moves into the house with Matt's mother and the family. With another man in the household, even at a young age Matt refuses to relinquish his self-awareness—of being a little man—by becoming small and childlike in the presence of George's adult maturity. This was fairly easy for Matt to accomplish because he did not respect George, who had been in the Navy, fought in the Korean War, and received "some kind of injury. So, even though he had moved in, he wasn't always there, because he had to go back and forth to the VA hospital. This guy was literally in the hospital a lot." On those occasions when he was not admitted to the hospital, George did not assume financial responsibility for or contribute money to the upkeep of the family. Matt considered George to be a "player"—that is, "I'm talking about guys who conned people out of their money. I'm talking about guys who were pimps. I'm talking about guys who were not necessarily players but because they had the gift of gab they would play for a place to stay; they would and find them a meal ticket."

During this period, Matt's mother continued to work full-time, and he recalls that she was going through a lot of "stress," both personal and financial. When George received "his check at the first of the month" from the veteran administration for combat disability, "he was like I'm going to go out and play with the girls and basically give his money away. Then he'd come home, and he'd be broke and that put us as a family in a bad situation." Matt's mother "was still working, but her bills were greater because now that she has this grown man and when he gets his money he disappears for two or three days and comes back when he has none and wants money for cigarettes and all the other shit, so we had to move around a lot because we can't pay our bills."

George "drank a lot," but, in retrospect, Matt does not think that he was an alcoholic. "No because when he didn't have money, he didn't drink, and he wasn't stressing a lot." But he does think that George was a "player" and presented himself to the community as such: "In terms of black men in the black community and how they demonstrate their manhood. I'm looking sharp, I got some money in my pocket, and put on some nice clothes and going to shave, going to get my hair done, my shoes are going to be shining, and I'm going to hang out with the other players."

George and Matt's mother got married, early in their relationship. Prior to George becoming his step-father, "My father shows up so that put a twist on a lot of stuff within a short period of time." His father's brief appearance was yet another notable and quite eventful period in Matt's young life. When Matt was only eight years old, his father "came to town [and] he asked mama to go out with him and she did." They went to a night club, and Matt believed that his parents made an effort to renew their relationship. But something happened while they were at the club, and Matt is still not exactly sure what occurred. Whatever happened that night, Matt surmises, "brought back memories" for his mother: she did not want that lifestyle anymore, and "she had an option because George was still there."

After Matt's mother rejected his father, he still "wanted me to hang out with him, so I did." Matt and his father stayed in room at the Belleclaire Motel, where "At that particular time, it's where girls were turning tricks. It's where the hustlers, the players, the pimps, the murderers, the robbers, the dope dealers, the users, and everybody hung out at. You had the Belleclaire Motel, but you also had a club, the Belle Lounge." During his stay at the Belleclaire, at eight years of age, Matt had his first sexual experience. He described what happened: he said his father and a friend were going to the Belle Lounge, and he asked this "girl to baby sit me."

> One thing leads to another and she's got my penis in her mouth, and there're two other girls there. I remember them laughing; that kind of shit. And I remember my father coming back, with his boys, his guys, and there's a discussion about what happened. The girls are laughing, and the guys are laughing. And one of the guys said to the girl "give him some money." And she gave me some money. These are pimps and players and whatnot. I can recall thinking I was going to get in trouble when my father came back. I can recall embarrassment. But nothing happened; they just laughed.

Seeing his father as a "hustler and a player," on reflection Matt said of that time: "He used me, and I can say now he used me as a prop in some of his scams. He recounted an incident during his father's visit:

> I'm hanging out with him and he's hustling. Even back then I recognized what was going on. I remember us going to get something to eat and coming back out and sitting in the car, and we took a nap, we went to sleep. And when we woke up, I remember us riding, and we ended up at a church rectory. He gets out and goes in and when he comes back out he has this white guy who's a priest with him. He introduces me and then they go back in. He comes back out sometime later and he has a white envelope, and I recognize that it had money in it because you know as a kid you're curious. I still didn't know for sure, but I knew something was going on. Even then I recognized something was happening.

In addition to his father's transactions, Matt was also taking note of his father's "interaction with other men," and it made an impression. His father "hung out" with "hustlers and gamblers and all of that; and that's what he was into. I'm talking about guys who owned hotels, motels, and clubs. These are the people that I got exposed to from my father." Matt took note of their style, their presentation of self—how they dressed, what cars they drove, how they talked, the confident ways in which they carried themselves and handled women. In this world of "hustlers and players," Matt was introduced to a way of doing masculinity that did not necessarily conform to patriarchal or hegemonic norms: manhood, in this instance, was not predicated on being either a responsible citizen or a good provider for family. Neither Matt's father nor step-father adhered to those fundamental expectations of manhood. Instead, both modeled the "hustler and player" identity. This identity is a different way of doing masculinity, but it is nonetheless linked to conventional manhood norms.

Matt learned the meaning and eventually embraced the identity of a "hustler and player." Violence connects this identity to the more conventional norms of manhood. In fulfilling the expectations associated with the role behaviors for a "hustler and player," inevitably violence comes into focus. This marginalized and subordinated masculine identity is predicated on the interactivity of violence; the use of power, control, and dominance—whether physical and/or psychological—define the qualities of a "hustler and player" lifestyle. During adolescence, Matt and several other men, raised with a masculinity according to the "hustler and player" norms, were lead down destructive paths that turns deadly. As an alternative approach, this path brought them face-to-face with not only the reality and consequences of rejecting the fundamental premise of established manhood standards but also the very real penalties imposed through social and cultural constraints.

WEAK BOYS

As the only male in his family, Bobby was clear about his identity as a boy. He understood what it means to be a boy from the rich and fertile ground of his family's interactions and experiences with neighborhood boys. He grew up in a single-parent household. Bobby, born in Philadelphia in 1958, lived with his mother and older and younger sisters. His family lived in public housing, The projects, where his mother had her own bedroom, and Bobby and his sisters shared a room: "I had my own bed and they had bunk beds." As the middle child surrounded by females, sex and gender differences were quite apparent to Bobby, even at a young age. He was different from his mother and sisters, and that difference shaped his interactions with them.

Bobby's mother was not a "nurturer." In fact, as a little boy he soon realized that she was distant, cold, and mean. He described his mother as "an evil ogre." "My mother made nothing easy for me! My mother beat me for exercise. She was evil, non-affectionate, non-nurturing, non-loving, or caring." To say the least, Bobby did not have a close relationship with his mother, but he also lacked a close relationship with his older sister, despite the mere eleven-month age difference between the siblings. Similar in personality to his mother, his older sister was "mean" and "a pain in the behind. She has been from day one and she still is." Overweight and physically the largest person in the household—for his mother was a small woman in stature and weight—Bobby's sister constantly hit or beat him:

> When she wanted to impose her will, she did it physically. She always beat me up. When she didn't get her way or when she wanted to enforce her way, because she was so much heavier. And I was programmed not to hit my sister. I recall being told by my mother "you're a boy, you're not supposed to hit girls, and you're not supposed to be aggressive." I took it to heart. I recall my mother saying something about being nice, being mannerable and respectful. I wasn't supposed to hit my sister. Even if there were times where I may have responded, my retaliation was met with greater force from my sister. And I would end up being the one hurt and crying.

The only person in Bobby's household in whom he took pleasure was his younger sister. Two years younger in age, he called her a "real sweetheart." According to Bobby, "She was calm and confident without being, like my older sister, arrogant—unjustifiably arrogant. When I was younger the main reason that I liked my little sister better was because she was my younger sister; she was always sweet in her demeanor and in her words. She always took the non-aggressive and less confrontation approach. "During his early years, there was no male present in Bobby's household to whom he could turn for guidance. Vaguely, he remembered his father while growing up: "I don't recall my father ever being in the household, where he would come home like a daddy is supposed to come home at the end of the day." Except for the time when he woke up in the middle of the night and found his father sleeping beside him, Bobby does not recall his father actually ever being in the house largely because he was an alcoholic. Bobby said that his father "was a full fledged alcoholic doing everything that alcoholics did—drinking, smoking, hanging out, and womanizing." As a child, Bobby knew little of his father, except his alcoholism and his army service. His parents were divorced when he was a little boy.

Upon later reflection on the family's dynamics, Bobby believes that his mother was indifferent and mean because "she was hurting. She was probably hurting because she had these children at a time when she wasn't ready. And had an irresponsible, alcoholic father to these children that she couldn't do anything about." His mother was saddled with three young children to feed, clothes, and shelter. Bobby was not exactly sure what she did to make financial ends meet, for when he was younger she was not working. When he was about five, he recalled "going to the line where you get the government cheese: It was in the projects. I stood in line, got the government cheese and some other stuff, and then brought it back to her. So maybe that's was part of what was going on at the time."

With a mother and older sister who physically beat him at will, Bobby did not see his home as either comforting or safe. By no means was it a refuge in which he could express his needs and aspirations, and in his neighborhood streets he did not fare any better. When he left his home and entered the streets of his public housing neighborhood, Bobby found "concrete and dirt where grass should have been; just concrete across the street and concrete to the right and left of me." But he also found other children. When he ventured out with his sisters, children from the projects took to calling them "Martians." For Bobby this meant that "we were different, that we were weaker, and that we were inferior somehow." This was not simply name-calling. There were implications: "It got to the point where they would not let us walk through the front door; we had to go through the back door" to get into their building. Describing himself as "very timid," when forced to go to the back of the building to get home, some neighborhood boys bullied and beat Bobby.

> I would have to fight, and I got beat up every time. They would really beat me up. They wouldn't beat my sister up. There was a reason for that. My sister was big. And even though those guys were tough, guys wouldn't really beat on girls. Girls came after girls and they didn't want to tangle with my sister because she beat them all the time. Even though I couldn't stand her, she defended me. She would step in. They just kind of beat me down until it got to the point where I would just walk around the back.

As a result of the bullying and beatings, Bobby said that "as a matter of fact I cried quite a bit." Although his older sister sometimes tried to defend him, his mother offered no sympathy for his plight. Yet, because of his mother, Bobby remembers the precise point in which he stopped crying after a fight. His mother sent him to the corner store to get milk and bread. "I came back home, and the milk was gone, and the bread was all smooshed up. I came back into the house crying and I told her what happened. She said, 'The next time you come in here crying over being beat up I'm going to beat you. When you get beat up you better use whatever you have to defend yourself.' After that my whole demeanor changed: I wasn't backing down and crying, and turning away."

Shortly after his mother had instructed Bobby to defend himself, he got into another fight. "There was one little boy who was trying to be with the tough guys. He was about my age. He was trying to be with the tough guys, and one day I just really got fed up with him. He was not one of these tough guys that can enforce his way. He's just hanging around them, trying to act like he was, and I just got fed up." Bobby decided that he was not going to take the boy's bullying anymore. As he said, "I'm feeling that I'm coming of age, I'm sick and tired of this—it's enough!" There was a "circle fight" between the two:

> The other kids formed a circle around you, and if you wanted to leave you can't leave. A circle fight is you ain't coming out until there's a clear winner. Somebody is going to have to submit, willfully or not. Mostly the older kids would eventually step in and stop it. However, they won't stop it until there was a significant amount of damage done. I got fed up with whatever he said, and I'm not going to take this anymore. A circle formed around us, and we started fighting and I just became somebody else. And I just tried to beat him into submission. I recall them pulling me off of him.

Early on, Bobby knew that physically he was a boy. Socially and culturally he learned what this meant, for that meaning was vested in the complex layers of his experiences: essential to his understanding were the various beatings he endured at the hands of his mother, older sister, and neighborhood boys. The patterns and stages of those beatings, and his own understanding and reactions to them provided a rite of passage in his developing self-awareness of masculinity. Physical aggression and violence took on an important role in that understanding. During his childhood, among his many "defining moments," Bobby instructively noted those instances when, for the last time, he was beaten by his mother, his older sister, and his childhood enemies.

Bobby grew up in a female-headed household where his father was largely absent from his life. On the surface, the mere composition of the family suggested that it fell outside of patriarchal and hegemonic family norms. But the actual family dynamics, based on Bobby's experiences, offer a different perspective to what was occurring in the household; again, violence played a significant role. Physical and emotional violence scarred Bobby: his experience suggests that early on this scarring was a result of the abuse he received from his mother and older sister. That abuse was rooted in the complicated and contradictory role that gender played in his household. Inside the home, his mother did not adhere to patriarchal and hegemonic norms of masculinity and did not tolerate Bobby's assertiveness and aggression in the house. Yet, she did expect for Bobby to "act like a boy," to comply with expected role behaviors outside the home. Contrary to logic, this contradictory message was by no means an antipatriarchal and hegemonic stance.

As a little boy, Bobby was expected to sort through the mixed or contradictory messages of what it means to be a young male surrounded by females. In the home, boyhood afforded no privileges. Bobby was expected to be nonassertive in addressing his needs and aspirations as well as nonaggressive in responding to his mother and sisters, despite their aggression toward him. To comply with established expectations for boyhood required that Bobby challenge the authority they assumed over him; but such challenge was apparently an unacceptable stance because he received only corporal punishment from his mother and beatings from his older sister.

It is difficult to discern whether his mother's and sister's attitudes and behaviors were rooted solely in rearticulated notions and norms of patriarchal and hegemonic dominance and control, for both facilitated Bobby's inability to conform to established role behaviors for a boy within the household. Perhaps their attitudes and behaviors toward Bobby were shaped by other influences altogether. Regardless, their vigorous attempts to maintain authority over him helped to shape what it meant for Bobby to be a boy in his family. That meaning was linked to violence through which Bobby saw himself as disvalued.

As a child, that disvalue extended beyond the home and was reflected in his peers' behavior toward him. In his neighborhood, Bobby was expected to behave in accordance with hegemonic norms. In the projects, Bobby was not respected by his male peers because he was not seen as a tough, strong, and independent boy. He was punished for their perception of him. They challenged Bobby's sense of boyhood through bullying and fist fights. In this childhood culture, only disrespect of others gains respect; intimidation and violence as well as retaliation and aggression in defense of one's personhood are expected role behavior for boys. His mother's harsh admonition about crying and defending himself, his sister's retaliation on his behalf, and the "circle fights" where he was forced to prove his worthiness evidenced this attitude.

Tears, avoidance, and allowing girls to fight his fights betrayed weakness in Bobby's childhood culture; all produced an enormous physical and psychological burden. Weakness is simply not an acceptable response for a boy, even a young boy, for it represents a lack of pride in and honor of the celebratory nature of who boys are supposed to be. Bobby's interactions with his mother, older sister, and neighborhood boys had a debilitating effect on how he saw himself as a boy. He came to believe that being physically big, strong, and muscular held the key to how he would not only change his image of self but also how he would garner the respect of others, especially his male peers. For Bobby his physique and physical prowess embodied masculinity. This physical change enabled him to offer a self-presentation, an image that unquestionably conveyed masculinity and manly strength to others. But this transformation occurred during adolescence when he finetunes his body and, as a result of his efforts, is rewarded by becoming a celebrated high school athlete. However, as a youngster, the violence continued to scar as beatings and emotional abuse at the hands of family members and neighborhood peers continued to bruise Bobby's young life.

CONCLUSION

This chapter introduces the dynamic family relations by which several men present early awareness of self and early ideas about what boyhood means begin to unfold. I focus here on the relations critical to the boys' early development and self-awareness. Families function in the broader social and cultural context of historical meaning; however, that meaning is actually experienced in the intimate space of personal life. As young boys they are absorbed into the many complex, individual layers of realities that shape the dilemmas, tensions, and contradictions of their parents' personal lives. Their experiences allow us to explore patterns of family interactions that are both similar to and different from one another. More important, the influences of gender and violence, shaping their varied realities, link those patterns.

In the family an early sense of self begins to emerge and forges identities. As children the men generally had affectionate relationships with their mothers. Some mothers offered a feeling of being "special" that helped to shape their early sense of self-worth. But it is unknown whether that sense of being special arose from their mothers' attempts to reinforce and bestow male privilege on their sons or whether they simply provided the care and nurture essential for the healthy well-being of their children. Regardless of the intent, as children the men display a general sense of being valued by their mothers and the other adult women in their families. Of course, Bobby's experience with his mother and sister offers a noted exception, given the particular gender dynamics at work in his household; as a result of his relationships with them, he developed an early sense of disvalue.

For several men, their fathers' early presence had an important effect on their socialization as boys within the family. Most of the boys were too young to fully appreciate their fathers' presence, until they returned from military service. We do not know the impact or effect that military service had on their fathers' lives or how they changed as a result. According to accounts, however, several fathers upon return, mostly from the army, were heavy drinkers or true alcoholics. Based on the men's accounts, their experiences suggest that their fathers played major roles in modeling a manhood that drew upon patriarchal and hegemonic norms of male behavior, even if it was unconventional.

By assuming authority over the family, their sons observed, internalized, and adopted core values that were associated with their fathers' particular way of doing masculinity in their household. A key observation that John and

Daniel could not help but readily recognize was their father's attempt to exert will over the family through the use of violence. For Matt this would be seen in his step-father's behavior. In chapter 2, I offer in greater detail the extent to which that violence was transformative in their early lives and the impact it had on their self-perceptions.

During their early childhood, the violence that the men experienced was physical in nature and accompanied by emotional wounding. From their families, they learned that being a boy was linked to violence. The resulting pain, frustration, and anger shaped both internal and external responses. Sometimes they adopted an image of self, such as tough boy or man-ish boy, a persona that allowed them either to feel good about themselves or to provide a minimal psychic defense protecting their senses of personhood when somehow threatened or jeopardized. At other times defenseless, they succumbed to pain, frustration, and anger. This often resulted in perceptions of weakness, disempowerment, and inadequacy that lead to compromised senses of self. Externally, they reproduced the model that they learned, and violence played a significant role. We now have a starting point for understanding how their childhoods began to influence the adults they became.

The boys readily found people to emulate in their neighborhoods—children and other adults alike, who taught what it meant to be a boy. Regardless of differences in geographical locations, all of the men grew up during the 1940s and 1950s, in predominately black working-class neighborhoods. As they began to venture beyond their homes and into the streets of their neighborhoods, they found excitement and fun as well as threats and dangers. And among the people with whom they would interact, they found different ways of being boys and men, of doing masculinity.

CHAPTER 2

The Souls of Black Boys

A DECLARATION OF HUMAN RIGHTS

In the aftermath of World War II, the genocidal atrocities that shocked the world led the Allied Powers of Great Britain, the Soviet Union, and the United States to form the United Nations (UN), a new organization dedicated to international freedom, justice, and peace. To represent U.S. interests, the Truman administration appointed Eleanor Roosevelt as UN delegate. Lending moral and political credibility to the position, she served as the first chairperson of the UN Commission on Human Rights, a body responsible for drafting an international declaration that affirmed basic human rights and fundamental freedoms. This declaration established moral principles that placed the value of life above all else.

After considerable debate among member states, the Universal Declaration of Human Rights was adopted in 1948. For the first time and unlike any other international agreement in existence, the Declaration recognized the inherent dignity and inalienable rights of all humanity. Roosevelt's commitment, guidance, and persistence were critical to bring this Declaration before a world body for approval. Her unquestionable leadership in this endeavor helped to position the United States as the moral leader of the "free" world. Yet hypocrisy cast a shadow over this well-meaning and unprecedented effort. Again, the ugliness of unbridled racism challenged the veracity of a U.S. claim to moral leadership.

While Eleanor Roosevelt was preparing the Declaration for consideration by member states, the National Association for the Advancement of Colored People (NAACP), under the crafty guidance of W.E.B. Du Bois, was busy preparing a petition for submission to the Commission on Human Rights. Du Bois meticulously documented the egregious abuses and injustices blacks were experiencing in the United States. Entitled "An Appeal to the World," the NAACP's petition was submitted for consideration to the Commission in 1947. It charged the United States with gross human rights abuses against Negroes and requested that the UN investigate its claims. As argued by Du Bois the petition noted: "There is a general agreement that the fundamental human rights which members of the United Nations are pledged to promote without distinction to race include education, employment, housing and health. And it is clear that the Negro in the United States is the victim of wide deprivation of each of these rights" (Anderson, 2006, Transcript of keynote address, p. 3). Because chairperson Eleanor Roosevelt, a "friend of Negroes" and a member of the NAACP board of directors, feared that the United States would succumb to international scrutiny and ridicule, she refused to allow the petition to be placed on the Commission's agenda for deliberation and action.

Excluding the NAACP's petition denied African Americans, at that time, an important opportunity "to articulate the struggle for black equality as a human rights issue" (Anderson, 2003, p. 276). In an international forum, the United States had once again actively intervened to marginalize the legitimacy of black grievances, and through this omission the country sent a message to the world that black life in America was insignificant. During this postwar period, racial segregation, discrimination, terrorism, and disfranchisement—accompanied by physical and personal violence—were taking an enormous toll on black life, as documented in the NAACP's petition. Even as the world was preparing to repudiate the "barbarous acts which have outraged the conscience of mankind," racism for many blacks continued to be a seemingly intractable yoke that shaped their daily existence. "African Americans were flogged by Jim Crow and lynching; disfranchised by poll taxes and white primaries; suffocated by 'goodwill and a white God;' and impoverished by 'charity,' when all they wanted was equality—social, political, religious, and economic equality (Anderson, 2003, pp. 8–9).

Eleanor Roosevelt used her moral and political prestige to get the United Nation to affirm the "dignity and worth" of all human beings, as inscribed in the Universal Declaration on Human Rights. And she used that same power to protect U.S. social and cultural interests in maintaining the rigid structures of racial polarization and inequality. But the world was changing: no longer reliant on the largess of friends, African Americans entered the dawn of the modern civil rights movement. Self-determined, they asserted their own right to dignity and worth, as they demanded "freedom, justice, and peace" in America.

As boys, the ensuing civil rights struggles set into motion a chain of events that influenced the trajectory of the lives of the men I interviewed. Moreover, the United States and the Soviet Union, no longer political Allies, entered a "Cold War" that also set into motion a series of international events, which later brought several of the men, as young adults, face-to-face with the dilemmas, tensions, and contradictions of war itself. Those domestic and international events provide both background and focus to the role that race played in how the men viewed themselves as both individuals and parts of a racialized whole.

THE VALUE OF BLACK BOYS' LIVES

The historical forces and events shaping the 1950s cast a shadow over the men's childhoods. As they went about the business of becoming boys, their experiences seemed far removed from the on-going struggles surrounding them, especially the civil rights movement initiated by blacks to realize their full human potential in the face of social and cultural constraints denying them that right. The movement's forces and events, though indirect, were no less effective, for they conveyed meaning about the value of their lives, as constructed by white society. As children, they too were a part of the black community, by racial and cultural affiliation: states denied basic human rights and fundamental freedoms, and the struggle for racial and social justice emanated. Thus, their particular and individualized stories are linked to a much larger historical narrative that chronicles the tensions, dilemmas, and contradictions of race relations in America society.

From the margins and through exclusion we began to understand what happens when large historical moments, formed on a worldwide stage, are played out in the everyday lives of black boys. They had no initial consciousness regarding political struggle, but as children they must grapple—to the extent that children can—with the realities that constructed meaning in their lived experiences. They either rebelled against that meaning or made compromises to it, as they sought to understand who they were as individuals and as part of a racialized group. Within this context the men assume a racial identity.

The importance of appearances based on perceived physical differences was often a difficult lesson for them to learn. To the world outside, as black boy, the meaning of perceived physical difference implied racial inferiority, either implicit or explicit. That racial meaning, however, did not necessarily extend to their home environment. In that environment, physical differences were significant to the construct of gender relations. As boys in their families there was no ambiguity; they knew all too well that they were physically different from girls. Even though different social and cultural expectations defined them as boys, that identity did not render them inferior, especially to girls. Blackness based on perceived difference in skin complexion and the social and cultural expectations that defined them as "colored" and/or "Negro," however, was another matter altogether. Initially, they did not know that by simply being born black, their lives held little value. An awareness of racial inferiority and its meaning was contrary to the image of self that was developed within their families.

As they ventured beyond boundaries of their homes and engaged in broader communities, they were no longer defined solely by their gender. Gradually, the boys acquired intersecting identities. They became black-and-boys, where their racial identity constructed a social and cultural lens that not only shaped how others saw them but also, more important, how they saw themselves. What does it mean to be a black boy in their communities? And what roles do gender and violence play in shaping their racial identity?

As W.E.B. Du Bois so keenly noted in *The Souls of Black Folk*: "This is the story of a human heart—the tale of a black boy who many long years ago began to struggle with life that he might know the world and know himself." In that struggle the men as boys confront three temptations: "the *temptation of Hate,* that stood out against the red dawn; the *temptation of Despair*, that darkened noonday; and the *temptation of Doubt*, that ever steals along with twilight" (Du Bois, 1989, p. 152). In confronting those temptations, family and neighborhood relations were ever-present and continued to shape their experiences. But, in their developing childhood maturity and independence, they began to engage the dilemmas, tensions, and contradictions of the broader community, for which the complicated intersection of race, gender, and violence played a critical role. Through those intersections they gradually learned the value of young-black-males in the eyes of both white and black America.

THE TEMPTATION OF HATE

After Richard's mother was arrested for murder, for stabbing a neighbor with an ice pick in the chest, anger and hate gradually began to grip his young life. At eight years of age he did not fully understand what was happening to his family, but he recognized that something serious was occurring. Richard looked to his grandmother for guidance, and she stepped in to assume responsibility for the three children following the arrest, but she was ill-equipped for the task at hand.

During the trial, his grandmother took Richard and his older sister to his mother's hearing. He wanted to testify on her behalf, to tell the judge that "it was true that my mother stabbed the man, but it was in self-defense." However, the "testimony of a child at that time was inadmissible." His mother was found guilty of murder, but her sentencing was delayed. Awaiting judgment, Richard and his sister visited his mother in jail, where she told them that they "needed to grow up really fast": "She explained to us that she was going away for a while. But it was really painful because I didn't understand. The big question was when are you coming home? Why are they holding you in this place? I didn't understand why she was in there. I felt bad. I don't remember being able to really express myself the way I wanted to." Richard's mother was sentenced to five years in a women's prison that was located two hours away from his home in Newark. Even though his grandmother took responsibility for the care and well-being of the children, Richard's family life began to quickly unravel following his mother's imprisonment. He realized that his grandmother "definitely had a drinking problem. She'd get drunk; mainly on the weekends. So we had to fend for ourselves." As his family drifted deeper into "real poverty," simply getting enough food to eat became a major concern for the children. Desperate, Richard started to take matters into his own hands, as he said: "Sometimes I would grab my siblings and we would steal meat from the market to survive."

Richard resented what was happening to his family, and increasingly he was learning the meaning of consuming anger and hate as a result: "I was filled with anger and hatred at that time, and I even remember going through this phase of blaming my mother for leaving us." Richard, conscious about what other people were saying about his family, started to take his resentment out on others. In his neighborhood it seemed as if "everybody in the projects knew and at school I can even remember hearing adults talking . . . they were 'saying be quiet because that's her son right there.'" Some children, however, were neither as mindful nor as hesitant in sharing their opinions about Richard's mother being in prison as the adults were in their reactions to the situation. When the children "started teasing, playing the dozens, and saying my mother was a convict," Richard responded by getting into fist fights: "Yes, I would get into fights with other kids or anybody who said anything about my mother or my siblings. 'You'll bums; you wear raggedy clothes.' That's not to say I won every fight because I lost a lot of them. But I just felt like we were going through enough to just let people antagonize us like that." Even with the upheaval in his family and the growing physical violence that he was engaging in, Richard was a good student. "I was an A student, but my behavior was horrible. I didn't care how I spoke to anybody; the teachers or the principal."

Although he continued to go to school, it was not a priority in his life. At the time, providing for his sisters and himself was his utmost concern. He started to work, shinning shoes and selling newspapers on the street corner, and there he began to notice the "hustlers and pimps" in the community:

Oh yes, at that time they were pretty easy to identify by the cars they drove and the way they dressed. I even knew a woman in the projects who had pimps. Some of the kids I grew up with, some of their mothers were prostitutes. I probably didn't have a name for it back then. We called them night ladies. But it was pretty evident what was going on. Bobby Bleau was a pimp that came from New Orleans. When he came it was like a caravan of cars, all these pimps and prostitutes. They had a pimp convention and a ball at the Paradise Hotel. I used to shine shoes in front of the Paradise Hotel.

Richard was changing. Not only was he stealing whatever he could get his hands on, but he also "started lying a lot because I felt I had to." He deeply resented being poor, "feeling less than," and the shame and humiliation that went with it. "So the stealing and lying continued for me because I wanted more. And I didn't want to be poor anymore." Initially, Richard's anger and hate stemmed from his sense of frustration and the utter powerlessness he felt in his inability to change the dire circumstances—the constant state of material need—under which he and his sisters were living. He was angry and filled with hate because:

> I associated a lot of pain in my life to being poor. If we weren't poor my mother wouldn't have been in jail if we could've afforded a lawyer. If we weren't poor, we wouldn't have gone nights without something to eat. We wouldn't have had those rent parties. We would have nice clothes like the other kids. To me poverty was really shaming. I wanted something. I wanted to have stuff like other people. I believed that I deserved more.

Roaming the streets of his community, Richard's anger and hate deepened with the realization that he was not simply poor; rather, he was black-and-poor. Race made a difference in how he was beginning to see himself. Richard "became mesmerized by all of the black people" he saw on the streets of Newark. He was especially impressed by those who stood on street corners and "talked to the community about what was going on in the world and what strong black men was supposed to do." One group was the Five Percent Nation; these people believed that 10 percent of the people of the world know the truth. Those elites keep 85 percent of the world in ignorance and under their control. The remaining 5 percent are those who know the truth and are determined to enlighten the rest. Richard thought the Five Percenters had a tremendous impact because they "used to tell us that we are black kings. So you felt a sense of pride in being black." Yet, Richard had to balance that growing sense of racial pride with his anger that sometimes when he entered white stores he was yelled at and called Nigger. "The store owners would call you Nigger just because it seemed like a good thing for them to say. 'What are you going to buy Nigger?'" The racial insults were not limited to white store owners.

As he moved within the broader Newark community he also encountered other white people, especially on the trains. Richard noted one particular incident during a train ride that occurred with a friend, when he was eleven years old:

> I had a friend, and we were riding the train one day. We were playing around the pole in the car and we were probably irritating them. This white guy said, "you porch monkeys need to sit down somewhere." My friend said, "what you say?" I said "come on man don't get in trouble." He said "that's right you little nigger take your porch monkey friend and sit down." He was turning red. I grabbed a hold of the pole and swung around and kicked him in face. The train stopped, and we ran off, laughing. That was probably the first time I retaliated. I felt like I had a victory.

This was by no means the last time Richard would use physical violence in retaliation to a sense of personal violation in the form of a racial insult, as evidenced by events in his adult life. But it is important to take note of this youthful hollow sense of "victory" that he felt from physically hurting another person. Richard learned that he was no longer powerless. He could exert power through violence: that knowledge became the lens through which he began to see the world and his place within it. From experience, physical violence—along with stealing and lying—became an integral part of the ways by which Richard would henceforth negotiate his life. Stealing, lying, and violence were readily available resources, for they only required Richard's desire to assert his will to get what he thought he needed, deserved, or simply wanted.

Those resources not only played a fundamental role in shaping Richard's life strategies for survival, but they also played a critical role in how he was beginning to interact with others as he moved through adolescence. After three years, Richard's mother was released from prison for good behavior. He believed that his life would change after his mother returned home. Or, as he said, "at least I wanted to believe that it was going to be a turning point." It did, in fact, prove a "turning point" in Richard's young life. The years that his mother had been away had taken a tremendous toll on him, and the lessons learned had become deeply rooted in his life. They were lessons, however, that his mother would not tolerate in her home, especially after she had become a dedicated Jehovah's Witness while in prison. But they proved essential lessons for living on the streets—for surviving on the streets of Newark when his mother kicked him out of the house—and Richard aggressively applied what he had started to learn at thirteen years of age.

Like Richard, the complex circumstances of several of the men's childhood lives made them vulnerable to the powerful emotional temptations of anger and hate. Those temptations were also readily available to John. Following his mother's early death, John relied on anger and hate as a way of expressing his grief, loneliness, and resentment over his profound loss. His anger and hate began early. On the night that his mother died, he remembers that "my aunt and uncle were there and they were arguing about something; I think that my uncle had been drinking." Resenting their lack of respect and reverence for the moment, at seven years of age, John took matters into his own hands:

> I remember that I pulled a knife on them. I was going to cut my uncle. I was going to cut him because he was arguing in my house and it upset my mother. My mother had been hollering at him to get out of her house. I pulled a knife on him and then I threw it at him. I almost hit him. I just didn't care. My mother was dying. She died that night. She died that night around 9:00 or 10:00.

Intuitively, John knew that following his mother's death, "my life was just going to be different. My mother was my protector, and I didn't think that anybody was ever going to protect me again." After she died, John became extremely angry. He said, "in a way I grieved to the point that I said that *I would never love any body again.* I said this to everybody, but mainly to myself. I said I will never feel this hurt again. I was very angry. I asked God why didn't he take my friends' mothers. Why my mother? I was real angry about that. For a while my anger consumed me and impacted everybody."

Following his mother's death, John's relationship with his father changed dramatically. During this period, his father quit his job at the lumber mill and "started drinking everyday because there was not structure." The more he drank the more physically and emotionally abusive he became toward John: "he drank everyday, and he would beat me everyday." Of his large family of siblings, the only person to whom John could turn to for help was his oldest sister. And he sought her refuge, but she was married and living away from the family home at the time. Furthermore, she worked full-time and could not provide him with the day-to-day care and especially the protection he needed. He had to get away from his father's abuse so John went to her house and sat on the front porch:

> I would go to her house, but there was no place for me to stay but on her front porch because I was too young to stay in the house by myself. So I would be on the porch the whole day. But that was her way of trying to keep me away from my father. She would give me fifty cent, so I could buy donuts and sodas and things. She was working like twelve and thirteen hours, so my whole day was spent with me on the porch.

Meanwhile, after his mother's death, John's other much older siblings began to gradually move away from the family home. With his father's unemployment, John's fear that there would be no one to take care and protect him became a harsh reality, for his father no longer provided for his immediate material needs. At eight years old, John started to take care of himself by selling "Jet and Ebony magazines, and I had a paper route." But his father stopped him. "So, then I started shinning shoes. A guy had opened a shoe shine place and I was shinning shoes on the weekends. There were people in the neighborhood who I would go to their house and shine their shoes and they would give me a dime to shine their shoes. I was making my own money. It was never beneath me to shine shoes": "You always got tips. And if you could shine shoes and pop the rag; if you could pop the rag and make it hum, guys used to love to hear that and they would give tips for that. I worked for a guy who had a shoe shine stand and he had about 10 boys working for him. I could shine two people shoes at a time and I was really fast, so I made a lot of money, and a lot of tips. I made enough money to buy my own clothes for school." As he moved within his segregated Albany neighborhood, John began to realize that he was tough and could withstand life's hardships, but he had to fight. John reflected on this part of his childhood: "When I was little I was really, really tough. I beat everybody in the neighborhood. I was just a tough little boy. Maybe, in thinking about it now, nobody could do anything worse to me than my father did." Not only did John fight the children in his neighborhood, he also "used to fight for them," especially children from outside of his neighborhood. Although his neighborhood was all black, whites lived only four blocks away, and the black and white children fought each other. From John's description it does not appear, at least on the surface, that those fights were rooted in racial animosity but rather in territorial or turf violations. Nonetheless, John started to carry a knife. He explained: "the first knife my father took from me was when I was about eleven, and I got another one. I always carried a knife. I was good with knives and I would cut you. I cut people in fights. If there was a neighborhood fight and I was a part of that I would cut you. I've seriously hurt someone, not kill anybody, but seriously hurt them."

John's neighborhood was tough, and in that environment John, knowing what it meant to be a boy, readily complied, despite his small stature, by taking on the tough boy persona: "at the time being tough meant that nobody was going to stop me from doing something that I wanted to do." Even though he fought white boys who came into his neighborhood, it was a completely different story when he ventured beyond the boundary of his neighborhood: he simply could not do what he wanted. Instead, John followed the rigid rules and complied with cultural and social expectations reserved for Negroes, under Jim Crow segregation, where, in the face of racial segregation and discrimination, he was no longer a tough boy. To the contrary, from experience he knew what it meant to go downtown as a black boy in segregated Albany, Georgia, and, as a child, he did not challenge that meaning:

I would go downtown maybe once a month. Downtown Albany was all white. I never had a run in with anyone because I knew my place. If you understand your place then you don't have problems. I fought white guys who came into my neighborhood. It just wasn't a passive neighborhood. But I knew where to sit on the bus. If I was sitting and a white person needed my seat, I just got up and if there weren't seats, you just stood up. When I went to the movies, we had to go around the back of the theater and go up the stairs to the balcony and sit. There were certain areas that we had to go in at the department stores; they had black areas that sold clothes. You just couldn't walk into the department stores and pick out things. You couldn't try shoes on; you had to know your size. In the white stores we had to always go around the back. We could never go through the front, and there were always sections setup for blacks. The way that I saw segregation was that it just was. I never thought about any of this, it just was. I do remember my father voting and paying poll taxes to vote. Blacks had to pay money in order to vote. I didn't realize that we just weren't getting our fair share. Black people were just born into this and you don't know anything different. It was all you knew, until the civil rights movement challenged it.

Through racial segregation, John learned that through the eyes of whites, he was a lesser citizen. But John came to realize that blacks in Albany, Georgia, were not getting their "fair share" of the city resources he later joined others as an activist in the civil rights movement. As a youth, however, his struggle was simple: to survive—to move beyond the anger and hate—in spite of his father's constant abuse. At an early age, John knew that he "had to learn to fend for myself." Yet, he "never, ever, complained to anybody because there was really nobody to complain to." All John wanted was to "be big," to be an adult. "I wanted to be grown. Because I thought that if I was big and grown, I could stop my father, and I knew that I would just get away from him. And when I was old enough to do so I did:"

> The last time my father hit me was when I was eighteen, and I pinned his arms against the wall. At that age, I said to him I was leaving, and that he was never going to hit me again. He hit me because he was drunk. I don't know what made me decide at that moment that that was the last time he would hit me. But it frightened me. And I really felt sick afterward because that was something that I never wanted to do to my father. I don't know why I did it because before I just took it. I just hit him. I left and went and stayed with a friend.

When John walked away from his father's house, he allowed himself to eventually leave behind the anger and hate that he had felt about the way his father treated him as a child. John reflected: "I didn't know about alcoholism and it being a disease, but when I did find out I learned how to forgive him." As a child, John did harbor anger and did hate his father's abuse, but as a mature adult he realized that he did not hate the man, who was his father, but rather his father's abusive actions. Unlike Richard, John tempered his expressions of anger and hate. In other words, he did not yield to their temptations or become driven by anger and hate. Gradually, the lessons he learned from those powerful emotions turned into a sense of self-determination. As John said, "once I got grown there were things that I knew: I knew that I would never get drunk and I would never beat my children." But John also knew, like Richard, that he would do whatever "was required of me, for me to make it."

THE TEMPTATION OF DESPAIR

Thomas did not grow up in a black community, but rather in a racially diverse community with whites, Hispanics, and blacks in Chicago, Illinois. Born in 1946, initially he lived with both parents and a brother who was three years younger. Thomas has only one "clear memory" of his father: "I don't know what it was in detail, but I know that there was a dispute, and that dispute could have been a fight. I just know that it was something between them that made me react to him in a negative way." During this incident, Thomas sicced the family dog, a German Shepard, on his father. Shortly, thereafter, his father left the family. For a long time, Thomas believed that his father left because of his action, and his mother never dispelled that notion.

Living in a single-parent household, Thomas saw his mother as "almost the male figure" in his life. She was "not a warm person," but a "strict disciplinarian" who made education a priority. Prior to starting school, his mother taught him how to read, write his name, and do simple math. "She used the method that if you didn't get it, you got hit. You couldn't be slow and dumb. She didn't know today's terms like learning deficiency and stuff like that. It was, 'boy what's wrong with you? You're not applying yourself.' I definitely could do basic reading, and could spell my name, and could count before going to school." And as a result, Thomas was ready to enter one of the most important community institutions, the public school system.

He started elementary school in 1952, but, unlike most of his black peers at the time, Thomas went to a predominantly white public school. In the 1950s most black children—whether living in the South or the North and whether living under de jure or de facto segregation—attended all-black public schools. Those segregated, racially discriminatory schools were inherently unequal; that inequality significantly curtailed black students' academic achievements and stifled their educational aspirations. Thomas found that his racially "integrated," neighborhood elementary school also offered a number of challenges.

Thomas does not remember specific teachers or the day-to-day details of the actual process of formal learning as he moved from one grade to another while attending elementary school. Thomas vividly recalled, however, that upon entering school he had his first memorable and meaningful encounter with white people. His "mother never talked about race. So when I went to school, I was not conscious about it." Consequently, he "was not real clear that there was anything special or different about being Colored until I got to school." For Thomas, initially that meaning was conveyed through some of his white teachers' actions toward him and other black students. As a dark-complexioned boy, he said: "They taught me my first real lessons in what was different about me."

During elementary school, Thomas does not remember being called derogatory names or racial slurs by his white classmates. But he soon realized that the indirect interactions, not necessarily the obvious encounters, held important lessons for how some whites responded to racial differences. This realization was based largely on intuition. He reflected upon his school experience: "I just knew that there was some stuff going on. I couldn't put my finger on it. It's like you're going to school happy, and then you're not happy anymore. Something has happened, and you don't know what it is, but people are treating you different." In this context, Thomas began to recall several incidents, and in some instances the pain and despair that resulted from those experiences was exacerbated by his mother's reaction to them. Thomas offered an example:

> A teacher lied on me. I asked a question in class, and the next thing I know my mother got a note from her saying I was misbehaving in school and challenging the teacher. In those days what a teacher says goes; it's true. My mother went to school immediately and she chastised me in front of everyone. I was stunned because I couldn't believe that my mother believed the teacher over me. I was shocked. She said, "The teacher got hers and you got to get yours. It doesn't matter what you say."

As a child Thomas "didn't understand" what this incident was all about, but intuitively he felt that he was being treated differently, and that difference was due to his dark complexion. He acknowledged that, even though he thought something unfair was occurring, "what really messed me up was that my mother believed the teacher over me." Feeling his powerlessness as a child, Thomas was enormously disappointed that the teacher's actions, as an authoritative figure, were unquestioned by his mother. From his accounts, it is not clear if his mother's failure to question the appropriateness of the teacher's response was based solely on a belief in the validity of the claim or if she viewed this incident as an important life-lesson that her son needed to learn, regardless of whether the teacher's assessment was right or wrong. Whatever the reasoning, Thomas was personally wounded by this experience. As a child, Thomas learned that he had to make adjustments to accommodate the unpredictability of white behavior toward him. This incident had an important impact on his sense of self and the lesson learned: he could rely on neither white people to tell the "truth" nor his mother to defend his developing sense of integrity.

Thomas pointed to another, more indirect, incident that also made an early impression on him regarding the roles that difference, authority, and unpredictability held for how he saw himself. A white teacher struck a black boy in the face and knocked his teeth out:

And nothing happened to the teacher. I couldn't believe that. I just couldn't believe that. The kid was black, and the teacher was a white male. He hit him in the face. In elementary school when you hit a young kid in the face you can easily knock a child's teeth out. I remember that his mother came to school, and they told her it was an accident; they told her that he fell. I didn't understand what that was about. I learned that white folks lie. But what really messed me up was that our parents believed them over us. I was clear that this was happening, so I decided that I had to do whatever I needed to do just to get through this.

On reflection, Thomas believed that he learned an important lesson about race relations while attending elementary school: his dark skin made him racially different from whites, and people treated him differently because of his color. Prior to going to school he "wasn't conscious that race meant anything." From his mother's tough guidance, Thomas "had a fairly developed sense of right and wrong," although, as a child, he did not fully understand the logic or rationale of why things happened as they did. Yet he knew—even if intuitively—that he, as well as others, was treated differently, and he attributed that difference to the blackness of their skin. Concomitantly, this difference meant that some whites saw blacks as unworthy or of lesser value. Thomas learned that racial difference could demean and, consequently, that difference could cause him pain and despair. From this and other early lessons regarding race relations, Thomas as a child gradually began to realize the meaning of race in his life. He retained these life-long lessons throughout his childhood and carried them into adulthood as well. Because of those lessons, Thomas developed a distrust of and kept a safe physical and emotional distance away from whites.

Although each of the men's experiences differed, as children they all learned lessons regarding the meaning of race in their particular lives. The meaning and the knowledge they acquired gradually unfolded as they proceeded along different paths toward the persons they became. Moreover, their early interactions with whites linked those lessons and paths together. Those encounters, in some instances, resulted in senses of personal violation that helped shape how they saw themselves. Like Thomas, their first interactions acknowledging the significance of race in their lives usually occurred at school. For some, those early interactions resulted in the unambiguous enmity that their blackness engendered from whites and laid a foundation for learning not only the meaning of racial hatred but also the value of black life as a consequence.

Similar to Thomas, Robert learned important lessons in school. But the important role that gender relations played complicated his school experience. Born in 1954, the youngest of nine children, Robert was raised in an all-black community in New York City. He grew up in a blended family, where his father had four children from a previous marriage and his mother had three children also from a former marriage. His father, born in 1898, was fifty-four years old when Robert was born, and his mother was considerably younger. In addition to his much older siblings, Robert also grew up surrounded by a large extended family: his father was the "second oldest of eleven brothers and sisters," and his mother "was the youngest of fifteen children." In addition to his nephews and nieces, who were around his age, he also played with many cousins.

His father worked primarily as a car salesman, selling cars to black-owned businesses. But he also worked at odd jobs as well: sometimes as a chauffeur for white businessmen and sometimes as butler in private observation boxes during football games, where "he was the person who laid out all of the food." During Robert's early years, he remembers that his mother basically took care of the family and did not work outside of the home. As the youngest, Robert recalls feeling special and loved by his large family. Affectionately, they called him "baby doll," and he said: "When I was little I got hugs and kisses from everybody."

Robert grew up in a black "middle-class neighborhood." When he started public school in 1960, the teachers were "predominately white." At school, one of the important early lessons that he learned was the distinction between feeling "special" and feeling "different." At home his large extended family treated him as special, but at school teachers and other students regarded him as different. Robert's teachers believed that he had a learning disability; he believes that he probably had a form of "dyslexia." So he was transferred to a "reading readiness program"—a program completely different from his elementary school. In that "special" educational program, the students were racially mixed, but the mostly white teachers "hated being there."

Robert said the teachers "were very mean to me and all of the other black kids. They were just hostile." In addition to the teachers' reactions to him, Robert encountered negative reactions from white classmates as well. In the readiness program: "The white kids started calling me names, they called me Nigger." Even though he was not familiar with and did not know what it meant, he "just knew it was a negative term and I didn't know why it was directed at me." But Robert gradually began to learn that it was a derogatory name: Nigger was a term of racial hatred, which implied that his blackness was of less value and inferior to those who were white. It was, as Robert said, "a negative term" intentionally used by whites to demean, humiliate, and hurt him; and it did exactly that.

Robert's enrollment in the reading program and his interactions within it were difficult, yet he learned how to read and write, and as a result returned to his old elementary school, where he entered the third grade.

Upon returning, he found that his school had changed, and the teachers now were mostly black. But this did not lead to a substantial improvement in his interactions as a student. He soon began to encounter new challenges that were more gender-based in nature. Soon after his return, Robert became the target of bullying from other children, especially the boys. For him, "it wasn't a question of if there was going to be a fight, it was when? I was fearful of fights on a regular basis." School violence and Robert's sense of fear, frustration, despair, and desperation became the prism by which he viewed his public school experience. As he said: "There were a couple of things that I liked about school, but I was so caught up in wondering what kind of violence was going to happen to me." Robert liked participating on the school patrol, but even here he engaged bullying. For instance, Robert described an incident in the fourth grade: "I had a street that I had to help kids get across. One of my classmates was picking on a kid that was two grades younger than us. I told him to stop. He didn't like it. But I told him to stop beating on this little boy. He went and got his cousins who were in junior high school. He came back and wanted to argue with me. They hit me in the head and knocked me out. I woke up in the parking lot."

As a child, Robert had difficulty explaining to adults the extent of the seriousness of what was happening to him. He said: "I hated the fighting and violence. But I couldn't convey to people my stress. They just didn't seem to understand it." He tried to tell his mother about the bullying, "but I'm not so sure how well I articulated it. I think she had an expectation that things happen in school and you have to work them out for yourself." He also found his black teachers unsympathetic to his needs and interests. Generally, he began to see them as "mean, hostile, and angry." Because of the teachers' attitudes, Robert found neither comfort nor solace in the classroom, as he said "in that environment the teachers were not on your side and didn't have your best interest at heart, except for a very few, if you were lucky enough to be one of them."

With the indifference of teachers and bullying by other students, Robert's boyhood simply meant "surviving" the emotional and physical toll violence was taking on his young life. His fear, frustration, despair, and particularly his desperation lead him to take dramatic action to protect himself. In the fifth grade, Robert started to "carry a knife to school. It wasn't a switchblade but one out of the house." His mother discovered that he was carrying a knife. Finally realizing the seriousness of the situation, she immediately started to look for a private school and was particularly interested in finding a spot at a religious school. But after Robert's experience in the readiness program, "she needs to know about the race thing":

She didn't feel comfortable with me going to a Catholic school. We were Protestant–Lutheran. She is calling and many of the Lutheran schools were white. She didn't want me in that environment. And all of them were giving her reasons why they didn't accept black kids. But she found one that was mixed. Twenty-five percent of the kids were black. So I started in the sixth grade. When I started school I was kind of watching because I hadn't been use to having friends. But in that environment, immediately, they started treating me as a human being.

As a reflective adult, Robert was unable to disentangle race, gender, and violence from his overall public school experience. Looking back, he said: "I now expect white teachers and kids to behave the way they did. But black students can be mean and hostile too. And black teachers didn't expect or want the best for the kids that they were serving. They didn't appear to have any racial loyalty or cease the opportunity to try to affect the well being of kids." The private Lutheran school appeared to be more welcoming, yet race, gender, and violence played an important role in shaping Robert's educational experience there as well. The dynamics of those influences were rearticulated to fit the context of that environment.

The complicated interplay between race and violence that Robert experienced at school undermined his positive sense of being special, as a boy, as formed in his nurturing family environment. At school, he was viewed and treated as different, an experience that did not render difference as something good or special. As a child, he did not fully grasp the reasons underlying why he was demeaned, humiliated, and treated with little regard, why he was physically and personally violated by children as well as adults. Immaturity denied him the opportunity to grasp the fact that public schools are key social and cultural institutions, which affirm dominant norms of race and gender relations. In his interactions with white and black teachers and other students, he was perceived as different from those established norms, and this likewise positioned his school experience as different. Those interactions gave meaning to Robert's school experience and developing consciousness. In spite of yielding to the temptation of despair and the powerlessness that accompanied it, to maintain a sense self specialness, Robert gradually began to understand "that a line had been drawn and I had to fight for survival."

THE TEMPTATION OF DOUBT

In following his own particular path, Matt's young life was full of twists and turns, and change was ever present. Shortly after his father's brief but eventful reappearance—bringing his "hustler and player" lifestyle with him—his mother married George, and soon thereafter she was pregnant with Matt's baby brother. During this period the physical violence between his step-father and mother began. The first time it happened, Matt remembers that he saw his mother "crying and George was walking down the street." In response, Matt picked up "bricks and kept throwing them at his ass." Even though George was physically disabled due to a combat injury while in the army, the violence continued, and his mother "was becoming a victim of domestic violence." When incidents occurred, Matt's tried to distract George to deflect attention away from his mother and onto himself: "Okay so you attack my mother, then I'm going to help her attack you. I was only about nine or ten years old. But I can remember picking up a broom and throwing it at him like it's a spear. It hit him and now his attention is on me and not my mother. So I began to realize that any time I heard him messing with my mother, I would go and find something to throw at him. He would start chasing me." Initially when Matt was introduced to George, he did not like him, and he "didn't respect him, I would never respect him." But now that George was physically abusing his mother, he liked and respected him even less. Matt was "angry" about the violence: "I was angry because I'm hearing my mother cry because some sucker was beating on her, and I have to deal with that. I was angry because I could not understand why she would stay with this guy. The way I looked at it we were worse off with him than we were without him. He would get his money and would go and get drunk and then would come home and want to fight."

The unpredictability of the violence and his mother's response were particularly disconcerting for Matt and his sisters. It was especially difficult for Matt to hear his mother's scream and the police constantly coming to their home in response to the violence that was occurring:

> My mother was a screamer. If he (George) acted like he was going to put his hand on her she would scream. I remember the police being at our house a lot, a whole lot. Neighbors would call them. They would usually be two cars. Sometimes they would take him away; sometimes they would just take him outside. Now I remember one time I was outside and the cop said, "look man we know how women can be but you gotta stop or I'm gonna have to lock your ass up." But I can also remember him being arrested and mama would go to the station and drop the charges and he would be right back. Like I said my mother was a screamer. She would scream a lot, she would make a lot of noise, but yeah she would fight him back. And as soon as something happened I was trying to help her. Whatever I could find I would throw at him. I remember a time when she was creaming and the police were coming. She said, "go pick that stuff up before the police come in here" and she went right back to screaming. As a kid, I was like wait a minute here. But all that screaming had an effect on me as a kid, because it made me nervous, it made me very nervous. My life was filled with those moments when I was nervous and frightened and scared and it had to do with him attacking her, with her screaming, and the police running through the house.

Yet amidst the jarring and constant physical and emotional violence he experienced in the home, as he was drawn into the fights between his step-father and mother, family life continued unabated for Matt. His baby brother entered his life, someone he loved and looked out for. But this child was George's son, and he was darker than Matt: this made a difference, not to Matt for this was his baby brother, but to George's dark-complexioned family, who treated the much lighter Matt different. Matt first realized the significance that skin complexion played in their relationship and the underlying resentment that they held toward him when "one time I ran out of the house—my mother was fighting this fool (George)—and I ran down to his brother's place for help and it was the reaction I got from him. Rather than helping he was talking about this high yellow shit, about my mother." As a light-skinned boy with straight hair, Matt was introduced to the racial acrimony of the black community based on skin complexion and hair texture. That acrimony is shaped by beliefs constructed under a color and caste hierarchy rooted in slavery and reconfigured in the ways race relations are articulated within the black community itself. Based on white standards of beauty and desirability, where the physical markers are light skin and straight hair, black cultural preferences are sometimes afforded to those whose physical features appear more whitelike. Those whose appearances differ can face disadvantages within the cultural milieu of the black community. As a result, acrimonious relations can sometimes develop between light- and dark-complexioned blacks within the same family and cultural community.

As he engaged the black community as a ten-year-old child, Matt learned that color and hair preferences held important messages for his growing understanding of what it meant to be a light-skinned straight-haired boy. He began to realize that George's family members were not the only ones who seemingly had problems with his complexion and hair texture. Rather than afforded privileges, especially from dark-complexioned blacks, because of the way he looked, Matt said: "I was treated differently, and I was ostracized because of my skin color. Because of my color, I mean I was the white Nigger, I was the yellow guy. It was common in the black community to hear that high yellow shit all the time." Yet Matt had no ambiguity about his racial identity. During the early 1960s, he knew that he was considered a Colored boy in the black community and a Negro boy by the larger white society.

Based on the messages he received from both as suggested by his experience, Matt developed a sense of uncertainty and doubt about where he actually fit within those environments, given the rigid racial divide of the period. As he said: "At the time I didn't know where I fit because black folks had as many issues with me as white folks had with me." Matt first encountered white racism after his family moved to a public housing project. As a ten-year-old in the fifth grade, Matt attended a racially diverse public elementary school and established close friendships with both a white and a Chinese classmate:

> So one day we decided we wanted to go fishing. This little white guy knew about a fishing hole that his parents had taken him to. It was a private fishing hole. So we planned on doing this, and I went home and told my mother. We planned on doing this on that weekend. We made all these preparations. It was something out of a story book because you have this black guy, this white guy, and this Chinese guy, and we all go to the same school. So we get ourselves together, and we had to walk about three miles to get to the fishing hole. So we get to the fishing hole, and there is this car going through the gate and it was an old white guy, and he stopped. So when we get to the gate the white guy looks at us and says, "you can come in but your little Nigger friend and your little chink friend have to go home." I remember that specifically. And we all turned around and went back.

Even as a child, Matt was well aware of what was happening in this encounter. "I realized then that I was being denied access to something because in this man's eye, I was a Nigger." This brief encounter with racism—the shame, humiliation, and powerlessness experienced—destroyed the boys' friendship with one another. They did not know how to talk about and move beyond their sense of embarrassment over what had happen to them. They walked home in silence, uncomfortable in each other's presence. Matt said: "Our relationship was changed forever. We didn't know how to be around each other, we didn't know how to interact with each other, and that was the end of that. We had been the best of friends, especially me and the white guy."

But Matt was not lacking in friendships or in finding activities to occupy his time. He played with children in his neighborhood and recalls that "we all were hanging out, in different ways, and at different people's houses. There was a house that was getting torn down and it had a garage. We turned the garage into a clubhouse and we would cut school and spend time there. We used to sneak off and smoke cigarettes together there." The more he interacted with other children, the more Matt became aware of the fact that the violence occurring in his home was not unique to his neighborhood; to the contrary, he remembers that while his mother "was going through that shit with George, the guy next door used to beat up his wife." One night, while sitting on the porch with his mother and her brother, his uncle, Matt said:

> We heard the door bust open, and this big black guy comes stumbling out. He's a big guy probably about six-two and two hundred and twenty pounds. When I say black guy, I mean a rugged hard dude. He comes

tumbling out and here come these two women, and it was his wife and his wife's sister and they were kicking his ass. I'm serious, they waited till he came home drunk, and they beat his ass. They beat him with baseball bats to the point where my uncle said "don't beat that man like that." This all made sense to me. I have been raised in my culture. Part of my environment, like so many of us in this country, at that time, and even today use violence to get people to do what you want. So you spank your kids. Men think that they can beat their women. So it made sense that if this man was going to be beating this woman that he deserved to be beat. And if they beat him to the degree that if he touched her again he knew that he would get that again. That might be the only way to make him stop because the police weren't making him stop. So it made sense that something had to be done. It was unusual that it was two women doing it, but then it made sense that it was her and her sister, and that's the way it should be.

The saliency of violence, as intersected by race and gender relations in his Baltimore community, was beginning to shape Matt's view of the world. Through his eyes the use of physical violence, as an important resource for getting what one wants, was beginning to make sense to him, especially at the time when he wanted to kill George, his step-father. As a child, however, he "didn't really have a frame of reference in terms of how to kill somebody. I knew I wanted to kill him and I was clear about that." Violence took on an added dimension in Matt's life, for it ultimately stopped George from further abusing his mother. Already physically disabled from a war wound, one night George went out and "got drunk and got cut up real bad. He had to get stitched up and shit and that kind of put a change in his game because he was fucked up afterward."

Matt was internalizing the important messages he received about the significance of violence as a useful tool. However, at this point in his life, other than reacting by trying to defend his mother from George's physical abuse, it is important to note that Matt as a child did not initiate or use physical violence against anyone. Even though he was an astute witness to the consequences that result from the use of violence, he avoided engaging in violence. In fact, as Matt recounted his experience of boyhood, although he was directly affected by violence and discussed his insecurities and fears as a result, never once did he refer to a childhood incident where he initiated some form of physical or emotional violence against another person. This restraint all changed dramatically when violence as a way of life not only made sense to Matt but also lead to destructive consequences for him as well as for others.

Unlike Matt, Jamie learned at an early age that violence was a useful resource in getting his way with others. The youngest of the men interviewed, Jamie was born in 1960 and grew up in Minneapolis, Minnesota.

As an only child, he was raised by a single mother and never knew his father. "He was never in the picture." But Jamie recalls being "raised in a nurturing household and felt loved, cared for, and where there was a lot of concern for me that extended to other family members."

As an only child, Jamie's mother indulged him, and he always seemed to have an abundance of his favorite foods to eat, clothes to wear, and toys to play with. He did not lack in material things. While his mother worked, she "did factory work at the time," Jamie stayed with a babysitter, who cared for several other children. At the age of four, he remembers the time when" the babysitter's oldest child used to try and strangle me. It was bad enough getting strangled, but no one would believe me. But I remember it to this day." Jamie readily admits that early on he "became a problem child because that was a reflection of what was happening to me at that house." And he recalls several occasions when he "fought the other kids" and was punished by the babysitter, who did not spank but rather isolated him from the other children when he was "bad."

Although she only had a high school education, Jamie's mother placed a priority on education and actively encouraged him to learn; at an early age he was an eager and bright student. He said: "My mother used to read to me before I got into school. We would read Mother Goose. I had a book with all the nursery rhymes in it. I had the Wizard of Oz, and Brer Rabbit. I had all those books." In 1966 when he started elementary school at five years of age, he could do basic reading. But Jamie's problematic behavior continued, and he "stayed in trouble" with his teachers. "If I couldn't have my way, I would throw a temper tantrum. I took my stuff out of the desk and threw it on the floor. I would fight. I would get into trouble for fighting mostly. My trouble came from being a disruption in class." Jamie's mostly white teachers viewed him as a "disciplinary problem" and as punishment for his behavior they made him put his head on the desk or stand in a corner.

However, the only black teacher at the school took an interest in Jamie's progress. In the third grade, Ms. Brown "actually let me know that I was intelligent. She was very encouraging and let me know that I was doing things that the rest of the students in my class weren't doing. But she would beat you. She was old school. You would get one of those black beatings from her." Jamie respected Ms. Brown and "didn't act up in her classroom." He was a good student and excelled in her class, and he began to lose the "the urge to start a ruckus." By the fifth grade Jamie settled down and largely complied with the rules of student conduct and behavior. He was becoming more mature and independent as a child. After school, he "started coming home by myself. I was what you called a latch key kid, with the chain around my neck with the key. The good thing about it was that I was mature and responsible enough to do it."

Jamie lived in a predominately white city, but his neighborhood was mostly black and poor. And as he walked from school, he saw "a lot of drugs addicts." He also saw older kids that he knew from the neighborhood "getting high. I had a friend that lived on the block with me. Him and his older brother were sniffing heroin. He didn't go to school with me he just lived on the block with me." At that time Jamie was not interested in drugs, and he wanted to live up to the responsibility his mother had entrusted in him. After school, he went straight home and did "my homework, sometimes I would go out and play, I would cook something, or I would have a friend or two over and we would watch TV." There was a lot to see on television because after all, as Jamie said, this was the "radical sixties." Although he had no particular consciousness about what it meant to be black, he did know that the color of his skin made him black. The television he watched reinforced his blackness:

> The family types and the events that went on were not my life-style. The things that I knew about life, I had no identification with that. I liked the life-style, but I didn't want to be the people in it. I wanted to be me in that life-style; the things that those life-styles were about. The house, the nice neighborhood, the little dog, you can leave the bike outside and no one was going to steal it, as it was portrayed on television. I did notice that something was amidst.

By the time Jamie entered junior high school, there was a notable change in how he perceived himself. As he said, "I'm the man, now." He readily admits that he had become "conceited," and the self-presentation he adopted left little doubt about his own sense of masculinity. As he said:

> I was one of the sharpest kids in school. I would willingly wear suits to school. I had the big guy coat, but for a little guy. I think it was shark skinned back then. I had silk pants and Italian knit shirts, I had a fur coat, and a leather coat with a Persian lamb fur collar on it. My mother would buy all of this for me. I was told that I had good looks from the girls. I had a lot of girls liking me and a lot of girls were attracted to me. I would have that one for about an hour and then use to quit her, and then I would get another one. I had an entourage of girls. It was all about me. Even if I didn't look good, my head was in the sky, so I was like whatever.

Jamie considered himself a "pretty boy," and others told him as much, especially the girls. He "dressed well, talked slick, and had a crazy Michael Jackson afro" hairdo. With his well-crafted style and presentation of self, Jamie was clear about who he did not want to be based on the models he saw in his neighborhood. "I didn't want to be the guy standing on the corner. I didn't want to be the guy that was nodding out in the street. I didn't want to be the guy that was drinking wine out of the bottle on the street. I didn't want to be the guy that was stuck, that had nothing going on. I didn't want to be that guy." Instead, Jamie wanted to be like the action characters he saw on television: he was influenced by media images of masculinity, even though those images were mostly white men. In comparison, he said:

> I wanted to be James Bond, not the person, but I wanted the life-style: the excitement, danger, lights, the notice, pretty girls, and cars. I say all of that to make the contrast here. That life-style was not what I saw in my neighborhood. Even guys who were supposed to be big time hustlers, there was something shady about them. You never saw them during the day which always amazed me. The daytime is the best part because that's when you can be seen, you're noticed. The nighttime you are creeping around in the shadows.

Jamie was clear in his own mind about the man he wanted to be. In junior high school, when he went from a boy to an adolescent, he developed a strong sense of his gender identity. Or, as Jamie said, at this point "I went from being a little kid to being a man." During this period, Jamie and his mother moved to the public housing projects, and she was now working as a secretary at a police precinct. Even though he continued to be a good student and was popular with his classmates, Jamie started to "hangout" with neighborhood boys: playing basketball in the park, smoking cigarettes and marijuana, drinking beer, and having sex with girls. While in junior high school, Jamie joined a street gang, "a neighborhood gang." This proved to be a fateful period in his life. Jamie continued to go to school and got good grades, but he started to make compromises to accommodate the expectations of the gang. Increasingly, he was fascinated and captivated with the gang lifestyle, to which violence gradually became an integral of his daily activities.

By the time he was fourteen years of age, Jamie's relationship with his mother changed:

> I'm seeking independence away from the nest. Being the only child, there's too much care and concern for my own good. I want nothing to do with my mother. Is the food done? I need some money. Bye. That's it. My mother didn't realize that something was wrong with that. I wanted to get a job, but my mother didn't want me to work. My mother said if you want something, I will get it for you, just focus on your school work, just graduate from school. The magic black folk formula, graduate and everything will be fine.

Jamie's relationship with girls was also changing during this period. Prior to this phase he saw himself as considerate and respectful of girls, but now, he readily admits, he was totally self-absorbed and self-indulgent in any interactions with them. Sexual pleasure became the main focus of any meaningful contact with girls. Although Jamie had had sexual intercourse and was not a virgin, at the age of fourteen he had his first orgasm. This experience provided an important turning-point in his perceptions of intimacy:

> I learned to separate feelings from desires. Understand that you can have good feelings, but feelings are passing. They too shall come again. I separated sex and desires from relationships. I am pursuing sex for a different reason. It is because of the good inner feeling I get and the pleasure. The fact that I was able to make that distinction and not get caught up in being sincere to the relationship allowed me to have many partners, and to do it with clear emotions.

In the absence of emotional commitment and responsibility, this stance allowed Jamie to treat girls as sexual objects, which allowed him to justify having sex with a lot of different girls; often Jamie did not use protection, and neither did his partners. As a result, two girls became pregnant: he persuaded one of the girls to have an abortion, and she did. But the situation with the other girl was decidedly more complex because "on two or three occasions I had sex with the mother and still had sex with the daughter. It was morally corrupt, but I didn't realize that this has to be damaging in some way. I got the daughter pregnant, and I'm having intercourse with mother. I think the only reason the mother stopped having sex with me is because the daughter got pregnant." Jamie tried to convince the girl to have an abortion: "how can you really bring a child into a family where this is happening?" Through his eyes, it was "the family who was at fault, I didn't do anything wrong. I just took advantage of the opportunity." The girl decided to have the child, but Jamie did not fully believe that the baby was his and so he assumed no responsibility. Reflecting on both relationships, Jamie concludes that he "was a total jerk" and that they "were all too young at the time" to be responsible for another life.

This period in Jamie's life produced tremendous change in his relationships with females, particularly with his mother and girls. Jamie's relationship with himself, however, as influenced by his gang activity and interactions with other males, proved to be even more defining during this time in his life. Although his body was changing, he was neither as tall nor as muscular as his peers. "I was one-hundred and ten pounds soaking wet, so I really wasn't too cool with it." Given his size, Jamie felt extremely vulnerable to physical attacks, especially after moving to the projects. "There's alot victimization in the projects. People were getting robbed. If you didn't know anybody you couldn't wear nice stuff, jewelry, a good coat, and your sneakers were stolen. Gun point, knife point, you got beat down, 'take it off.' Guys fighting, guns, however they would come at you. My neighbor was getting robbed like clock work," he said.

To compensate for his size and the possibility of becoming a victim, Jamie took on a tough boy persona: he became extremely violent. He became known in the projects and got a reputation that said: "You don't want to mess with me because I'm somebody that will get you." At the time Jamie was running with the gang, but he was also hanging out with the "other bad guys" in his neighborhood. Between the two, in his words, he became "buck wild":

> I was a monster. Violent, I became very violent. I would throw something at you or hit you with something because I was smaller. The guys would say leave him alone because he is touched in the head. Now I have a position in the social order. I was the person that was looking to vent on others. I didn't take no mess from anybody. I would proceed to hurt you. I got robbed and that was the key, the victimization piece that turned me. It was the boulder that sent me tumbling down hill. I was weak, and that was not how I saw myself as being. The person that I saw myself to be was not supposed to be robbed. I said I should have died. At least I would have been dead, and it would have been known that I went out as opposed to someone taking my stuff and I'm still living. It shattered my self-esteem being taken advantage of. I really felt scarred. I really, really felt scarred and I didn't like it at all. I felt scarred and I didn't like that feeling. I said to myself this will never happen again. It happened one more time, and that's when I became who I am today.

By the age of fourteen, Jamie had become a "monster." He describes himself as a "Frankenstein monster living a dual life," where along with the violence he tried to continue as a successful ninth-grade student. But balancing the two lifestyles proved difficult. With his gang activities, increasing drug use and sexual escapades, Jamie said, "I messed up a semester. But even though I had messed up in school, I found esteem in being in a classroom setting." After dropping out for a term, "I straightened myself up and went back to school." Jamie wanted to "salvage" what he could of his education and "focused on being in class and doing my assignments so I could graduate because I wanted to go to college." He had a clear goal in mind; he would graduate from high school and go on to college. This decision, however, was not clear-cut: self-centered and full doubt, the "monster" Jamie created also accompanied him to college, as he plunged headlong into the maelstrom of violence. The powerful lure and destructive force of that violence forever changed his life.

CONCLUSION

Childhood experiences do not necessarily determine either the course or the outcome of the men's lives. Over time they change: Men will develop new needs, aspirations, and new ways of seeing and being in the world as they journey through life. Amidst the inevitability of physical and personal change, continuity exists. That continuity is often created by recurring patterns of cultural and social constraints, which limit rather than affirm the possibilities the men's lives hold. Race relations provide fertile ground upon which change and continuity often meet. As we have seen from the men's boyhood experiences, the tensions, dilemmas, and contradictions that change and continuity sow, as a result of those relations, began to take shape early in their lives.

Change brought about a developing maturity and independence, and their childhood lives became denser and more complex. That maturity and independence allowed them to engage the broader dimensions of their cultural and social environments, and they, in turn, began to learn the meaning of hate, despair, and doubt in which race relations played a significant role. Those powerful emotions signified a growing awareness of their sense of cultural and social estrangement; not only did the boys increase their understanding of the difference by which they were seen and treated by others, but, more important, they began to see themselves as shaped by their interactions with others. Hate, despair, and doubt did not simply evolve "organically." Instead, those emotions came from someplace; they emerged as a response to events occurring in their lives. Hate, despair, and doubt were created within and against the context of their lived experiences, and a developing sense of anger linked those powerful emotions together.

Whether that anger was expressed or simmered just beneath the surface as evidenced by experience, it embodied feelings of hate, despair, and doubt. As children, their anger suggests that they were developing a view of the world. Although that view was shaped largely by looking through an intuitive prism reflecting experience—after all they were children—it allowed them to gauge how they were positioned in relationship to others and how they saw themselves in the world. In other words, their anger played a critical interpretative role. Anger helped them assess and make sense of what was happening to them, while conveying to others their dissatisfaction with the circumstances and arrangements under which they experienced their lives.

To articulate their dissatisfaction, their anger and the myriad of ways it was expressed in their interactions and relationships became their symbolic voice of disapproval. For some of the men as children, that anger was both necessary and unavoidable, given the circumstances of their particular lives. It articulated a stance that expressed what was unacceptable to them. Increasingly unacceptable was a growing sense of disvalue, and anger expressed their sense of both estrangement and malcontent. As their interpretations and experiences suggest, there were legitimate reasons for expressing anger, an anger that articulated their sense of agency.

As I discuss in chapter 3, some of the men, as they continue on their journey of becoming, form their sense of agency in the context of anger, which drew them deeper into a reality that limited their expectations of self.

Gradually, they became trapped into a racialized existence, borne of cultural and social expectations that constrained their reality. They became inseparable from the trappings that a reality of disvalue imposes; they began to embody an "angry-black-male" persona that ultimately became destructive to others as well as to themselves. Other men traveling along similar paths toward becoming, while not immune to this deep sense of anger, found that anger in a slightly different form accompanied them on their particular journey as well. They too were drawn into a racialized reality where anger was also shaped by limits. They struggled in their attempt to avoid being consumed by the "angry-black-male" persona, as they seek to become self-determining, but anger still imposed its reality on their lives as young men.

CHAPTER 3

Manhood

THE COLD WAR

By the 1950s, much of the postwar world was divided among the former Allied Powers. Despite enormous death tolls, human suffering, and infrastructural devastation experienced on the home front, in the aftermath of World War II, England and France were again firmly committed to maintaining an economic grip on their African and Asian colonies, through violence if necessary. Moscow and the Soviet Union solidified their communist grip on most of Eastern Europe through violence, as their political influence expanded into Africa and Asia as well. In Washington, D.C., and throughout the United States, fear of spreading communism persuaded the country to position itself as the chief arbitrator and protector of Western values and ways of life and fully prepare to use violence in this endeavor. As the world powers realigned their political, economic, and military interests, they largely ignored the desire for freedom, self-determination, and independence by oppressed and nonwhite people around the world.

Emboldened by the spoils of World War II—wealth, territorial booty and, the important capacity for nuclear annihilation—by the 1950s the stakes of the former Allies were clearly demarcated. A new world order was born. But in men's desire for greater power, control, and dominance through the use of violence, a new martial song trumpeted throughout the international community. Again the world was at war. This time, however, given the ability to wipe enemies off the face of the earth, the newly equipped nuclear powers waged a Cold War. The battles were fought largely on the continents of Africa and Asia.

Meanwhile, oppressed African and Asian people did not stand idly by as the nuclear powers asserted economic, political, and strategic interests on their homelands. Indeed, a new generation of nonwhite men emerged to press their claims to freedom, self-determination, and independence. Anti-imperialist struggles were afoot, and a new international manhood asserted itself. On the continent of Africa, Kwame Nkrumah challenged Great Britain's colonial rule in Ghana. In 1935, as a student, Nkrumah had gone to the United States, to study at the oldest U.S. black college, Lincoln University in Philadelphia (Birmingham, 1998). There he established relationships with black intellectuals, most notably W.E.B. Du Bois, for whom the strategic and cultural importance of African to the black world was of increasing interest. Following World War II, Nkrumah left the United States and moved to London, where, in 1945, he and Du Bois convened the Fifth Pan-African Congress. For the first time, more than ninety delegates from Africa, the Caribbean, and the United States came together to develop an agenda for the future independence of Africa.

With an agenda in hand, Nkrumah returned to Ghana and organized the Convention People's Party (CPP) to challenge Great Britain's colonial rule. Following Mahatma Gandhi's nonviolent direct action campaign for self-rule of India, the CPP mounted a series of civil disobedient protests. In 1957, Ghana became the first black African country to gain independence, and later Nkrumah became its first president. But Nkrumah knew if Ghana was to survive as an independent state, her independence was "linked up with the total liberation of the African continent." Nkrumah argued:

> Divided we are weak; united, Africa could become one of the greatest forces for good in the world. I believe strongly and sincerely that with the deep-rooted wisdom and dignity, the innate respect for human lives, the intense humanity that is our heritage, the African race, united under one federal government, will emerge not as just another world bloc to flaunt its wealth and strength, but as a Great Power whose greatness is indestructible because it is built not on fear, envy and suspicion, nor won at the expense of others, but founded on hope, trust, friendship and directed to the good of all mankind. (Nkrumah, 2006, p. 12)

Following Ghana's lead, by the mid-1960s more than thirty African countries had gained independence from British, France, and other colonial rulers. The former colonial powers and the United States were highly skeptical, however, of the economic and political systems adopted by many of the newly formed independent countries. With a plundered economic infrastructure and a public sector designed for political expediency to facilitate that plunder, the former colonies sought alternative models for economic growth and development from the ones they had inherited. Nkrumah argued that "capitalism is too complicated a system for a newly independent nation," such as Ghana. Instead, he was inclined to adopt African socialism: this system combined modern economic growth with traditional values.

African socialism as envisioned by Nkrumah was not based solely on a free market economy or a democratic governing structure. His economic and political vision for Ghana's future brought him squarely into conflict with the West. More aligned with his country's needs and interests, Nkrumah turned to the Soviet Union and the People's Republic of China, both communist countries, for assistance. This fateful move brought Nkrumah into the throws of the Cold War conflict. In 1964, while Nkrumah was on his way to China, a Central Intelligent Agency (CIA)-backed coup d'etat staged by Ghanaian army officers overthrew his government. Nkrumah spent the rest of his life in exile in Guinea under the protectorate of Sekou Toure, another African leader who, following his country's independence, adopted African Socialism.

As newly formed African states struggled for self-determination during the 1960s, they were not the only countries seeking release from the structural injustices, inequalities, and oppression faced under colonial rule. Liberation struggles were occurring on the subcontinent of Asia, particularly in Vietnam. Following World War II, the French tried again to assert their rule over Vietnam. Led by Ho Chi Minh, the French met fierce opposition. Minh had lived in the United States, Great Britain, and particularly in France, where he became a staunch ideological socialist. His beliefs about and commitment to socialism as a revolutionary force for Vietnam's liberation took him to the Soviet Union and the People's Republic of China, and they, in turn, provided military assistance to wage a communist war against France's colonial rule (Kail, 1973). In 1954, after almost a hundred years of colonial rule, the Vietnamese forced France to leave their country. Before the French left, the warring factions reached an agreement under the Geneva Peace Accords. That agreement divided Vietnam into two countries, North and South, and authorized an election two years later to vote for reunification.

South Vietnam, backed by the United States, refused to take part in the election. Ho Chi Minh's Communist Party controlled North Vietnam and mounted a vigorous armed assault against the South, which sought to reunite the country. Vietnam became a critical "domino" in the Cold War conflict between Moscow and Washington. From 1954 to 1975, the United States fought one of the longest and bloodiest wars of its history (Williams, et al., 1975). Eventually, the United States could no longer sustain a protracted and costly war: there were simply not enough volunteers to fight, and the draft proved unpopular as antiwar protests erupted on college campuses and in cities across America. The "Great Society," envisioned by President Johnson, slipped into bankruptcy as the economic cost of the Vietnam War escalated. The staggering cost in human lives became untenable for many Americans. The price was high on all sides; of the dead, an estimated three million North Vietnamese and South Vietnamese were killed in the struggle, and 58,000 U.S. soldiers died (their names inscribed on the haunting black granite panels of the Vietnam War Memorial in Washington, D.C.).

By the end of the 1950s, the meaning of freedom, self-determination, and independence was deeply entangled in the political, economic, and military realities of the Cold War. The essence of that particular war was no different from any other war: war hinges on the divergent thoughts, practices, and behaviors of men and the uneven power that exists between them. In other words, war is about men asserting or defying the will of other men. On a contested terrain often race and gender relations lay somewhere at the root of that entanglement; fundamentally, war tests the superiority of manhood, and a bloody battleground test the inferiority of masculine toughness. During the Cold War race, gender, and violence were critical factors that structured a dual reality among men; they buttressed as well as transformed existing social arrangements. That reality was by no means formed on opposite ends of a social and cultural continuum, where total domination exists at one end and absolute subjugation at the other end. Rather, that reality was intertwined and interconnected as men struggled over the meaning of freedom, self-determination, and independence. The battle lines were drawn, and within and against the chronicles of history, in too many instances, those struggles resulted in the loss of human life.

COLD WAR WARRIORS

The men interviewed in this book came of age as adults, as young black men, in the midst of the Cold War during the 1960s. Stepping into a world that was made by and for men, they could not avoid the political upheaval and turbulence of the period. The United States was not only deeply embroiled in a war abroad, but it was also engaged in war at home, where the struggle over ideas and ways of life were fought in the neighborhoods, homes, and on the streets of America. As young adults, several of men participated directly (albeit on the fringes) in the events that altered the social and cultural landscape, both at home and abroad. Some entered the military and found that the enemy was not the North Vietnamese, but rather racism. Others were drawn into the civil rights movement and later the black power movement, where they too engaged the struggle against racism. Some men did not participate in either struggle, but they, too, could not help but be affected by the bloody battles challenging the existing state of affairs in their homes, neighborhoods, and the country at large during this period of social and cultural turmoil.

The men were drawn into ideological and political struggles over freedom, self-determination, and independence, even if on the very margins of historical events. Those struggles were not solely external; many men struggled within themselves. At a time when blackness and maleness was undergoing fundamental changes in both black and white America, each man sought to give meaning to his own particular understanding of manhood. The men played active roles in shaping their own individual identities. Each of their experiences was set within and against a broader reality, where ideas about freedom, self-determination, and independence assumed a particular meaning in their lives.

The men were neither fully autonomous nor self-directed. Nor were their thoughts and actions predetermined by external social and cultural arrangements. Rather, there was a reciprocal interaction: they acted, but within and against circumstances imposed on their daily lives. This mutual relationship is revealed in the tensions, dilemmas, and contradictions of their experiences. They made decisions and acted on behalf of as well as against their self-defined needs and interests, given the particular circumstances of their lives. At times the men were complicit in the arrangements under which they acted. At other times they simply accommodated or adjusted to the social rules and cultural expectations imposed. Sometimes they were defiant and actively resisted; sometimes they attempted to create anew the circumstances for their lives. Ever fluid and always engaging, at any given moment in time, the men reflected many different behaviors.

This new generation of black men, attempting to assert new ways of doing manhood, was restless as the men eagerly greeted the uncertainty that newness creates. Leaving the dependency and restrictions of childhood behind, they engaged the world of men as young participants: social and cultural expectations, along with standards of conformity and accountability, and the important actions and consequences differed from those of their childhoods. Yet the world of adult men was not altogether unfamiliar because, after all, they had been groomed as black boys upon that terrain. But in seeking freedom, self-determination, and independence as young black men, they found this adult terrain treacherous as race, gender, and violence shaped their experiences of manhood.

FREEDOM

Education represented freedom for Daniel. It was a priority in his family life, and he was an excellent student. Although his father completed high school, his mother dropped out of school to give birth to Daniel. Yet both were "very committed to education": they believed that once obtained, it was something that could never be taken away from their son, and their hope was that it could better Daniel's life chances as a young black man. In a household where his father's controlling behavior and violence loomed over the family's interactions, Daniel found that education was also an important outlet for self-expression, not because it held possibilities for his future but rather because it was an acceptable and accessible outlet that allowed him to express himself in ways that afforded a sense of freedom, particularly from his father's control and abuse.

As long as he maintained good grades in school, Daniel realized that he could do mostly whatever he wanted, especially outside the home. An added benefit, however, was that he could avoid interacting and getting into conflict with his father, which was a real concern. His mother proved a strong ally, and she sought to protect her son whenever she could from his father's aggression, even if it meant that she became its target instead.

As a child, Daniel became known in his community as a "smart kid." He won the fifth-grade spelling bee in the city and later set a record for reading the most books at the Indianapolis Public Library. With an uncanny determination, he remembered: "I set a goal and I read about forty books a week. I went there everyday and got eight books and read them. When you check out your books, they would keep track of them, and I read the most books."

Because he was "smart" and excelled especially in the areas of math and science, Daniel was recruited to attend a largely all-white, all-male private high school that was sponsored by a highly respected Jesuit college. Initially, he was hesitant about attending: of the twelve hundred students enrolled, he was one of only fifteen black students attending. His mother strongly encouraged him to go, and, although he received a scholarship, she worked a second job in order to help defray some of the tuition cost. Yet Daniel "really didn't want to go. I didn't understand why she was making me do it. But I ended up going. And it was probably the best thing I have ever done."

Daniel's school was located about ten miles away from his home. He took an early morning bus so he could work in the school cafeteria as a way of helping to cover some of his own educational expenses. In this all-male school environment, in addition to pursing his academic interests, Daniel actively participated in sports where he played football and ran track. He also became a state-champion wrestler. Daniel saw himself as a "scholar/athlete." His academic achievements and extracurricular activities were notable, and he excelled on all fronts. Even more noteworthy is that his very busy school schedule kept him away from home for long periods of time; he left early in morning and usually did not return home until late at night. Consequently, he avoided meaningful contact with his father.

Daniel was no longer a child in a boy's body. Physically, he had gotten "bigger and stronger." He was not tall, but rather "broad." As he said, "I was at that point pretty thick, and for lack of better words, I had an aggressive posture." Even though as a child, he considered himself tough, as a young man, he now had a muscular and athletic physique to match his sense of toughness. With his physique, Daniel was definitely committed to a posture of not "backing down," particularly when it came to his father's aggression. Daniel embraced the person he had become: "I felt a greater sense of control to affect things. I'm now very aware of my intention. My intention was to get stronger, and kill my father, or at least beat him up really bad." Daniel recalled the "first direct fight" he had with his father:

He wants to impose a curfew on me. I'm pretty much coming home, eating something, and leaving. So he wants to impose a curfew and I'm like, no way. I was pretty defiant. I said I'm not going to do it. It was one of those weird exchanges, like "be home at a certain time." I didn't say anything. He said, "did you hear me?" I said, "I'm listening." He really wanted to keep me from leaving or for me to acknowledge that I heard him and was going to obey. He grabbed my arm and I pushed him as hard as I could into the refrigerator. He jumped on me, bit me, and I threw him down the stairs and left. I felt like a man. I could make my own decisions. No longer was he going to be able to make a decision for me, and physically I am not intimidated or afraid of him. My mother and brothers were shocked because they all observed this. They saw this as two men fighting.

By the late 1960s, Daniel was not the only one in his family undergoing significant change; his mother and father were changing as well. Daniel used school activities as a way of distancing himself from his father. Similarly, his mother also used education as a means of lessening her husband's control and gaining greater independence for herself. After dropping out of school to have Daniel at sixteen years of age and two other sons shortly thereafter, his mother had managed to get her high school diploma. And while Daniel attended high school, she worked two jobs while enrolled in a local college. One of her jobs was that of a nurse's aide, and she wanted to become a licensed nurse. Good at math and science, Daniel helped her with "algebra and chemistry classes," and through their mutual love of learning they became even closer, as mother and son. Although his father valued education and made it a priority for his children, unlike Daniel's mother, he did not return to school, but continued working as an auto mechanic. Daniel said: "My father was committed to education and academic excellence, but he didn't have the capacity to experience it in any joyful way."

Around this time, Daniel started to notice a change in his parents' relationship. To him, they seem to be moving in opposite directions and occupying different worlds. Daniel said from 6:30 a.m. to 3:30 p.m. his father's world was that of work. After work, he focused on "clothes, cars, and alcohol." Daniel discovered that his father's world also included a relationship with another woman. He had seen his father with her, but he had never told his mother because he did not want to hurt her or exacerbate the existing tensions between his parents. Beneath the surface of the changes that he witnessed in his parents' relationship, on reflection, Daniel believes that his father was growing increasingly jealous and resentful of his mother, as she pursued a more independent life:

My mother was focused on her intellectual development and being exposed to new environments. She was starting to make these different decisions and doing things independent of him. There is a tension and he is now feeling on the outside, and feeling very judged. He had a chip on his shoulder. My mother was very physically attractive and she was taller than my father. My father had short man's disease. He was five-five and he was shorter than me. And my mother was really young. She was really wide-eyed, excited, open to learning, and people were really attracted to her; people really liked her. And that was a problem for my father. It was all about power.

One time Daniel and his mother were visiting a neighbor, and "she was white and married to a black man. It was a Friday evening and it was summertime. My father came home and no one was there. We had lost track of time. He stormed into the women's house and immediately started hitting my mother. He threw her down and started kicking her. It was a real mess; it was real violent and a public episode. We spent the night there and that morning we walked home. I remember, on the way home looking my mother in the eye and saying, why are we going home? And she said, 'to fix breakfast.' And that's what she did." But she also was waiting for an opportunity to leave. Daniel experienced a series of separations between his parents, where his mother would leave and take the children with her. But she always returned to his father.

By the time Daniel entered the twelfth grade he had gotten his driver license. Using his mother's car, he said, "I'm free." But as he drove around the streets of Indianapolis, he is "starting to have these odd events. I am now starting to see men fighting women a lot. I don't know if that was the year where I said enough is enough. If anybody is going to get their ass kicked, its going to be me kicking somebody ass." Daniel described one of several incidents he recalled:

> I was not going to watch another woman get beat. It was not going to happen ever again on my watch. When you pre-frame your brain to watch out for something, all of a sudden you see it everywhere. I was driving down the street and this woman comes out of the house in a bra and panty. This dude comes walking out of the house calmly. She is knocking on people's doors. He grabs and drags her back to the house. She breaks away and makes a run for it. He catches her and drags her back to the house again and closes the door. I can't leave. She comes out of the house again. I get out of the car and I put her in the car. I drive away and this dude kicks the car. I take her to the hospital.

To Daniel it started to seem as if physical violence, especially between men and women, was all around him. In this awareness, it seemed like the "violence was normal. For a long time I thought it was only my family.

The shame part when you are younger is because you don't think anyone else is doing this. Nobody else's parents are on the porch fighting." Returning late at night from his long school days, there came a point when Daniel was forced to monitor the level of tension between his parents. "I don't go to sleep until everyone is sleep, and it's completely quiet in the house." Emotionally, Daniel was growing fatigued and wanted to be free of the violence in his life. In his desire for freedom from both supervision and violence, Daniel realized that he "can't save my mother."

Again education becomes the vehicle, the outlet that Daniel uses to try to escape his parent's violence. He received acceptance letters from all of the colleges to which he applied. Awarded a scholarship, Daniel decided to attend a major college in Michigan with a highly ranked chemical engineering program. Determined to leave home, he said: "I'm getting the hell out of Indianapolis. I am really clear about that. There is nothing that can hold me now." He graduated from high school on "May 12th and I was in Michigan on May 18th."

While Daniel was away, the tension and violence between his parents "kept escalating and getting worst. Supposedly, my father's best friend had an affair with my mom. This was absolutely absurd." During that conflict, once again, his mother decided to leave his father. Taking her sons, she also moved to Michigan to stay with friends. For Daniel, "it was a huge burden lifted off of my shoulders. Now I knew where everybody was and they were safe, although it was messed up. We started going through this whole thing of my father trying to find them. It was just crazy." Daniel's father discovered where his wife was staying and sought her out in an attempt to reconcile their relationship, but this time his mother refused to return home.

At the end of his first semester in college, for Christmas break, Daniel, his mother, and younger brothers returned to Indianapolis for the holidays. On New Year's Eve, Daniel went to visit friends, "my brothers were with their friends, and my mother was at church with her friends. My father comes to the church and wants to talk to her and show her something he has done to the house." Daniel's mother decided to go with him to look at the remodeling he had done on the house, but on the drive home:

> At some point they get into an argument, and he pulls a gun on her. I don't know the real content of the conversation, but "you're not going back." He shoots her in the car at close range five times. She tried to get out of the car and opened the door. She falls out. He pulls away, leaves her on the street to die, and goes home. This is major news. I get a call from my aunt. Somehow my mother recited my uncle's phone number. They took her to the hospital. I get a call from my aunt, and she tells me that my mother has been shot. I borrow a car. I leave, and I'm going to

find him. I don't tell anyone exactly what I'm going to do. I drive past a few places. I drive over to our house, and his car is on the lawn, and the door is open. I go in the house, and he is dead. He has killed himself. He is bleeding on the kitchen floor. I was angry that he had killed himself. He had done this and left everyone to deal with the damage. I didn't call anybody. I just left. I walked out of the house. I drove to my uncle's house. From there I tried to find my brothers and we went to the hospital where my mom was at. She was in intensive care. Lots of tubes; lots of IV's . . .

Daniel's mother was extremely lucky; the bullets did not hit any of her major organs, and, although she survived, she was critically injured. Meanwhile, other family members depended on Daniel to take charge of this crisis. At eighteen years of age, he was forced to handle all of the inquiries and arrangements with doctors, police, and the funeral director, and he also took responsibility for his two younger brothers. Outwardly, he calmly went through the motion of getting things done, but inside Daniel was seething with anger. He was extremely angry at everyone, including himself. Through his tears, Daniel's past and present converged as he tried to convey the depth of his emotions during that period:

I was angry at all of us for being in Indianapolis. What the hell were we doing in Indianapolis, like we're on vacation? This is not Disneyland and he is not Mickey Mouse. Everything in our lives has said this is what comes from violence. I was angry at my father. I was angry at my mother. What the hell was on your mind? What the hell did you think was different? What is it that makes people think that one and one is all of a sudden four?

Daniel was now the man of the family, and he took control over the situation, as best he could. He said, "I know that I have to take charge or nothing is going to get done." While standing at his father's grave with his two younger brothers at his side and knowing his mother was fighting for her life in intensive care, Daniel realized that he was finally free of father's violence. Yet that freedom came at an enormous price. That freedom committed Daniel to a life of nonviolence. But even twenty-five years after his father's suicide, his freedom from his father's violence has not given him a sense of peace.

In 1960, as a young man, John too was finally free of his father's abusive behavior, but, unlike Daniel, he eventually found a sense of peace with that freedom; he still continues to ponder the reasons why his father so resented him and physically abused him as a child. At eighteen, following his only physical fight with his father, John left home determined never to live under his father's roof again. He wanted to be rid of his father's abuse and was committed to doing whatever was needed to survive independently. Given the seemingly stark and unambiguous reality of his life, John had a clear understanding of certain truths. John could only find work as a common laborer; there was always an odd job, here and there, to make ends meet. He wanted something more out of life, but he knew that as a young black man living under racial segregation in Albany, Georgia, his life-options were quite limited.

When John left his father's house, initially he took a room at a boarding house for five-dollars a week. Extremely resourceful, he worked odd jobs to pay his rent and buy the things he needed. John worked as a caddy for local white golfers, manually set up bowling pins at an all-white bowling alley for a penny a pin, cleaned and mopped floors for local businesses, and, if he had to, continued to shine shoes. Through tenacity and hard work, where he saw no "honest job" as demeaning or beneath him, John made about fifty dollars a week, which for him, was more than adequate to meet his immediate needs.

Limited in what he could and could not do, under Jim Crow segregation, John, like other blacks in Albany, was denied basic physical, personal, and social freedoms. Their physical movement, personal choices, and political participation were severely restricted by both law and custom. Seen by whites as racially inferior, as less than, blacks were relegated to second-class citizenship and treated as such. They were forced to endure the shame and humiliation of separate toilets, drinking fountains, waiting rooms, parks, schools, and other public facilities and accommodations. Segregation was not just a patterned system of discrimination and exclusion denying blacks constitutional rights and guarantees; it was a system of racial oppression designed to strip blacks of their dignity and worth as human beings. That system was firmly maintained through intimidation and violence by white police forces, terrorist groups, and individuals. As a young black man, this was the world that John engaged.

Denied fundamental freedoms, it was difficult for John to envision a future for himself under racial segregation. He reflected on the roles of black men in his community at that time:

> You could be a postman, you could work at the lumber mill, you could be a teacher, and you could be a minister. What else? You could be a black funeral director. So there were few jobs that you could have. But then if you don't see yourself in any of those, you don't see a lot of what your future is going to be like. I never dreamed of going anywhere. Nobody told me at the time that you could go places and do different things. Albany was my world. I was just who I was in it. I understood some of the abilities I had, but to understand myself in the world beyond Albany, I didn't have that.

In a world where his life-options were severely restricted, John was not deterred because he also knew that education could, perhaps, hold the key to a better life. And so he decided to go to college: a small historically black college located in Albany, where "tuition was free, but we had to buy books and things." In that college environment, John gradually began to see possibilities for his life because people cared. He discussed his educational experience:

> It wasn't a school where you went and you just stood there waiting for something to happen. It wasn't simply up to you to get it. They gave you what you needed to know, and they made sure you got it. They gave us everything that we needed, plus they cared whether or not we got it. The faculty was all black, and they would sit with you one-on-one if need be, for as long as you needed. They put an emphasis on what you gonna do in your future, but you had to make the decision. We had black history, and we were taught a lot about what blacks had done, and I took pride in being black. We were taught that you stand up and be a black man. That black men were strong; that men took care of their responsibilities. It's about strength and about being in charge. We as young black men were taught how to be men and what it meant to be a black man.

In the early 1960s, for John there were no clear social and cultural distinctions between the college he attended and the community in which he lived. They were one and the same. What linked the two was the presence of the black church and Jim Crow segregation. In an ironic way, racial segregation in the South through marginalization and exclusion, spurred the creation and development of two of the most venerable institutions in the black community—black colleges and black churches. Similar to his peers, John was positioned on the cusp of both. He had grown up in the church and as an adult continued to attend Sunday services on a regular basis. As he said: "It was disrespectful if you didn't go to church. It was just not done. You had to go to church. Church was always a part of my life," and so were the people with whom he lived and interacted. For instance, the minister of his Baptist church was also John's math teacher in college.

His church was affiliated with the Southern Christian Leadership Conference (SCLC), lead by Dr. Martin Luther King, and his minister spoke out against the oppressive social conditions of Jim Crow segregation from the pulpit. Many of John's fellow students also attended church, and together they formed a campus group loosely affiliated with the Student Nonviolence Coordinating Committee (SNCC). These two organizations, along with the National Association for the Advancement of Colored People (NAACP), were critical to the struggle for civil rights, especially in Albany. As a part of that struggle, students began organizing nonviolent demonstrations. Discussing this period in his life, John recalls his first protest; students boycotted and led daily pickets against a white-owned grocery store located in John's neighborhood: "We didn't necessarily want to shut it down. We wanted better treatment.

We found out that one of the sons of the owner of the store was a member of the Ku Klux Klan. And that was one of the reasons why we picketed the store. And the store ended up, after about six months, closing because the only people that really went to the store were black." Prior to the civil rights movement, John had never seriously questioned the legitimacy of racial segregation in Albany. He "never thought about any of this, in one way or another, it just was what it was at that time. It was all I knew until the civil rights movement started to challenge it," he said. Initially, he was not committed to nonviolence as a proactive strategy for obtaining equality because it was usually met with hostility and violence from whites in general and the police in particular. John reflected, "I realized that if somebody hit me I was going to hit them back." But the ministers offered guidance to the protesters. "They told us how important it was that we abstained from violence, from retaliation, and that we had to stay focused on our cause." Intellectually, John understood how important a nonviolent posture was to the movement, but, even as a child, he had not backed down from a fight. For John, a nonviolent political stance in the face of violence was a struggle in itself, one that required enormous inner strength: "it took me some time to realize that if somebody hit me, that it was important not to be angry; not to fight; not to let them get the best of me; that you had to take whatever happened to you." In that realization, John, like other students at the time, knew that nonviolent demonstrations could result in injury or even death.

But after hearing Dr. Martin Luther King speak at his church and "heard how important it was to abstain from violence," John realized that "I can do this and it's okay to do this." He was selected to participate in the student "sit-ins at the five and ten-cent store downtown." Describing what happened when he along with other protesters attempted to sit at the lunch counter in Woolworth's, John said:

We've always gone to the back of restaurants to pick our food up. We could never sit down and have a meal. The ministers said it was time we sat down. I was picked. I guess we all had to do our part, so they would choose different people for different protest, at different times. You are supposed to go in the store, you have to sit there, and whatever happens, you have to take it. We went down, and the cops stopped us at the door. The police had been waiting. They didn't put us in paddy wagons, they had trucks, and there were all these cops on both sides of trucks on motor cycles and in cars. They took us to the county jail, but we didn't go in the jail. They had a fenced in area in the back of county jail, and we had to go in that area, the county jail was pretty small. We were put into this holding area, and we started to sing, and that's when they started putting water hoses on us. They said, "we have to cool these niggers down."

It worked for a minute or two, and then we started back singing again. We stayed until that evening. A lawyer came down and got us out. I don't think anybody ended up actually staying in jail. They just took our names, and it was more like harassment than anything else. For us, it wasn't traumatic. It wasn't a thing that we felt like we were going to change the world because of what we did.

It is important to note that black students participating in the lunch counter sit-ins throughout the South faced enormous risks to their personal safety and jeopardized their college careers. Many were idealistic and believed that they could indeed change the world. But after centuries of development, changing the deeply entrenched racial status quo of the South was both a courageous and a daunting task. Each step in the civil rights struggle toward the goal of racial equality did not necessarily produce tangible results—that is, results significantly altering the political and economic well-being of black life at the time. Simply stated, fundamental change was slow and in most instances not readily apparent, especially in the day-to-day lives of southern blacks. Therefore, it was difficult for John to grasp that not only was the world changing around him as a result of global and local freedom struggles taking place during the 1960s, but he too was changing as a result of his direct involvement in the civil rights movement. He actively participated in boycotts, protests, and other demonstrations. He voted for the first time after passing a literacy test, and, along with college classmates and church members, attended the heralded 1963 march on Washington led by Dr. King.

John was in fact gaining self-confidence and developing a broader consciousness of the possibilities of black life. The notion of physical, personal, and political freedom began to resonate for him, and he wanted more out of life. Yet the stark reality imposed by race on black life at the time—even amidst gradual and incremental change—continued to limit his life-options. He graduated from college in 1964, with a Bachelors of Arts degree in business administration and a sense of accomplishment. Even so, John still could not envision a future, one that afforded a sense of worth and value, especially in Albany. With a sense of pride and a college education, John took a job as a clerk in "the stock room of a jewelry store." He said, "I really didn't have a sense of what I was going to do." Lingering, one day he received a telephone call from his "brother who told me to come to New York." John decided to leave Albany and asked his best friend to join him. With his brother's call, he started to imagine a world beyond Albany, Georgia. In 1965, John arrived in New York City.

John's and Daniel's experiences fit into a broader narrative about physical, personal, and political freedom and its meaning for doing black masculinity. Their experiences were tied to the structural ways race, gender, and violence influenced different and convergent realities of black male life during the 1960s. Through their decisions and actions, each pursued life-strategies that sought greater physical, personal, and social freedom. Those strategies, however, were highly dependent on the possibilities and choices, or lack thereof, available for them to pursue. Change, whether minor or significant, occurred in their individual lives. That change, however, reflected a reality imposed by existing social and cultural arrangements, where the meaning of freedom took on an illusive and deceptive quality in both of their lives.

For Daniel, the meaning of freedom was deeply personal but attached to a larger narrative that connected patriarchal manhood with that of abuse and violence. Daniel's father valued education—if not for himself, then for his son. That value did not necessarily rest in a purely intellectual pursuit of knowledge. Rather, he saw education, once obtained, as a socially acceptable device, a mechanism that could perhaps mitigate some harsh realities of racial oppression. But, presumably, his father did not envision that education could also be used as a mean for lessening some harsh realities of patriarchal oppression. As such, education became an acceptable outlet for self-awareness and expression that allowed Daniel to mitigate some of his father's power, control, and dominance over his life.

In Daniel's desire for freedom, he used education as an important pretext, a guise that provided an effective cover in attempts to avoid, manipulate, and resist his father's abuse and violence. Education was a tool that he used to assert his own personal power. By no means do I imply that Daniel did not understand the importance of academic achievement in obtaining his life-aspirations. Instead, I suggest that in the immediacy of his life-circumstances—in a household where violence was constant—education was a means-to-an-end that enabled Daniel to gain greater sense of freedom. Perhaps, in an ironic way, the value his father gave to education actually resulted in him losing a grip over the lives of both Daniel and his mother. and that loss of power, control, and dominance led to violence and self-destruction. Free of his father's violence, Daniel's memories of what happened continue to shadow his life, and the experiences surrounding what happened shape how he sees himself as man.

Similar to Daniel, but in a different social and cultural context, the meaning of freedom for John was also deeply physical, personal, and political. However, that meaning was attached to the larger narrative linking racial injustice with violence. Jim Crow segregation imposed its reality on John's life, and as an individual he was virtually powerless in his response. Segregation severely constrained and limited John's physical, personal, and social being. In so doing, this system of racial oppression denied his very humanity. As his experience suggests and John well understood, his freedom was linked to collective, rather than individual, action. The civil right struggles were hard fought, and changes were slow in coming. Racial restrictions that prohibited access to public institutions and accommodations were eventually legally abolished. But during the 1960s John realized the most fundamental question: what is the value of that access, the meaning of that freedom, when manhood itself is denied?

Self-Determination

As young black men, also coming of age in the 1960s, Richard's and Matt's experiences carried them down different paths than those of Daniel and John. Their sense of manhood took on a different meaning. They did not engage in a struggle for physical, personal, and social freedom. For them, that freedom was assumed. Living their lives on the edge, seemingly on their own terms where they determined the rules, manhood for them was whatever they wanted it to be. But they learned that there was a tremendous physical, personal, and political price to be paid for the illusion of self-rule. Three years after his mother was released from prison, Richard, at thirteen years of age, discovered himself homeless on the streets of Newark. Determined to survive by any means necessary, he now found lying, stealing, and violence at the center of his way of life. What was morally right, correct, or fair was of little concern to Richard, for he found those coveted social values and attitudes unrelentingly denied to him. Free of conventional restrictions, he abided by his own standards. Richard had no reservations whatsoever about what he needed to do—in a seemingly uncaring world—to simply survive. Coming of age as a young black man during the late 1960s, he lived his life as if he had nothing to lose, except life itself. He determined the rules, without considering either restrictions or consequences to his actions, and engaged the world on his own terms. But, in so doing, he repeatedly paid a hefty price for that determination.

Living on the margins, Richard was well aware of his immediate surroundings and attuned to potential hazards and dangers threatening his well-being. He was also acutely aware of the presence of racial injustice and the threat it, too, posed to the value of his life and the general disvalue of black life. This fact was made painfully clear to Richard in 1968, when a black man whose life was the antithesis of his own, Dr. Martin Luther King, was brutally assassinated.

Richard vividly recalls when and where he heard the news of Dr. King's assassination: "It's something that I will never forget," he said. He has strong memories, because, in his anger over the killing, he sought retribution. Richard was not alone in his feelings; many young blacks across the country took to the streets in rebellion. Richard joined them and actively participated in the Newark riot, immediately following Dr. King's death. With a friend,

Richard "steals a truck and we are riding around looking for stores," and they decided to loot a Pawn Shop:

> It had gates on the window, so he drives this truck through the Pawn Shop window. It was bent, so he said "you just climb in there and pass the stuff out to me." They had leather coats, jewelry, and gun cases. Whatever I could grab I'm just handing it to him. He's throwing it into the back of the truck. He said the police are coming. He leaves me and I'm scared to death. They're shinning lights inside. They had all these cashmere coats on this rack, so I pulled the coats over me and I hid under them. The cops are walking all on top of me. They were searching the store. "Nobody is in here." I stayed under the coats until about daybreak. I said, I'm not going to leave here with nothing. So I packed me some bags up with watches and rings. I crawled out of the store and run to my mother's home. I'm knocking and knocking, but she wouldn't open the door.

Because of his unruly behavior, Richard's mother kicked him out of the house when he was only thirteen years old. Periodically, he would return to the projects and stay with his family. But the stays were usually brief because he did something unacceptable, and, refusing to tolerate his behavior, his mother again kicked him out of the house. Finally, he remembered the time when his mother came to the door and said: "You can't live here anymore." Richard said that he did not "care. I'm a man and I can take care of myself. I don't need anybody." Not only did his mother "throw" him out of the house for good, she also called relatives to say: "I put that boy out and don't let him live in your house. And they followed that to the letter." Initially, Richard bounced around from one friend's house to another, and sometimes he even slept in subway stations or trains. Forced "to fend for himself," Richard "was really bitter. I'm mad at the world. And I blamed my mother for everything that was happening to me."

To survive, Richard "joined a gang shortly after I got put out of my mother's house." He described the gang as a "bunch of runaways, all of us were pretty much in the same situation: runaways, homeless, young people, looking for love, and family." Gang members provided protection, solidarity, and an alternative family. Finding what he needed, Richard moved into a building the gang had taken over. In this male-dominant environment where aggressive masculinity was prized above all else, Richard thrived and rose quickly through the ranks. He became the War Lord "because I enjoyed the violence, and there was a lot of it." As the War Lord, Richard positioned himself as the ultimate arbiter of the gang's activities, especially over when, where, and with whom they would do violence.

Violence was not only condoned but also expected, particularly in settling disputes and in asserting one's will over others, for whatever reason.

Primarily, the violence included "fighting rival gangs" and extorting money by "terrorizing individuals and businesses who owed us." As the War Lord, under Richard's leadership, the gang grew from "probably about fifty of us, to close to two thousand" members. What Richard liked most about his gang activities were the status, prestige, respect, and especially the power he enjoyed among its male peers: "I saw myself as being a powerful person. My power was in manipulation and controlling other people. I was good at it. It was about fear. Nobody really knew where I was coming from. And I didn't care if I got hurt, but I knew I could hurt you." Yet that violence neither appeased his anger and bitterness, nor did it provide a sense of comfort for his unspeakable pain—his family's rejection and his deep sense of loneliness as a result: "I really didn't have anyone to talk to about a lot of the things that bothered me. It just seemed like, at that time, whatever happened you just shove it under the rug. You hide whatever is going on. You don't have a right to discuss your feelings. In fact you don't even have any feelings." But he was deeply troubled, and to relieve his anguish and numb his pain Richard turned to drugs. At sixteen, Richard was a drug addict, taking drugs intravenously through his veins. After his mother kicked him out of the house for good, he started selling drugs—heroin and cocaine—for his cousin. Richard was "skin popping heroin and mainlining. But for me, I didn't want to believe I was addicted because I never was sick. I had drugs all the time. Being addicted to heroin I still played basketball. It didn't affect my ability to do things." Yet when he started to sense that his addiction was becoming a problem, Richard "would go buy Methadone from other people on the street," to ease his cravings, and "chill out for a couple of months." Although he developed the ability to stop using heroin for long periods of time, Richard continued to "smoke weed and have a drink on a daily basis." He always drifted back into using heroin and cocaine.

In addition to his gang activities and drug involvement, around this time Richard had his first serious relationship with a young woman. He described his relationship with this "girlfriend":

> I believed that I was in love with her. It felt like love to me. But love for me was being very controlling. Where are you going? Where have you been? Why were you in that place? What did he say to you? I was physically abusive to her. At that time I felt like I had some power over a woman. I felt that I had power and control over outcomes. I used to see the pimps and be around a lot of those guys. I used to see the reactions or the response they got after they treated their woman like that. And I guess I picked up a lot of that stuff from them.

Richard and his girlfriend moved into an apartment together, and he used drug money to pay their expenses—"the rent, utilities, buying the food."

He believed that their relationship "worked" because she was "really street smart" and "we were getting high together." But in that relationship, similar to his relationship with gang members, "there was a lot of physical abuse and a lot of fighting." He described what happened:

> A lot of older guys liked her. I was very insecure. I always felt like people were going to let me down. I am not having it. Through violence and manipulation, I tried to control her. I tried to buy her. I was trying to hold on to her. We clearly understood each other as far as our experiences go when we were growing up. Nobody loved us, no support from family members, and cut off from our families. We had a lot in common when it came to that. But I guess as time went on I became more and more brutal. I didn't know how to deal with her, how to communicate what I was feeling to her, or why I felt that way. I always tried to apologize and make up. After every violent incident it always led to sex afterwards. And that was a control situation, because I knew she felt like she didn't have a choice. She was afraid of me. I know she was for sure. It was pretty violent. I was full of rage. It seemed like every time I was trouble, I would be violent, and a lot of time it was misdirected. I was enraged. It seemed as if I couldn't control it. I was powerless over it. We probably lived together for about two years. This was the first woman that I had truly assaulted.

This girlfriend was by no means the last woman whom Richard brutalized. Given the pattern of his life thus far, he wanted to change his behavior, but he did not know exactly how to go about it. Searching for alternatives, he began to notice how members of the Nation of Islam presented themselves as black men on the streets of Newark. Richard "thought they were sharp and articulate. They moved as if they had control over themselves. When you see them you reacted to them," he said. Impressed by their dignity and the ways they carried themselves on the streets of Newark, Richard started to attend the Mosque and later converted to Islam. But he was not necessarily attracted to the religious teachings, the codes of conduct governing behavior, the deference to leadership, or the self-discipline that was required. Instead, he was attracted to the Black Muslim's presentation of masculinity, and so, he "wasn't into it wholeheartedly."

The streets offered "real opportunities," especially for making money, which Richard did not find by standing on corners selling *Muhammad Speaks*, the Nation of Islam newspaper. So he drifted back to what was more familiar to him. As a gang member and drug dealer, Richard liked the fact that he "was somebody to be reckoned with" and took great satisfaction in the power, money, and especially the violence that came with the status he received. When he returned to the streets, however, Richard was not as active as he once was in the gang; he was no longer the War Lord. He continued his heavy involvement with drugs, both selling and using. Through that involvement, the opportunity that he had long waited unexpectedly presented itself one day:

A guy, who I was selling drugs for, came to me one day and gave me a briefcase. I said what you want me to do with this? He said, "If I don't come back it's yours." That scared me. I said, I work for you and if some people are after you, they may be after me too. I knew who was after him. It was Bobby B and his people. It was a take over. They wanted to take over my projects. The word on the streets was either you get down with Bobby B, or you lay down. And those that didn't get down with him laid down. He had a lot of people murdered. I didn't want to get caught up. I had this guy's briefcase. It was a lot of money in there, about $250,000. I wanted to get away. It was an opportunity to get away. Fear, money, and deep down inside I really wanted another chance at life. I wanted another chance to try and start over again. To try and figure out where I was going in my life.

Richard decided that the Army National Guard was a good place to hide himself and his new-found wealth. The added benefit, he believed, was that it just might be a good place to try and start life over again. He "didn't want anyone that was involved in my street life to know that I was leaving," but he knew that he had to get away. He decided to "clean" himself up by getting the drugs out of his system so that he could pass the army's physical examination. Once that was done, he signed up for the National Guard and was sent almost immediately to Georgia for basic training. Although Richard had burglary charges pending against him, a deal was struck between the Army and the Newark prosecutor's office, and "they gave me a second chance." Richard took a commercial flight to boot camp; on the way he had a lay-over in Atlanta, and there he found a bank branch, where he opened a small savings account and rented a safety deposit box. He put the bulk of the $250,000 in a safety deposit box, about $4,000 in savings, and carried $2,000 with him to boot camp.

While riding the bus on his way to an army base in rural Georgia, the safety deposit key securely around his neck, Richard started asking himself: "What did I sign up for? I didn't know anything about the military or what's it going to be like. I was worrying about basically what did I get myself into?" Upon arriving at the base, "immediately they started barking orders at me. Who in the hell do you think you are hollering and spitting in my face? I wasn't used to taking order so right then and there I knew it was going to be rough. The Company Commander says something about he doesn't take crap off of anybody. He said, 'This is Uncle Sam's Army and we now own you.'

I was pissed off. I didn't expect anything like that. I felt I was in a lot of trouble. I said what the hell did I get myself into? This is going to be a real problem. I had to figure out how to get the hell out of there."

Richard was no longer in a position to exert independence. In this all-male environment, his freedom was compromised, and his personal power was threatened: he had no control over the situation he found himself in, and no longer could he do whatever he wanted simply as he pleased. Initially, Richard had problems adjusting to the military codes of conduct and following army rules. Deferring to the authority of his white southern sergeant was a major hurdle that Richard had to overcome. But Richard did not lose sight of his needs and interests at the time. Begrudgingly, he complied with the rules and orders because, as he said, "they told me they were going to give me a dishonorable discharge and send my black ass back to Newark." But something changed. Late one night his sergeant came into the barracks and said, "I want to talk to you outside right now":

> I was like what is this guy up to. He said that he had read my file, and he understood that I had had it rough. "That the discipline is created to teach you how to become a man, and I want to help you to do that." I don't trust this white man; I don't trust no white people. Today I can say that he had my best interest in mind. I became a project for him. Not so much that he was going to break me, but that he was going to help me become a man. For him being a man meant showing me what it took to be responsible.

Gradually, Richard realized that he liked this all-male competitive environment. As he said: "I began to enjoy it. I was in the best physical shape of my life, and I was drug free. I loved the competition. Everything was designed around winning, being a leader, or excelling in whatever you did." Richard did excel; upon graduating from basic training he received "the top award for soldier discipline and training," and as a sign of accomplishment he received the rank of Private First Class (PFC). At that time, he described himself as "truly a soldier. I believed in everything in the military, and whatever the military said, that was pretty much it. I felt like I was really an American, and it was my duty to fight for my country."

The camaraderie he felt toward the military was similar to what he experienced as a member of his street gang. Also similar was a nagging sense of distrust. As Richard said, "even though I have excelled, I still had this thing about trust. What is really going on here? What is really the plan? " But the distrust he sensed in the Army was clearly different. Richard's leeriness about the Army stemmed from his view of racial disparities: "I saw the disparities between the black soldiers and the white soldiers, and I was distrustful. A lot of times we always got the demeaning jobs, while the white soldiers would get the cushier jobs. I viewed those things as racist." As Richard continued his military service, he indeed had reasons to be distrustful.

Following basic training, Richard wanted to attend "airborne school," and with his record of accomplishments in Army thus far, he thought that he had a good chance of getting accepted. He was waiting on base to receive his new orders for that training, but there was a delay. Meanwhile the base commander sent him to Missouri to be trained as an auto mechanic on military vehicles. About a month after Richard had arrived in Missouri, while working in the motor pool and awaiting new orders, his National Guard unit received activation orders "to go to Vietnam to ship bodies back to the states." Richard was "scared because there is still a war going on and I don't want to go over there. There's a lot of fear. They didn't explain to us exactly what our detail would be doing. They only told us that we would be there for six months." Upon arriving in Vietnam, Richard found out exactly what he would be doing:

> Twelve-hours shifts dealing with body parts all day. I said no big deal. My cousin was a mortician so I used to help her out. No big deal because I've done that before. There was a crew, a squad of us, and what we did specifically was build bodies. We would put body parts together; arms, legs, heads, torsos . . . it wasn't a thing of accuracy, it was about returning a body to the states so that the family could bury a body. If it was Caucasian, and if the arm looked like it could have been about the same size we would put all that in one body bag until we had a whole body. There was a building that they were using for storage, and they delivered so many parts from the freezer to us. They may have a freezer full of arms and a freezer full of legs. . . .

Richard found a macabre, gruesome and ghastly assignment far removed from his aspiration of airborne training. Contrary to his initial impressions, Richard was not immune to the human destruction and ravages of war and sorting body parts was indeed a big deal that took an emotional toll on him. Once again, to numb his feelings toward what he was experiencing, he turned to alcohol, but it was not enough to deaden his emotions. Along with other guys in the crew, he started buying "marijuana, heroin, and opium" from the women who worked at brothels. The drugs allowed him to develop insensitivity to handling the body parts: "I just wanted to block it out. Twelve-hours a day, everyday, constantly doing the same horrible things. I just wanted to shut it out. There was a lot of smoking of opium and smoking of heroin: probably to the point where I was hallucinating; nodding out when I would do stuff; and so high that I would do crazy stuff. I had no regard for the bodies that we were handling. Ain't nobody going to look in the damn body bags, just throw any arm or any leg into it!" Finally, one day a lieutenant came into the area and saw how "stressful" Richard had become. "He asked me if

I wanted to do this anymore. I said there's nothing you can do about it. He said, 'yes it is, I'm going to take you off of this detail' so after about five-months into it, he took me off the detail." Because Richard had some training in auto mechanics he was transferred to Germany, where he received several promotions. "I became a sergeant, and I was probably one of the youngest." Richard soon discovered, however, that there were increased expectations attached to an increase in rank. One day his lieutenant "told me that there are drugs being sold in the company and that they wanted me to infiltrate the people who were selling the drugs and come back and inform them. I told them that's not my job." He refused to play the role of a snitch, that request violated the code of conduct Richard developed not only as a gang member but especially as a drug dealer.

Even though he was an enlisted soldier, Richard was also a sergeant and "expected to go along with the program. You're either a part of the program or you're a problem for the military." Almost immediately following the conversation with his lieutenant, Richard started to experience major problems in the army, and from his perspective racism lay at the heart of his experience. He started noticing increased racial insults and menial job assignments. Richard felt disrespected and decided that "I'm not going to keep letting these white boys call me Nigger and keep doing these crappy details." At that point, he decided that he "really didn't want to be in the military anymore." Subsequent to that decision, Richard did not complete his required "four years of military service."

Richard thought that he was being harassed, and he "was angry all the time." He also started drinking heavily and again smoked heroin. He described his overall "attitude and demeanor":

> I'm argumentative with officers on base. I'm getting these things called Article Fifteens for not reporting to duty. I had a lot of days coming, so I said the hell with this. I'm getting written up for bad behavior, and I'm getting into all kinds of conflicts. They are taking my money. I didn't care about that because I had money. I remember telling an officer I make more money in a day than you make in a month. I got a couple of guys selling drugs in the company, now. I go back to the old life style. You take my pay and I'm going to get as many of these white guys strung out on drugs as possible. So I'll take their pay. So it got even crazier. I'm at a point that I really don't care. I'm disoriented and in a lot of pain, and no one to talk to about it. Even if I did have someone to talk to, they wouldn't understand what I was going through. I just felt alone, and I was very lonely. I didn't think I had any control over my life. I didn't care about life. The only thing I wanted was to get out of Germany. I just wanted to get away and go somewhere else and start over again.

To get out of the army, Richard drew upon a familiar resource for getting his way—violence. As he said, "I was going to be destructive. That was my plan to be destructive." Through a series of very violent encounters, Richard put his plan into action. In one incident, he hit a white soldier over the head with a guitar. Rather than locking him up in the brig, the Military Police (MP) took him to the hospital. "The psychiatrist tells them they can't press any charges against me because I was so high that I was temporarily insane. That I was not responsible for my actions, so they let me go." But Richard was not deterred; "I put myself in a position where it made them justify their actions":

> I was on crappy detail and on restrictions all the time. I couldn't leave the base. I tried to leave the base and that would create other situations for me. One night I came in—I wasn't supposed to leave—I was totally inebriated, drunk and everything else. I entered these guys' rooms, and they were sleep. I assaulted them in their sleep. I despised the company. So I go from room to room assaulting people. They finally call the MP's. I get into a big fight with the MP's with a baseball bat. They are assaulting me, and I'm assaulting them. I wake up in the morning in the brig. I'm pretty beat up, and they bring me before my Company Commander. We go to the base commander's office. I can't stand at attention. I'm hung over, sore, and I can't do it. "Are you refusing to follow direct orders?" I was like, whatever you want to call it. Just send me to prison or whatever, just come on with it. He said, "You heard me nigger." All I can remember is leaping over his desk. They beat me pretty bad.

Richard was charged with assaulting a commanding officer, a colonel. He was found guilty, stripped of his rank, given a bad conduct discharge, and sentenced to "two years in a federal prison in Kansas." But all Richard wanted at the time was to "go back to the states." And the Army did not hesitate in sending him back. Two days after he was convicted, with "legs and hands shackled to the seat" Richard was on a military plane headed to prison, in the United States. Flying back, Richard said: "Ironically, all I was thinking about was that I was free. I'm out of that hell hole. I'm free. I'm going to be in prison for two years. I can do these two years and move on with my life." Until this point, Richard had not spent any length of time incarcerated, although he had been arrested on several occasions. While in prison, however, he found it extremely difficult to simply serve his time and then move on with his life.

As a young black man, Richard fully participated in his life. He attempted to live life on his own terms, regardless of what was considered social and culturally acceptable. Gradually, however, he began to embody a reality that was imposed upon him—a reality that positioned him on the very margins of society where he lived his life largely under antagonistic circumstances. Alienated from social and cultural expectations and defying constraints, as Richard interacted in the world of men, he carried continuous anger and unexpressed pain with him. Although his anger may have been viewed as "manly," especially by other men, Richard knew that expressions of emotional pain were unacceptable; such expressions were sure signs of vulnerability that exposed weaknesses that could diminish the respect he received from other men.

Amid fears, doubts, and hurt, to repress these feelings, Richard resorted to self-medication. Numbing his pain with alcohol and drugs, Richard's addiction allowed him to avoid taking responsibility for his decisions and actions, and in turn, this made him both damaged and dangerous. Under such circumstances, Richard gradually began to lose his sense of self-worth and value. As a result he cared little, if any, for self or others. As he moved on with his life he continued to rely upon destruction as a life-strategy that would eventually have deadly consequences.

In looking back over this period, Richard recognized that he "did not have control over my life," that he was not determining the rules. That lack of control is reflected in his social and cultural alienation and in the enormous emotional pain undermining his sense of self-value and self-worth. Consequently, Richard believes that while living life on the edge he was "a deeply troubled young man. I was very troubled and in a lot of pain." He attributes his troubles and pain to estrangement, a sense of deep loneliness, and to the racism he experienced. Richard, however, readily admits that these and other experiences were merely the effects of, rather than the root cause of, his troubles and pain. What lies beneath these experiences reveals the "real" source of his troubles and pain, as seen in his interpretations of what happened to him as a young black man.

On reflection, Richard thinks that some of his troubles and pain stemmed from the fact that he was forced to fend for himself, in whatever ways he could, when still a child. For this abandonment he harbored anger toward his family, particularly his mother. He said, "I just didn't know what to say to her at the time. I was very bitter with my mother. I was torn between an apology for my behavior and being really anger with her. At some point I realized that some of my behavior had to do with her putting me out, even though I didn't want to fully own it. I wanted to blame someone else for my life and what was happening to me."

Of his deep sense of loneliness, Richard said: "I think a big piece of that loneliness came from what I associated with what it was for me to be a man. I couldn't tell any one what was happening to me. I was really concerned about what other guys thought of me, and not so much of what I thought of myself. I wanted guys to perceive me as this real hard guy that could pretty much deal with anything. But that was the furthest thing from the truth. So I was living that lie and going through the pain of it at the same time." Of the racism he experienced, particularly while in the army, he said: "Because of the drugs and my state of mind, when I look back, I probably should have gotten a medical discharge at that time. But racism didn't make it a consideration for the powers that be in my company. It was about being with the program and not about how do we get this guy some help? He's angry and defiant. He has assaulted people in the company. We don't care about what kind of pain he's going through; he just needs to be punished."

Similar to Richard's experience, Matt's life gradually followed a path that increasingly became to difficult for him to alter. Coming of age as a young black man in the late 1960s, Matt too was seeking to live life on his own terms: terms that eventually alienated social and cultural expectations and defied constraints. Self-determined in his decisions and actions, Matt fully participated in making his experiences. But those experiences brought him face-to-face with the reality that race, gender, and violence imposed—the consequences of what it means to be the arbiter of one's own life as a young black male in America.

In 1968, Matt was living with his family in the projects of Baltimore, which he called Brick City. Matt no longer relied on his mother for economic support. While going to school, he worked several odd jobs and provided for himself and helped his mother with household expenses. Yet a strain had developed in their relationship. Matt was increasingly intolerant of his step-father's presence in the household. Even though the violence between his step-father and mother seemed to have declined, owing partly to George's deteriorating health, Matt still hated him. Because of George's unavoidable presence in his life, Matt developed a "love/hate relationship with my mother. The hate part was the fact that she continued to stay with this guy who was a detriment to everything we were doing." Yet, he loved his mother, and to show his affection he bought her gifts: "Christmas, birthday, mother's day, you name it."

As a young man feeling a sense of his own personal power, Matt was now able to say to George, "fuck you." There was on-going tension in the household so during one summer vacation Matt's mother sent him to Chicago to stay with her two brothers. Matt respected and admired his uncles, unlike his step-father; for him they represented "strong black men, who stood up for they believed in." From his relationship with his uncles, Matt "developed a sense of black consciousness. These were black men who were veterans and had college degrees." His uncles were Vietnam veterans; one had been in the Army, and the other in the Marines. Matt listened closely as his uncles and their friends' debated political issues, namely the state of racism and the Vietnam War: "I remember all the discussions they had about the Vietcong asking black soldiers why they weren't in their own country fighting the same enemy they were fighting." Not only did his uncles discuss politics, but they were also active in social movements, and Matt went on demonstrations with them. That political involvement, Matt said, had an "effect on me as a young man, and it had an effect on me when I went back to Baltimore, and it has an effect on me now. I understood that my sense of blackness was linked to them and my sense of manhood was linked to my uncles." When Matt returned to the projects of Baltimore after visiting his uncles, to his surprise his mother decided that the whole family would move to Chicago: "Mama decides that it's time to get the hell out of Brick City because it was becoming too violent." Matt was delighted with her decision. Relocating to Chicago represented a new beginning. He started high school and shortly thereafter got a part-time job working at a unionized supermarket. He made friends, and "the girls liked me." Life seemed hopeful and unproblematic, until one day Matt and a new friend, Jay, decided to cut woodshop class, which was the last period of the school day. The woodshop teacher "was a black guy," and the next time Matt and Jay returned to class, the teacher wanted to punish them for cutting class.

> This was during the time when they used corporal punishment. He wanted to paddle us. Lean over on the table, I'm going to hit you on your ass with a piece of wood. He told us to "bend over and take it like a man." We said no, and it turned into a huge thing. I had a problem with someone who wanted to hit me with a piece of wood. It wasn't going to happen. The teacher wanted to fight. So he pushed Jay, and we ran out of the classroom.

Unbeknownst to the teacher, Jay was a member of the Black Gangster Disciples, a street gang, and his brothers were part of the Royal Disciples, the leadership of the gang. Jay had grown up in the Disciples' royal family. Therefore, when Matt and Jay returned to school after the initial confrontation with the teacher, they were accompanied by Jay's "older brothers and his guys, and everybody was strapped. They had weapons—guns—and wore their blue berets," symbolizing the Disciples' color. As a result of Disciples' intervention, Matt and Jay were moved to another class, and the teacher was told by the administration not to have contact with them, and "that was that." And Matt liked the fact that the Disciples had power and could determine certain outcomes.

This was Matt's first, but certainly not his last, encounter with a street gang. There was gang activity all around him, and he too became involved. Matt started to notice that a gang periodically came into his high school's cafeteria and "start smacking people around, everybody including women."

One day, while walking home from school, Matt was passing "this taco place, where we used to hang out, and somebody hit the window and says come in." What happened next is:

> I go in and there's a group of black men that I know from the Disciples. And they asked me, what are we going to do in terms of the gang that's running into the school and slapping women around? One of these guy's girlfriend had gotten hit in the mouth. They said it's reached the point where, what are we going to do about it? They said that they were sanctioned by the Disciple Nation to form a branch of Folks. We ended up having the 116th Street Disciples. The gang was formed in the taco restaurant that day, when I was just walking by. This was like the day after the other gang had run into the school, for the last time. They asked me to join because of what happened in the woodshop class with the teacher, and they knew I wasn't a coward. They also asked me to join because I dressed well, and the women liked me. There was no initiation, it was just we're going to do this. We formed in defense of the school and in defense of ourselves, that's what this was all about.

As a member of the 116th Street Disciples, Matt was now a part of the Folk Nation, which included the Black Gangster Disciples, the Black Disciples, the Black Gangsters, and the Disciples. These gangs were all members of the Folk Nation, they were Folks, and to signify their affiliation they wore blue berets, in contrast to their chief rival, the People Nation, whose members wore red berets. For Matt, the two current gangs, "the Crips and the Bloods are the children, the descendants of the Folk and People Nations of Chicago." Matt's involvement with the gangs introduced him to a new political reality:

> You could go into certain neighborhoods in Chicago and see three to five hundred young black men wearing different berets. During that time the gangs were becoming political; they in some ways had a sense of social consciousness. It came from the black movement, where black folks no matter who you were, were just being political. But the gangs were used by Cointellpro (counter intelligence program). They got almost a million dollars from federal and state governments to disrupt some of the Black Panthers stuff that was going on in Chicago. They gave them the money, during the late 60s, so that these street gangs could develop summer programs and give stipends to the kids in the neighborhood. But it was the leadership of the different street gangs who were the ones that were empowered to run these programs, and they were paid to do it. They were also paid to be disruptive and it had an effect on the Panthers' activities at the time.

During this period, Matt continued to go school and work and liked the rewards he received from both. Increasingly, gang activities took up his time as well because Dock was "the peewee coordinator for the shorties, and I became the coordinator for everybody." As such, Matt's gang involvement introduced new levels of violence into his life. Prior to his gang membership, he had experienced only the violence between his mother and step-father—now nonexistent with the family's move to Chicago and George's failing health. In other words, Matt's direct involvement with violence outside the home was relatively limited. But as the coordinator of 116th Street Disciples this changed dramatically: "that put some stuff in motion." Matt recalled his early involvement with the gang:

> I'm on my way to work and I see three guys with the other gang. I'm by myself and I take off running. I knew that I couldn't handle all three of them. But I also knew that right inside my house, like a vestibule, we kept a shotgun. I knew it was there. So when I see them, I'm not just running, all I got to do is get to the house. They're chasing me and I could run. It's only about ten blocks, and all I wanted to do is get to the house and get the gun. I did. They saw this little gun and they left. I grabbed the shotgun and they take off. I don't think I would have shot them; then it wasn't in me. If they were beating me I would have shot them, but in that situation I didn't have to shoot them.

Matt became known in various communities for his gang affiliation, and because of this when he walked the streets of Chicago he was often accompanied by other members of 116th Street Disciples. He also started carrying a gun on a fairly regular basis:

> I was strapped. I had a gun in my pocket. I got the gun from Folks. Once we became the 116th Street Disciples, we were sanctioned, and Folks gave us weapons and shit. There was a War Lord. The War Lord is the person who kept the guns, so if something is going on he would bring whatever he had. He's the one that kept all the weapons for all of the groups. The guns were kept in one central place, and the War Lord was responsible for that. Just like the treasurer was responsible for the money. He had to be accountable for those guns, like the treasurer was accountable for the money.

Even though he carried a gun and participated in gang activities during this period, Matt did not shoot anyone, and no one shot him. In Chicago, he had settled into a new way of living, but his mother had not so she "was ready to move back to Baltimore." Matt thought that George "wanted to move back because Baltimore was his home." Regardless of whose decision it was, Matt was "not ready to leave" because he had "status within the gang." Additionally, he was going to school and working, and he had a girlfriend and a car. Given this, Matt had no incentive whatsoever to leave Chicago and return to the Brick City. But one of his uncles "tells me that he thinks I should move back to Baltimore and be with my mother and sisters, to look out for my family. I didn't want to go, but I did." Matt went back to Baltimore with his family, but rather than returning to the projects "we moved into a white community, into a house."

Upon returning, Matt entered his junior year of high school. Because his family lived in a predominately white community, unlike their place in Chicago, he attended a white school, and his uncles' influence on racial matters came to the forefront. He was conscious of his new surrounding and the racial disadvantages it held for him and the other black students:

> When I get there, there're 2,500 students, but there are only 150 black students. Now my political awareness from my uncles starts to kick in. In school I'm very political. I say to them, look as black students we don't have any representation. We don't have the numbers to elect our own to the student government. We need some form of representation. My biggest nemesis was the only black man in the administration, who was the dean of boys. He thought that I was the worst thing he had ever seen. For him, I was the most arrogant nigger he had ever met, because I refused to cooperate. It's not that I refused to cooperate it's that I refused to be dismissed. I had become a student leader, so to speak. Eventually they allowed us to form an organization, but they would not allow us to call the organization Black Students United. They said that we couldn't use the word Black because that would suggest that only black students could be a part of the organization. They told us to call it another name. So we said what about Ebony Students United. They said okay.

On the day black students held an election for officers to this newly formed student organization, to which Matt was "probably going to be elected president [was] the day I literally walked off campus and walked into an army recruiter office." Reflecting, Matt said that he enlisted because he was "running away" from something. He was running away because he could not determine the outcome of circumstances that he thought were beyond his control.

On returning to Baltimore, Matt had developed an intimate relationship with Janice, a girl he had known in Brick City, "but something happened and we stopped seeing each other." He was also involved "with a couple of other women. I mean I got a life, and I'm moving forward." Matt discovered that he had not only his life to worry about, but also another; Janice was pregnant with his child, and there was a new life for him to consider. Furthermore, he did not want to be in Baltimore, and the tension at home escalated between Matt and his mother, especially when she found out that Janice was pregnant. The confrontation with the school administration over the new student organization representing the interests of black students placed added stress on Matt as well. There was "all this stuff in my face and I can't deal with it." Going into the Army for Matt seemed like "a legitimate way to escape, and I wanted to get away."

Toward the end of the Vietnam War in 1971, Matt at seventeen years of age went into the Army. Once again, he entered an all-male environment where competition, aggression, and violence were expected and rewarded. In basic training, Matt found symmetry between gang life and army life. He discovered that there were black men in his company who were also gang members, who were also Folks. He said: "Understand this was during a time when the criminal justice system was giving black men the choice of going into the Army or going to the joint. They needed soldiers, so they began to give black men going to prison the option of going to the Army. There were groups of men from Newark, DC, and Chicago, many of them gang members, and many of them knew each other. We came to the Army with a gang mentality, so there was a lot of violence" among rival gang members as a result.

Similar to the group dynamics that occurs in street gangs, during basic training, Matt was socialized into the male culture of army life, where he learned techniques for warfare and killing. He described some of the training activities: "There're a lot of push ups, sit ups, pull ups, running through obstacles courses. They were trying to get us fit: building our muscles and getting us to work as a team. We spent time on the firing range, running with fire arms. You're trained on weapons: M-16, 45, 50 caliber machine guns, and grenades. There's gorilla warfare training and night training." Matt was clear about the purposes of basic training: "I learned to be a killer. They taught me how to kill. They helped me to rationalize killing." As time past, these skills and lessons would not be lost on Matt. For now, however, his focus was on graduating from basic training and getting his permanent assignment. Receiving the rank of Private First Class (PFC) for his accomplishments during basic training, Matt was assigned to an army base in California, where he underwent six weeks of training to become a security clerk. He was trained to handle confidential information, for which he received a top security clearance and was assigned full-time to the message center. His job was from nine to five, and, other than the occasional guard duty, Matt was free to live off base and pursue his interests unabatedly.

The Army base was located in a small California army town that commercially catered to the needs of soldiers. Except for the daily routine of doing his job at the message center, the Army was now different for Matt because "you could disappear and you could now wear street clothes." Along with his guys, after work or on the weekends, Matt went to the black section of town and "hung out" with the hustlers and players. Matt described one fateful weekend:

> A couple of guys and myself go to this club, but it's a restaurant too. This is where all the players, hustlers, pimps, dope dealers, dope users, prostitutes, and everybody hung out at. So the hustlers and players bring their dope, their girls, their product to the area because they have a market. So we're sitting at a booth, and we're eating and it's like 2:00 in the morning. I'm sitting on one side of the booth and they're sitting on the other side. Again everybody is hanging out. I hear someone say, "I'm more woman than anyone in here." It's a gay guy, who is made up in the face but not really dressed in drag. He says the same thing again, "I'm more woman than anyone in here," and he turns and look at us and says, "Where're you boys from?" Obviously we are new, but the thing is we don't have short hair, so you don't really know that we're in the military, but we are in the military. He knew that we were, but he could recognize that we are not suckers by the way we were dressed. So the guy comes over and starts this conversation. I get uncomfortable, and as they are talking I grab the glass salt and pepper shakers off the table, I put them in my lap and take a handkerchief, and I put them in the handkerchief, and wrap them up. I'm thinking in a defensive mode. This was from the streets. This wasn't from anything I got from the military. This goes back to the streets of Chicago. So this guy comes and asks if he could sit down, and he probably weighs about 220/230 pounds, a fat guy. So I said let me get up; I didn't want him to pin me inside the booth. I get up and I let him sit down. One thing leads to another, and the guy puts his hand on my leg. I said, "Don't do that." I don't suffer from homophobia, but at the same time I'm not gay. I know this at my age, I'm nineteen. So one thing leads to another, and he grabs my leg again. I tell him, don't do that, and he says something stupid. I remember elbowing him in head, and I cracked him with the glass salt and pepper shakers. I hit him in such a way that his head split open and blood splattered all over my white two piece suit. He's hollering and screaming. He gets up, and I hit him again. My guys are ready to start whooping him, but the table booth is in the way. Everybody in the place is seeing what's going on. So when they see this happen, they're like oh shit, and everybody's trying to break down the only door to and get out. Cars are moving fast because they know the cops are on their way.

Was this brutal and bloody incidence a case of homophobic violence? During this period in his life, Matt does not acknowledge it as such. But he does recognize this incident as a "crucial point in my life." Not because he had any inkling of regret or remorse for hurting and injuring this person, but because of what happened next. In this environment of hustlers and players, some people were carefully observing Matt: his demeanor and presentation of self, his clothing, physical prowess, emotional detachment, and, above all, his ruthlessness. In this environment those qualities were highly respected, for they attested to Matt's toughness as a man. Matt's actions left little doubt to restaurant observers that he was someone to be reckoned with, that he too could defy conventional rules and was well-suited to play the game, on his own terms. That violent incident was indeed a "crucial point" in Matt's life. Displaying toughness, Matt's violence facilitated his initiation into the world of hustlers and players. He became a pimp. He described how he got into the "pimping game" that night, while still working full-time for the Army:

> My guys and I make it to the door, and a girl says, "get into my car," she was driving. So I hop in the back and another guy hops in the front, and she takes off. I didn't know who she was. She looked good. She took us to this after hours place. People were talking about what I did. The same people who had been at the restaurant were now at this place. I'm getting caught up in the accolades, in the status that I just whipped somebody. That night I got the tag, "Young Blood." This girl clearly wants to be with me, and we leave. The next thing I know, I wake up and we're about fifty-five miles north of the Army base. So we check into the Hilton Hotel. We spent the day in bed drinking and eating, and it getting towards evening. She gets herself together and says "I'll be back later. I'm drunk on wine." She had been out all night and day. She comes in and goes into the shower, and comes back and asks me how my day was. We have a conversation and then she put some money on the bed and says it was mine. Her name was Marie, and she begins to tell me about herself. She was in the prostitution game. So she throws this money on the bed, and it had to be $3000. She tells me that she's choosing me. I don't know what the hell to do, but I'm like okay, I'm all about that.

Marie introduces Matt to "the game of prostitution and everything that comes with that." At eighteen years of age, Matt becomes a pimp, and Marie is his "girl." This world of hustlers and players was not altogether unfamiliar to Matt; as a child from afar he had seen his father play in this world as a hustler. But it was Marie who groomed Matt as a pimp. She had chosen him as "her pimp, not because I knew the game, she knew she could control that, but because I put the fear of God into people and I had heart."

Marie also brought another woman, Karla, into the stable. Now Matt had "two girls and I still don't know what I'm doing." But he quickly learned the game. Known as "Young Blood" in the community of hustlers and players, Matt was taking in about $1,500 a week, plus receiving pay from the Army.

Living in a house together, Marie, Karla, and Matt were all enterprising: Marie prostituted herself. Karla's job was stealing and boosting stolen goods, conning men out of money, and occasionally prostitution. And Matt sold drugs, namely marijuana and acid, and he was "passing paper, I'm writing bad checks." Although Matt was still learning his role as a pimp and all that came with it, he knew that his chief adversaries were other pimps. For protection, Matt was regularly "strapped"; he carried a gun. And over the course of about five months, he was now firmly rooted in the game.

Matt was noticed in the community of hustlers and players, but the Army began to take note of Matt, as well: the expensive house, flashy clothes, and car drew attention in a small town. There was talk on the base. Matt recounted the situation, "I'm still going back to base. I'm now encountering racism on base. There were these Master Sergeants, white guys from Texas, who had issues with me. I'm experiencing a lot of racism, which was making me feel like I didn't want to be there anymore. They were discriminating against me and talking to me real stupid, making racist remarks." After about a year, Matt decided to leave the Army. He called his "mother and said I want to get a hardship discharge. So I put together a petition saying that as the oldest son, I was needed at home." The petition was approved, and Matt received "an honorable discharged with full military benefits."

While Matt was awaiting the Army's approval of his hardship petition, another pimp disrespected him, and he had to deal with him or lose street credibility. The pimp intruded on Matt's turf by inviting Marie and Karla to work for him. In the pimping game, Matt's credibility was being tested, and "it was a test that I was going to have to pass" to maintain his status, prestige, and especially respect among the other players in the game. "If you let people disrespect you, then they know that they can do whatever to us, and part of my job was protection. Guys in the community knew I would respond," he said. Disrespect simply was not tolerated in the game. Matt had "to make an example out of this guy"; he had to respond promptly and decisively. With Marie and Karla, he hatched a plan. "Okay, this is what we're going to do":

> Karla tricked him (the pimp) to the hotel room. The lights are already off and we (Marie) go into the bathroom. We hear Karla's voice and she says, "Let me go to the bathroom." He was doing his thing. I stepped out of the bathroom with the pistol. And when I stepped out, he got his clothes off and is in his shorts because he thought he was getting down with Karla. So when I come out, I put the pistol on him. Then they hand-cuffed him, with his hands behind his back, and they tied his feet together, and they gagged him. I sat down with the pistol, and they began to do what they did. Marie got some coat hangers and twisted them, and she began to beat him. That came from some pimp boys, who would beat

their girls with coat hangers; that's the worst thing that can happen because the corner of the hanger would go into the flesh. I saw her acting out this behavior, beating him. She was venting her frustration, for all the men who had ever done anything to her; she seemed to be venting her frustration on him. And the way she was talking to him, "bitch, punk motherfucker, disrespecting my man, I'm gonna teach you a lesson." She was very vocal. Karla was less vocal, she was just, "yeah motherfucker what did you think this was," and she was hitting him with her hand and her shoes, that kind of stuff. So this shit is going on for about an hour. I mean he was beat up bad, and there were some holes in his body where the hanger hit him, it left welts on his body. He had been humiliated by women, and within the code, you're supposed to be a pimp, and you just been beat up by two women, who also pissed on you. So it was all about humiliating him and making an example of him. We dragged his ass to the car and put him in the trunk naked, and dropped him off in a sand dune and left him handcuffed. We found out that he and this girl had disappeared and went to L.A.

With this brutality, Matt realized that he was now "consumed with the life" of hustlers and players and that increasingly he had no control over that life. He was playing a dangerous game where the stakes were becoming too high. Matt sensed that his freedom was threatened and again, he "was ready to run because I thought the police were going to be looking for me." Four days after the assault on the pimp, he received an "honorable discharge" from the Army. He decided that it was a good time to run, and so he did. Matt returned to Baltimore and brought the lessons learned from playing the game with him. In Baltimore, where those lessons became his guide, playing the game lead Matt down a destructive and deadly path.

As a young man, Matt had a strong sense of his own self-worth that was affirmed though his interactions, especially with other men. Through those interactions, he was introduced to and became a player in the game of men. For Matt, the game is a metaphor for describing men's interactions with each other based on power relations, where control and dominance often mediated through violence characterize the degree of manliness. The game begins with a simple declaration of manhood: an unquestionable acceptance of the norms and standards of masculinity.

Race and gender relations, however, positioned Matt as a subordinate player in this manly game. The opportunities and options available for playing the game are shaped by social position, and this determines the particular form and content of the games that different men are allowed to play. In declaring his manhood, Matt assumed a marginalized masculinity that, increasingly, was alienated from social and cultural expectations and formed in defiance of social and cultural constraints. Although marginalized, this did not prevent Matt from being an active player in the game of men; to the contrary, he readily accepted subordinate membership that carried limited opportunities and options for playing the game and aggressively pursued them nonetheless.

In the variety of social, political, and economic games that men play in their interactions with each other, access is based mainly on either hegemonic or subordinate manliness. Performance varies depending upon the context and setting, but, as in any game, there are rules, strategies, stakes, competition, personal choices, alliances, and, above all, winners and losers. Even though the games men play differ, the overall objective is similar. The point, whether expressed, is to increase one's positional power: to impose one's will in seeking to gain an advantage, where the payoff is usually increased status, prestige, respect, and, depending on the nature of the game, money and/or other resources of power. At each ever-fluid level of success, greater levels of performance, investment, and risk-taking are required to continue playing and increasing one's chances of winning even larger payoffs in this game of men.

Asserting a marginalized masculinity, Matt initially entered the game through membership in the 116th Street Disciples, later as a soldier in the military, and then as a pimp among hustlers and players. In those interactions, a major feature of the games Matt played was proving his veracity as a man; otherwise, he ran the risk of losing manhood credibility. In playing the game, Matt became proficient in the use of violence. Threat, mastery, and actual use of violence were important skills, whereby he received status, prestige, and important respect from his male peers. The payoff of money and other resources were important prizes to be sure, but they were not necessarily Matt's main attraction or motivation to play the game. What drew him into the games was apparently the excitement of competition and the challenge that they posed. The games tested his credibility as a man—a test to his sense of self-worth and value—an image that required vindication, especially from other men. When the excitement of competition became too daunting and the challenge rose to dangerous levels or, more important, when he could no longer either play by his own terms or determine the outcome, Matt ran away from the situation. He knew that playing the game meant risking the possibility of losing.

As Richard and Matt entered the world of adult men, they gradually assumed the posture of "real men." The meaning thereof evolved from experiences shaped by race and gender relations for which the saliency of violence played a defining role. To prove their worth in largely male-centered environments, they unquestionably and actively embraced codes of conduct that governed and reinforced what it meant to be a man: seemingly tough, emotionally detached, self-reliant, and uncompromising in the use of violence.

These qualities reaffirmed their senses of self-determination. They went about the business of living their lives on their own terms; they refused to accept vulnerability, acknowledge weakness of any kind, or adhere to constraints and limitations. But as Richard's and Matt's experiences suggest, social and cultural consequences attached to the decisions they made and the actions they took. Those consequences reveal that, for young black men, self-determination was illusive.

INDEPENDENCE

As a young black man, Bobby also became a player in the game of men, during the late 1960s. But he played a different game. Bobby embraced a manhood stance that drew him into the celebratory culture of organized sports. His game was football, a team sport that fell within the boundaries of social and cultural expectations and conformity, where structured conflict, competitiveness, and especially violence were expressed within acceptable limits. Similar to an athletic performance, race and gender relations shape players' importance to the team and position them differently on the field of play. Playing the coveted position of running back brought Bobby a sense of enjoyment; more important, it brought him a sense of independence, for he relied solely on his own ability to do exactly what he wanted to do, play football. That independence also brought him face-to-face with the reality of power; reality differentiated and marginalized his value, even as he received accolades and praises for his athletic prowess.

Bobby no longer lived in the projects of Philadelphia. Abruptly, the family fled to North Carolina to stay with his maternal grandparents. Prior to that move, unbeknownst to Bobby or his sisters, his mother remarried. She married "a man who was a Vietnam veteran and an alcoholic." Bobby does not recall a courtship between them, "a wedding or any ceremony," or even a conversation about him with his mother. In fact, he had only met her husband once prior to their marriage. Bobby did recall that one night, shortly after their marriage, his step-father "was drunk and got into some kind of argument" with his mother:

> They were fighting. We (Bobby and his sisters) came out of the room, and my mother's eye was cut, and she was bleeding and sitting on the couch. He was pressing his will over her. Being intoxicated he was being very aggressive, not physical anymore. But being real aggressive in what he wanted. "Get my cigarettes, go do this, and go do that." It was a horrible night. I went to the neighbors and tried to get them to help her, and they refused to help. I went into the kitchen to get a knife to kill him. For whatever reason my mother looked at me, and with some kind of non-verbal communication, she implored me not to do it. Somebody called

the cops, and they came but did not take him away. My mother was able to call my uncle. We left in the middle of the night going to North Carolina.

Having grown up in an all-female household with a seemingly distant and uncaring mother and an older sister who routinely bullied him, Bobby was still extremely protective of the females in his family. Amidst the constant tension in their relationship, as the only boy in the family, Bobby felt compelled "to protect my mother. I needed to let her know that she can find some safety in knowing that her son will be there for her." At that time, Bobby still had the body of child, rather than that of a man, a fact that he thought limited his physical ability to protect her. This was an important consideration, for Bobby wanted a body that was bigger and stronger than the one he possessed.

As a young man, Bobby's perception of his physical being—his body—became an increasing concern. Having lived in the projects of Philadelphia and then moving to North Carolina was a major cultural change for Bobby. Immediately, he took note of the emphasis that some blacks placed on his body, particularly the color of his skin complexion. As he said, "One of the first things that I wrestle with was that I'm an outsider." He thought that this was due in part to the darkness of his skin:

> I got teased a lot because I was darker than the other boys. They used to call me twelve o'clock in the alley, pitch back, and black stick. Those are three names that readily come to mind. You know as a young man playing in the summer sun, you just get darker. I was darker than most everybody else. In some sense I felt that I was different but maybe not in a good way: maybe I was inferior because I was darker, but I really couldn't put my hands on what was going on. This had me puzzled for a while.

In this new environment, Bobby saw himself as an "outcast," as not good enough, and a major issue for him was his appearance. With a sense of insecurity about his body, he wanted a change. As a child, because he was small in stature and timid in demeanor he had been vulnerable to bullying from his older sister and other children, particularly boys. Also, because of his size he had been unable to protect his mother from her abusive husband. Now he was ridiculed because of his body, the darkness of his skin. Although he could do nothing about his complexion, with hard work however, he knew that he could change his physique. He wanted a more manly body.

So Bobby went to the YMCA and started lifting weights. There he was introduced to men's locker room culture and the unspoken attention that is placed on the body. He said, "I was kind of timid about being seen. But there were men walking around naked. So I'm looking at these guys and I'm like, hey these things (penises) come in all shapes, colors, sizes and hairiness. This is kinda cool. If I did get in the shower, I just dried myself off real quickly and got dressed. But some guys would walk around and waited until the last moment to put their underwear on. I'm sure it was a by-product of how they felt about themselves."

Lifting weights, Bobby's goal was to "get bigger, get stronger." And he did just that: "I'm really tight and muscular, and I'm getting longer and so I look slim. And I'm okay with that." With a sense of self-satisfaction and confidence about the way he looked, Bobby was now ready to play a game he loved, football. For him, it was the most physical of the manly games. "Not basketball because it's a sissy sport, like soccer, I needed to hit something." Fundamentally, football is a game that is predicated on physical violence of the most primitive form: on the ability to hit an opponent with as much force as possible as well as take the force of a hit from others, but the hitting must be within the rules. On the field of play, football positions are largely determined by an athlete's "physically gifts" or size or strength. With combat as a metaphor, men's bodies are used as weapons on a contested terrain, and performance is a public spectacle, where physical courage, bravery, valor, and superiority are applauded. The physical demands of football, in this all-male arena, are no less than a public affirmation of manhood.

Bobby was now fully prepared to engage this arena, but he needed permission from his mother to play. He felt a strong sense of independence; "at this point, I wasn't asking her; I was telling her I'm going to play football." As an "outcast," Bobby was determined to prove that he was "a better athlete," a better man than the other guys. Entering his freshmen year of high school, he tried out for the football team. He recalled that first day of practice: "I remember the feeling I had going out on the field and seeing forty, fifty, or seventy guys all doing our stretches. I looked around and said man this is really cool. I like this. I liked the team. I liked the feeling of brotherhood, camaraderie, everybody doing the same thing at the same time. I'm not a morning person, but for whatever reason, I liked being up in the morning with the guys." With confidence in his physical abilities, Bobby made up his mind to tryout for the running back position on the freshmen football team. For him, "running back is the premier position on the football field. You would think it would be the quarterback. But the running back is the star, because when the ball is in his hands, he is usually the most talented guy on the field as far as being able to run with the ball. And he's the one that will more than likely score points." Bobby's major competition for that position was a popular guy who was also known as a bully. During school he "wore double knit paints, and a dress shirt, and had an attitude of being a tough guy and he was a bully. But after school he was a stud athlete. He could do everything," Bobby said. Even so, Bobby was "committed to showing him and everybody else" that he was a better player: "I'm bigger than him. I'm taller than him. I'm faster than him." Nevertheless, Bobby's competition was selected as the starting running back for the team.

Even though he did not start, Bobby did have an opportunity to play, and "every time I got a chance, I always proved that I was just as good if not better than the starter." While waiting for the chance to start as running back, Bobby took great pleasure in simply being a member of the team, and he especially liked the physicality and permissiveness of violence that was much a part of this all-male culture. For him, there was something "real masculine" about football that he took enormous pleasure in and thoroughly enjoyed. As he said:

> It feels good to manhandle a man and not be told you can't do that. As a matter of fact you're being encouraged. So when you knock somebody off his feet and you get praised for it, that's just the greatest feeling in the world. Because outside of the football field you can't do that; inside the field and until the whistle blows it's all legal. So if I take your head off it's literally within the scope of the game; if you take mine off I can't be mad at you. I got knocked underneath the bench one time. I almost got knocked out, where I'm seeing birds. You know what, that's in the scope of the game. I think, for a young man that wants to get the violence out it a great way to do it. It's much better to do it that way because other ways can literally cost you your life or your freedom.

Bobby had a passion for this manly game and was consumed by football. "I would even carry my football to class because as a running back, you're responsible for carrying the ball. The thing that is important about being a running back is that you always know where the ball is because it's in your hands, and you can't lose it. So I take my football to class," he said. And if something was not related to football, such as girls, Bobby was uninterested. With a single-minded focus and narrow vision of life, he was determined to become a starter on the team. During his second year on the sophomore football team, Bobby "started every game." He was living his dream. As he said, "I lived every experience I could have ever wanted, to the point that there were times when I wanted to come off the field and the coach said, 'We need you out there.' So I played running back; I played quarterback; I ran back kick off returns; I was everything. And I loved every moment of it."

During practice one day, Bobby was rewarded for his efforts when: "The coach hollered my name as said 'you're playing varsity on Saturday.' Yes, that's what I'm talking about!" Moving to the varsity football team, Bobby was introduced to a new group of guys, who were physically bigger, manlier, and more intense in their interactions. Bobby went though initiation, a hazing, to become a full-fledged member of the varsity team: "They beat you into submission. Oh my goodness. And they don't come at you one at a time; it's three, four at a time. Everybody that's coming at you is bigger and stronger. There's nothing you can do but take it."

On the varsity team the stakes were higher. The high school expected the team to win the state championship each year. Moreover, the star athletes were auditioning for the next level of competition, the rewards of which were athletic scholarships to college. With these expectations, Bobby was introduced to and "experienced the politics of sports." He quickly realized that there was a "pecking order," and to make matters worse the head varsity football coach, who was white, "did not like him." Although promoted to the varsity team, Bobby did not start as running back. Instead, a white guy whose father had played for the school and who "gave money to the school," was the starter.

But Bobby took advantage of the opportunity given, and he played by the rules of the game. He ran the football back after each kickoff from the other team, and he "breaks all kinds of records, written up in the newspaper, talked about, and teams develop defenses just to stop me." He receives little acknowledgment from the head coach, but the assistant coaches praised Bobby's accomplishments on the field of play as well as the public attention he received as a result. The running back coach for the varsity team, who was also his gym teacher, was particularly impressed with Bobby's ability. This coach "felt like the head coach had made a bad decision in not starting me; he clearly knew my talent," Bobby said. Even so, he was not prepared to advocate on Bobby's behalf because "he was what's considered a brown nose to the head coach, and he had aspirations for when the head coach retired." Still the coach admired Bobby's athletic abilities. In gym class one day, Bobby's coach/teacher asked him to demonstrate a routine on the gymnastic horse, and what happened next would prove to be fateful for Bobby: "He puts the horse up three feet, then four feet, and five feet, it's really high. He had a hard on. So he puts the horse up to six feet. I get on the horse, and when I come down my right knee goes out. He heard something, but I didn't really hear something, I just felt something. That was the moment that I tore a cartilage in my knee. This injury would affect everything I've ever done, from that point forward." Bobby spent the summer rehabilitating his knee. Also, given the success he had during the past season, Bobby began to think seriously about the possibilities of going to college on an athletic scholarship. Although he was a B student, his guidance counselor told him to consider "going to a trade school, because you're not really college material. How're you going to tell me I can't go to college? I've got good grades." During the fall semester of his senior year, in the absence of encouragement from teachers or his mother, Bobby applied to eleven colleges. Given his family's financial situation, to attend college he needed a scholarship, preferably an athletic scholarship.

Meanwhile, Bobby had rehabilitated his injured knee and was ready to play football for his all-important senior season. "Now it was clear to everybody, including the head coach—whether he wanted to admit it or not—that I was the MAN. They knew who the star was, so when the starting team lined up for practice, I'm the running back." But on the third day of practice, things started to unravel for Bobby:

> We have triple practice sessions, and I'm on this knee. It's swelling up, it's tough to move it, and we run a routine play. I go to push off and there's pain and I had no strength. And the defense pursued and caught me, and just tackled me to the ground. I couldn't get up. I had to be helped up; basically they carried me off the field. And for the next three weeks I didn't practice. I lost my starting job. The head coach couldn't have been happier; he put somebody else in my place. First game of my senior year, I couldn't play.

By the second game of the season Bobby was again ready to play, his knee was heavily taped, and he was hoping that it would withstand the physical pressure of playing football, even though there was swelling. But he had lost his starting position, and now Bobby waited on the bench. Again, an opportunity arose for Bobby to prove his worth to the team: "The guy they put in to take my place got hurt. The people in the stands started screaming for the coach to put me in." And the coach did:

> My leg isn't better. My knee is swollen. I haven't been practicing. What am I going to do? I'm going to do what I do. I get this pitch, I'm about 45 yards away from the end zone, and I realize I have one guy to beat, the quarterback this little white guy. And I said on my worse day I can beat him. But I just don't know if I can do it, and it got to the point where he's catching me, and I gave him the slip. I got to the end zone. I had ninety-six yards in one half. It was a good game. But from that point everything started to go downhill. I started the next game, but the coach took me out after only four plays. I recall him saying that I had an attitude that he didn't like. I don't care if you don't like my attitude. If I can come out here and play and perform well, I should be playing. What he was trying to do was totally kill my spirit. My best friend said, "You know everybody knows that you're the best out here. Don't quit because if you want to play college ball he will black ball you."

Bobby, however, did not heed his friend's warning and quit the team. That decision came with consequences. Most notably, he was not recruited by scouts to play college football and, as a result, did not receive an athletic scholarship to college. Upon graduation from high school, Bobby's faced limited opportunities and options for playing football, ever again. Playing the game, up until this point, had been Bobby's "whole world." As a young black man, it had anchored his identity. Through his eyes, football was the thing that defined who he was and tested his worthiness as a man. For Bobby, it was the vehicle for assimilating into masculinity and providing a sense of redemption and affirmation from other men. Football had positioned him in the world of men and developed his sense of self-confidence and independence, especially from his all-female household. Bobby's identity was rooted in his ability to play the game. Ironically, he walked away from football to sustain his sense of self-worth, but without that anchor he began to falter.

Bobby accepted the rules of the game as given, and his needs and aspirations were built around football. In the face of athletic success, he believed that physical prowess was enough to achieve his goals. He thought that physical ability alone was enough to even the playing field. But Bobby never became an "insider" in the game; he was always marginal, expendable, and there was always someone else at the ready to take his place, regardless of his ability. His physical presence and performance was not enough to mitigate constraints and offer him advantages in this highly competitive manly game of football. Upon reflection, Bobby realized that "the best man doesn't always win. Sometimes you got to play the game long enough to get what you want out of it. And, then, when it's time to leave you better leave the game before it breaks you."

Although they differed in age, Thomas like Bobby also grew up with a single mother, and she too remarried. Similarly, his mother's marriage was unexpected and never discussed with Thomas: "in those days nobody told you anything, people just popped up in your life." Thomas also did not have meaningful interactions with his step-father; their relationship was "distant," to say the least. Thomas's mother, however, continued to maintain a strong presence in his life. By 1965, as a young man, his mother could no longer give Thomas what he wanted or needed at the time—the guidance and companionship of "strong" black men. He said that "my mother meant good, but she was not a black male." He wanted independence, to be free of his mother's overbearing control so "at that time, the most important thing that happened is that I started going to the Community Center." Through his relationships with men who ran the Center Thomas "was beginning to get a sense of myself as a man, in the sense of how I was going to conduct myself":

> I'm seeing black men who have education, who have jobs, who for the first time are strong people in my life. Up until that time it's was my mother who is the dominant force in my life. They worked with youth. They were the first males who were saying "don't do that, but do this." That was my first notion of hearing about going to college, and that there were black colleges that you could go to as opposed to going to white colleges. I wanted to go to Lincoln, the oldest black college, because one

of the men went there so that's all he would talk about. I'm like yeah, that's where I want to go.

In addition to supportive relationships with men at the Community Center, Thomas was also developing a strong relationship within his church, and the head minister took him under his wing. At this point Christianity became important, and his Presbyterian faith had a profound influence in his life; he began to think that "God had a plan for me." During this period Thomas's sense of being black-and-male began to crystallize in his life, for which his faith played a major role. Through what he viewed as "positive interactions" with other black men, he began to construct both an intellectual and cultural image of self:

> I was fortunate enough to have people in my life who pointed me to the areas I needed to go to create an identity for myself. I was proud to be a black man. My role models were these men and images from the stuff I was reading. My images of black men and how they carry themselves is not the gangster stuff from the guys on the streets; it wasn't the uneducated; it wasn't the bigger Thomas. I didn't want to be him. So my image was of W.E.B. Du Bois. I wanted a moustache and a pipe and a tweed coast. That's what I wanted. I wanted to be responsible. I knew I had a responsibility to the community. I had a responsibility to our race. I knew that, and it was real clear to me.

At the time, for Thomas "all of the things that I knew that was done correctly were coming out of the black church." Thomas channeled his clarity of purpose to the black church. He became very active in his church's Young Christian Life (YCL) group where he started working, as a part-time counselor at its group home facility for homeless youth. Meanwhile, Thomas was going to school and getting good grades. However, during his senior year, he "got into a confrontation with a teacher over a paper." As a result he refused to write the term paper; "I said I'm not doing that." His teacher informed him that if he did not write the paper, he would not graduate. "I said, well, okay, I won't graduate, but I'm not doing that." Even though Thomas was well aware of the consequences of his decision, he said: "At some point in my education I decided that I wasn't going to allow teachers to have that kind of power over me. I thought I was real bright and I could learn whatever I wanted to learn. I absolutely refused to play the game, and I wasn't going to let teachers intimidate me. So I refused and I didn't graduate. I was going to stand by my principles." Thomas did stand by his decision, but he also "had an ace to play." He knew that the YCL not only had a group home facility, but it also administered a nondenominational alternative education program that enabled youth to get a high school diploma.

In addition to getting his diploma from YCL, Thomas also studied to take the college entrance examination. He got accepted and received a full scholarship to a church-sponsored private community college located in Los Angeles. He "felt real good about leaving Chicago because I was doing exactly what I was expected to, and I had no second thought about leaving home." Leaving home for the first time, Thomas had a strong sense of self-assuredness: "I was in control of my life. I knew a lot. My convictions and positions were real and strong. I knew what I was going to do. I was going to change the world." In 1967, at eighteen years old, Thomas headed off to college seeking to change the world.

Although the student population at his community college was mostly white, "twenty-five percent black and the rest were white," Thomas was impressed with the beauty of the campus. What was even more impressive was the black political climate he found upon arriving on campus. He "ran right smack into the black power movement." In this highly charged political climate, Thomas began to focus on the notion of freedom, self-determination, and independence that meant the liberation of black people from political, economic, and cultural oppression. When Thomas arrived on campus, the politics of "Us, the Black Panther Party, and the Black Student Union" dominated the intellectual and political climate of the college.

United slaves, known as Us, was an organization founded in 1965 by Ron Karenga, who extolled the virtues to a Sevenfold Path of Blackness: think black, talk black, act black, create black, buy black, vote black, and live black. Celebratory of an African heritage, ideologically Us was based on a philosophy of cultural nationalism. As such, its members actively organized black students, particularly on college campuses in California, around the development of Afro-American Studies Programs. But Us had a fierce political rival: The Black Panther Party for Self-Defense, which was founded in 1966, by Huey P. Newton and Bobby Seale. The strong ideological and political tensions between the two groups sometimes led to violent confrontations. The Black Panthers at that time embraced a Marxist-influenced philosophical stance: a Ten-Point Program that included a call for land, bread, housing, education, justice, and peace, and exemption from military service for black men. The more socialist oriented Black Panthers condemned the racial exclusivity of the cultural nationalist advanced by Us. The intellectual and political tensions were clearly demarcated; both Us and the Panthers competed for members from the same population, black students.

When Thomas arrived on campus, without hesitancy, he embraced the intellectual and political climate of this new environment and immediately began to change with the current. As he said: "Of course I thought the revolution was tomorrow, and I wore an afro and a dashiki. This is the way it's going to be." Yet, he did not fully embrace the programmatic agendas of either Us or the Panthers. Instead, taking what he needed from both organizations, Thomas was developing a black nationalist's political stance with a socialist's influence that was highly racialized and gendered in content. With an independent streak, he devoted his political activism to strengthening the Black Student Union. Highly opinionated and intellectually "clear" in his political views, Thomas "started having a lot of clashes with folks" over the issue of race and gender, especially concerning black men dating white women and the disrespect of black women in the process. Thomas described his thinking:

> There was a community of black and white couples, and that was weird to me. Their world was diametrically different from mine. I started to notice that when black men got with white women they weren't black anymore. I never could figure that out. How can you be with someone from another race and they don't know anything about who you are? You're a black man! These are your people! This is who you are! Nothing about white women attracts me. I thought they had an odor. I know it was just in my mind. It was a whole psychological piece that is not scientific. In my mind black women and Hispanic women have different stuff going on. When I was young I said that's why white women use so much perfume, but sisters are natural.

When Thomas became president of the Black Student Union during his first year at college, many active members and those in leadership positions on whom he depended were black women. His views on the importance of black women's involvement in the movement contrast with the organizational stance of Us and the Panthers, where black women were usually restricted to supportive roles. Thomas explained that "because of my mother I held black women in a certain way. It wasn't intellectual at that time, but I treated them with respect." And when it came to criticizing both Us and the Panthers over the treatment of black women, Thomas did not hold his "tongue":

> I voiced my displeasure about dating white women. I would say stuff like, why are you saying that all the sisters can do is have babies for the nation? When I'm reading that Vietnamese women are carrying arms and doing revolutionary kind of work; I had problems with that contradiction. Why should we be limiting the sisters? I raised questions like that. The brothers didn't like the answers, but the sisters did. I would have a lot of sisters around me.

In assuming leadership over the Black Student Union, Thomas focused his political energy on making the campus more welcoming of black students. In so doing, black students called for change, but faced with administrative resistance to their demands they became "disruptive." Confrontational, the Black Student Union held a series of campus protests demanding greater inclusion of the history, culture, and intellectual contribution of African Americans into the college curriculum and insisting that "the campus newspaper call us Black, rather than Negro." Similar to demands made by black students around the country, Thomas and the Black Student Union at his college called for an increased number of black faculty, additional courses on African American history and culture, and "space for our meetings." Furthermore, lead by Thomas student union members took over the president's office: "He wanted to tell us how the majority of students were walking around being called Negro and they didn't have a problem with that. I said, yeah, but we're the ones in your office, so you got a problem with us." Admittedly, Thomas relished the fight with the college administration and "going up against power." In the process, he realized that as a part of a group he was not powerless. Of this realization, he said, "for me it reaffirmed that you had a sense of self, as a group. The group was made up of individuals, but it was the group that had power."

Maturing as a political activist, Thomas was developing "some ideas about what I didn't want to be." He carried himself in high regard, and he explained his thoughts: "All the stereotypes that black people were ignorant, powerless, and poor, I refused to be any of that. I thought I had power; thought I could create change; and I thought that I was a strong black man. I knew I was a decent guy." Guided by a strong sense of political consciousness regarding what was right and wrong about the world and an independent spirit, Thomas was also developing some ideas about what he was not going to do. During this period, going to Vietnam to fight in a war against nonwhite people was one of those things. But he "got drafted the first year I was in college." Thomas described what happened:

> For me the Vietnam War was peripheral to the Black struggle. But you couldn't get away from it because almost every Black man in L.A. was getting drafted. Guys were coming up with broken arms and all that stuff to try and avoid getting drafted. And I got drafted. I was going to refuse induction. I was clear about that. I got drafted with this white guy who was playing basketball; he was six-nine. We went to the draft center together, which was downtown L.A. He got exempted immediately because he was tall. I told them that I wasn't going. They said you still have to take a physical. They had these different color tags that they put around your neck. I didn't know what that meant at that time, it seemed random. They put a red tag around my neck. I said what's the red tag, but they wouldn't answer me. I'm blind in my left eye and I told them that I have a bad eye. I can't see out of the eye. I told them if you make me

go over there I'm shooting everybody I can see. I was just nervous and scared. With the red tag I'm now going through the physical part twice as fast as everybody else. Now I'm really upset, why am I getting this special treatment? I go through the whole physical, and I fail the eye test. The Doctor tells me, "Oh, you're blind in that eye." I said what was the tag about? He said, "That was the Green Beret tag; that's what happens when you talk too much. You go right to the Green Beret, to the front of the line."

Following his first eventful year at college, Thomas went back to Chicago for the summer, but that "summer went by quickly," and he soon returned to California for his second year. Rather than living on campus, this time Thomas decided to "get my own apartment" off campus. But, "it seemed like every place I went people kept saying no, no, no. That was my first real experience with housing segregation. White people were literally saying you can't live here; you have to live over there. I knew that I was never going to stay in California." But Thomas found an apartment in the "ghetto," in a building where many of the tenants were members of the Black Panther Party. He discovered that his apartment building was closely monitored by the Los Angeles police department. Periodically, there would be police raids in the building. Thomas recalled an incident when he was leaving the building one day:

I came out and the police had surrounded the building. I started to walk away, but decided to go back and tell the guys. I turned around to go back, and they (police) told me not to go back in. Because of my hard head I went back anyway. They ran in after me. They pushed me up against the wall and held me. During all the commotion the panthers opened their doors and they all had guns. I almost got shot.

This was Thomas's first encounter with the police, but it was not his last. He described Los Angeles as a "police state," during that period: "you had to carry ID (identification) if you were a black male, and the police were white officers and had a lot of power." In another encounter, one night a friend was driving Thomas home, and they were on the freeway:

The police pulled up behind us and pulled us over. We weren't doing anything. They told us to pull over. My friend was driving and he had to show ID. My ID was in my gym bag. It was dumb on my part. I reached into my gym bag to get my ID, and as soon as I did it I knew I shouldn't have done that. Something told me . . . The lord really has a plan for me. Something told me not to move. The next thing I heard was a click. I didn't move and I turned my head slowly. The officer had a 357 pointed right at my head. He said, "Take your hand out of your bag slowly." I said I was just reaching for my ID; I don't have anything. I knew that

I could have done a number of stupid things that black guys do everyday. Well bang! I was mad partly at myself because I knew it was a dumb move. The other was why did they stop us? He said, "I have a right to stop you." In L.A. they do. They found out that I had a ticket for jay-walking during my first semester that wasn't paid. Yes they were serious out there. This is not Chicago. They took me to jail. I stay there; I spent the night in jail until the guys could get the money to pay the ticket. You get real clear about the police. The cops are real serious, they are aggressive and you don't need to be messing with them unless you are prepared to get your behind whipped or get killed.

Thomas was "clear" that in a "police state" the cops operate as authorized agents of social control, and through constant surveillance black men are often presumed "guilty" of something in the eyes of the law, which provides a legal justification for police intervention. Following this incident, Thomas became even more committed to the black political struggle, but he was torn between Us and the Panthers. He "believed in the revolution and that we were going to change the country." But the Panther's notions of the "violent overthrow of the government didn't make any sense to me." And, Thomas could not join Us because he "could not do all the praises to Kurenga," which was required of members. He said that "there was something wrong with that. In my eyes he was not a god, but just another guy." Thomas resisted becoming fully involved with either group and avoided the violent clashes that were developing between the two. He tried to stay centered: "My center was it had to make sense to me, their actions had to be consistent with my vision and how I saw the world. Because I didn't see any of them as enemies: if you don't believe what I believe that doesn't make you an enemy. Everybody thought they had the solution. And I didn't necessarily think that no one group had the whole solution. But I wasn't taking sides, so I was able to maneuver with all of these folks."

During his second year of college, Thomas began to struggle. "I'm still going to school, but I'm not really going to classes, anymore. I spent more time struggling with the philosophical stuff." By becoming more Afro-centric in his world view, the people and cultures of Africa were becoming important, and his "Christian faith got all out of whack." As such, Thomas stopped going to church: "I was cut off from the church." He stopped attending church not because he no longer believed in God but rather because he discovered a new avenue for expressing his faith, one more attuned to his intellectual and cultural ideas.

He began to gravitate toward the Yoruba religion, based on the spiritual beliefs of the Yoruba people of West Africa; this religion has devotees on both the African continent and the Western Hemisphere, particularly in African American communities. Yoruba is rooted in traditional religious beliefs and practices: in addition to the worship of one God, named Olodumara, devotees also recognize lesser deities known as Orishas. For Thomas, Yoruba provided a strong spiritual link between his political ideas and cultural sensitivities. He adopted the Yoruba religion but refused to adopt a traditional African name. "My position was whatever name I have, I'm going to make it stand for something. Changing it to an African name doesn't mean anything unless you make it stand for something," he said. But Thomas did not hesitate to adopt changes to the way that he dressed, and today he continues to wear African garb on a regular basis.

Thomas founded a new sense of spirituality among those in the Yoruba religious community and continued to "hang out" with black political activists, yet he felt "isolated and alienated" in California. "Things were falling apart for me. I didn't feel as if I was a part of any particular group. I had lost my focus on school, and there wasn't anything for me in LA. I just wanted to work in the black community, that's all I wanted to do. I didn't see myself as a California guy. I wanted to bring my skills and everything that I had learned back to Chicago." And in 1969, at twenty years of age, Thomas did just that. He returned to Chicago and brought with him political knowledge and experience, as he went to work in the black community.

During this period for Thomas and many other young black activists, freedom, self-determination, and independence took on a sociopolitical meaning: it meant an end to racial, economic, and political oppression in the United States. But the competing strategies advanced—of the various black groups and allies in the struggle that made up what is widely known as the black power and cultural nationalist movements of the late 1960s—were too limited in scope to realize the systemic changes, the revolution, needed to transform society's social and cultural institutions to bring about "black liberation." Simply put, that liberation could not be obtained within the prevailing social and cultural order. Internal turmoil befell many of the groups, often based on patterns of racial and gender exclusion and marginalization that privileged the needs and aspirations of black males over others in the black community; the external ideological and political conflicts between the groups often turned warlike and bloody as a result. Also, on-going surveillance, incarceration, and, in too many instances, murder by various federal and state law enforcement agencies as well, undermined the emancipatory objective embedded in the black power and cultural nationalist movement. Given these and other considerations, black freedom, self-determination, and independence as envisioned by black power advocates, such as Thomas, became increasingly illusive aspirations.

CONCLUSION

During the 1960s, new forms of black masculinity were expressed on the social and cultural landscape of the United States. As in the past, those new expressions of manhood emerged largely in response to the continual racial and gender oppression. As in the past, they too were marginalized masculinities. Yet those seemingly new forms of masculinity were expressed differently. Generally, they were more assertive in presentation and more aggressive in articulating needs and aspirations. Self-defined, those new ways of doing black masculinity embodied strategies of both nonviolence and violence in attempts to bring about greater freedom, self-determination, and independence from oppressive social conditions and cultural practices and to bring about political, economic, and cultural change in the United States.

Externally, those more assertive and aggressive black masculinities projected a progressive political stance aimed at sociopolitical transformation. But, internally, they were often unfortunately riddled with regressive tendencies: the interests of men were usually privileged in ways that often marginalized and excluded the needs and aspirations of others in the black community. Consequently, even though the forms may have differed from past expressions of black masculinity, difference did not necessarily denote fundamental changes in the ways of doing black masculinity. Just beneath the surface of those new expressions of black masculinity, the content of those new forms often revealed an adherence to the norms and practices of hegemonic manhood in black men's interactions.

As young black men, the men I interviewed stepped into the political worlds of adult men during the turbulent 1960s. Their ideas of physical, personal, and social freedom, self-determination, and independence—not unlike those that emanated from the broader geopolitics of the period—were interwoven throughout their day-to-day experiences. Similarly, their complex and multilayered experiences suggest that it was not enough for them to conceive of those ideas as "autonomy, self-ownership, or nonalienation." As the men discovered, those ideas operated in a larger social and cultural context where powerful constraints were imposed on their individual decisions and actions, regardless of what they felt, thought, and did as they asserted agency in their individual lives.

The men actively participated in making their experiences. In so doing, they engaged social arrangements and cultural practices that limited their abilities to assert their will over their lives, whether in their interactions in the home, community, or larger society. As they sought to participate, they were brought face-to-face with the harsh realities of their lives as young black men and the consequences of the decisions and actions they took. They experienced the tensions, dilemmas, and contradictions of what it meant to be black-and-male in America, particularly when agency and constraints are in conflict. This conflict gave the meaning of freedom, self-determination, and independence an illusive quality. In each of their individual lives, to varying degrees of reality, that illusion resulted in pain, fear, frustration, and uncertainty as they went about their own particular ways in doing manhood.

Continuing on their particular journeys, the men attempted to negotiate within and against the realities of their lives—negotiate the insidiousness of race and gender relations and the engendered violence. In those negotiations, some men began to move toward a definition of manhood, even in the boundaries of oppressive space that allows them to seek alternative ways of doing black masculinity. Other men, as I show in chapter 4, for a time become imprisoned by those boundaries.

CHAPTER 4

Imprisoned Manhood

CIVIL AND POLITICAL RIGHTS ABROAD

During the Cold War, the United States sought to halt communist expansion by imposing democracy on Vietnam through violence. For many Americans, the loss of that war represented a crushing military defeat to U.S. stature as moral leader of the free world. To regain its prestige, in 1977 the Carter administration set a new course for America's foreign policy. A human rights agenda became the focal point of international relations. On October 5, 1977, Jimmy Carter signed the UN's International Covenant on Civil and Political Rights (ICCPR). This was indeed a significant international development. For twenty years, the United States had refused to sign this particular covenant because past administrations feared that taking such a moral stand on international affairs would inevitably raise embarrassing questions about America's commitment to racial, gender, and social justice at home.

The ICCPR extended the intent and scope of the Universal Declaration of Human rights by identifying fundamental civil and political freedoms to which each human being was entitled. Differing from the Declaration that emphasized economic, social, and, cultural rights, the ICCPR focused on five categories of rights to which member states were expected to adhere: protection of individual's physical integrity against execution, torture, and arbitrary arrest; authorization of procedural fairness in law that includes rights upon arrest, basic conditions of imprisonment, rights to a lawyer, and rights to an impartial process in trial; protection against gender, religious, racial, or other forms of discrimination; guarantee of individual freedoms of belief, speech, association, press, right to hold assembly; and guarantee of the right to political participation, such as organizing a political party, voting, and voicing contempt for political authority.

By placing human rights as the "fundamental tenet" of the U.S. foreign policy agenda, the Carter administration recognized that a new, more complex world was emerging from the vestiges of the old, as symbolized by America's stunning military defeat in Vietnam. For the Carter administration, the Cold War and the on-going tension between the United States, the Soviet Union, and China continued to be a major consideration in foreign policy matters. The interests and aspirations of nonaligned countries—many of whom were former European colonies—were, however, also making their presence known in international discourse. In his attempts to reposition America as a world power, in the eyes of both aligned and nonaligned countries, Carter relied upon principles of human rights as the foundation for establishing a common understanding for peace, freedom, and social justice among nations. To affirm his commitment he appointed Andrew Young, a former advisor to Martin Luther King and political strategist for the Southern Christian Leadership Conference (SCLC), as the U.S. ambassador to the United Nations, the point person for his administration's human rights agenda.

To the utter dismay of many conservatives at the time, Carter, giving voice to his vision, announced to the world a new international reality that called for change. He responded with pragmatism:

> The Vietnamese war produced a profound moral crisis, sapping world-wide faith in our own policy and our system of life, a crisis of confidence made even more grave by the covert pessimism of some of our leaders. In less than a generation, we've seen the world change dramatically. The daily lives and aspirations of most human beings have been transformed. Colonialism is nearly gone. A new sense of national identity now exists in almost 100 new countries that have been formed in the last generation. Knowledge has become more widespread. Aspirations are higher. As more people have been freed from traditional constraints, more have been determined to achieve, for the first time in their lives, social justice. The world is still divided by ideological disputes, dominated by regional conflicts, and threatened by danger that we will not resolve the differences of race and wealth without violence or without drawing into combat the major military powers. We can no longer separate traditional issues of war and peace from the new global questions of justice, equity, and human rights. It is a new world, but America should not fear it. It is a new world, and we should help to shape it. It is a new world that calls for a new American foreign policy—a policy based on constant decency in its values and on optimism in our historical vision. (Carter, 1977)

Carter recognized that the world was indeed changing, and, as a result, America's approach to international affairs required change. As a signatory of ICCPR, the United States was obligated to uphold civil and political rights, and this obligation, as Carter—son of the old segregated South—fully recognized, was not limited to foreign affairs. He told the Organization of American States (OAS) no nation "can claim that mistreatment of its citizens is solely its own business. I am convinced that all the peoples of the Americas want a world in which citizens of every country are free from torture, arbitrary arrest, and prolonged detention without trial. . . . The rights and dignity of human beings concern us all, and must be defended and enhanced" (Cohen, 1982, p. 216). Yet, during the mid-1970s, as Carter advanced a foreign policy agenda based on principles of human rights, at home the U.S. prison population began to surge, and the death penalty was reinstated after a ten-year moratorium on executions. As political opponents predicted, the seemingly omnipresent race and gender relations, shaped by violence, again undermined America's position as the moral leader of the free world.

CIVIL AND POLITICAL RIGHTS AT HOME

The disproportionate rate of black male imprisonment in comparison to their overall percentage of the U.S. population was abhorrent to fundamental principles of rights and morality. As documented by Pettit and Western, the incarceration rate for black men born between 1945and 1949 was 10.6 percent; as shameful as this percentage was, it almost doubled to 20.5 percent for those born between 1965 and 1969. By comparison, the incarceration rate of white men grew from 1.4 percent to 2.9 percent over the same time period (Pettit & Western, 2004). During those years, black men as a group constituted only 6 percent or less of the total population in the United States, but they accounted for 30 to 40 percent of the overall imprisoned population in the country. Why, it must be asked, has such a small group of men loomed so large in the U.S. penal system?

The racial and gender disparities in black men's imprisonment have often been explained by their participation in criminal activities. Yet, as Pamela Oliver points out, the large number of black men in prison was not explained solely by the fact that they commit crimes or commit more criminal acts than others; something other than their criminal activities was occurring on the social and cultural landscape. She suggests that, "to tease apart the reasons for the high racial disparities in imprisonment, the first question one wants to ask is how much of the disparity is due to real differences in crime, and how much is due to bias" (Oliver, 2001, p. 29). In attempting to address this issue, her analysis reveals that "crime rates were high in the 1970s, but have fluctuated several times since then, while the rate of imprisonment has steadily risen." Oliver argues that "the rise in imprisonment since the 1970s is not explained by crime rates, but by changes in policies related to crime." Therefore, as she concludes, crime must be seen in a relational context; it must be linked to "different kinds of relationships to social and economic factors, to political factors, and to law enforcement," factors that contribute to ever larger numbers of black men going to prison.

Amidst racial and gender disparities in black male imprisonment the fact remains that "nearly everyone in prison has committed a crime," as Oliver observes. But why do some black men commit crimes? Some social theorists argue convincingly that the reasons for criminal behavior are linked to deindustrialization, residential segregation, and poverty (Wilson, 1987; Massey & Denton, 1993; Oliver & Shapiro, 1997). Economic inequality, which results from structural racism, makes poor black men especially vulnerable to criminal activity. In turn, their lack of social and political capital increases their risk of arrest, prosecution, and sentencing, which ultimately results in high rates of incarceration (Brown, Carnoy, Currie et al., 2003). These explanations are insightful for they point to the role of broader social forces in shaping black men's experiences, and they are useful to an understanding of the social organization of structural inequality. But such explanations fail to capture what I believe to be some underlying reasons about why it has been so important for the United States to impose rigid social and cultural constraints on this particularly small group of men.

It is, therefore, also important to explore what some purposes served by black male imprisonment may be, in order to get a more complete picture of what else might be contributing to the racial and gender disparities in black men's increased incarceration. I put forth two interrelated, historically linked purposes for additional consideration. First, the ever-increasing institutionalization of forced labor creates an economic incentive, for which the U.S. prison system has historically played a critical role. Following slavery, southern whites were "convinced that free Negroes would not work steadily or effectively." After regaining power, white lawmakers authorized jail and prison officials "to lease the labor of convicts to the highest bidder," and this, along with the promulgation of black codes designed to restrict black behavior, had a devastating effect on freed blacks.

Predictably, as freed blacks violated racially restricted codes—for the first time in increasingly large numbers—black men began entering the penal system for crimes and misdemeanors, and the state started trafficking in convict labor. During this period of "neo-slavery," W.E.B. Du Bois argued that the state became a trafficker in crime, where the "sole object was to make the most money possible" (Du Bois, 2005, pp. 3–8). In 2008 Blackmon's *Slavery by Another Name: The Re-enslavement of Black Americans from the Civil War to World War II* provided facts to bolster Du Bois's claim that black male imprisonment was big business. Blackmon found that during Jim Crow segregation: "In fifty-one of Alabama's sixty-seven counties, nearly one thousand prisoners had been sold into slave mines and forced labor camps the previous year—generating $250,000, or about 2.8 million in modern currency, for local officials. The state government pocketed $595,000 in 1925—or $6.6 million today—selling about 1,300 men to Sloss-Sheffield's Flat Top mine" (Blackmon, 2008, pp. 368–369).

Today, the convict lease system—as constructed in the past—has been abolished. This is due largely to the influences of the Ashurst-Sumners Act passed by Congress in 1935, which made it illegal to transport prison-made goods across state lines. However, under the Carter administration, Congress passed the Justice System Improvement Act of 1979, which granted exemption for Prison Industry Enhancement (PIE) projects. As a result, the use of exploited inmate labor for commercial profit reemerged. Black male incarceration rates, which started to rise during the Carter administration in mid-1970s, have helped to spur what we are witnessing today, a reconfiguration of an industry in crime—an industry yielding billions annually.

Today, as in the past, increasing black male imprisonment has become a matter of dollars and cents: the cost of incarcerating and supervising black men is less a matter of how much it takes to house prisoners, but more a matter of the profit margin yielded from their labor. A mass prison industry, based on public/private ventures, has emerged, and the linchpin shaping this purely commercial endeavor is cheap and controlled prison labor. Although broader in scope, this modern prison industry is similar to that of the past, for the intent as Du Bois already noted is to make the most money possible. Also, similar to the past, this modern "prison industrial complex refers to the tripartite relationship binding private enterprise, government officials, and political leaders in a mutually beneficial relationship that has fueled the construction of prisons and jails at a record pace" (Booker, 2000, p. 213).

With a growth in penal industries, many prisons in the United States virtually operate as domestic "Free Enterprise Zones," and businesses that employ inmate labor are granted enormous federal and state tax incentives. Prison industries are hidden behind security walls, housed usually in rural areas, and shielded from public view; there tens of thousands of inmates are forced to work for pennies because they are not protected by minimum wage laws and denied the right to form a union, instigate a strike, or collectively bargain. As the prison population explodes to its current 2.5 million people, incarceration is a booming business, whereby cheap and controlled prison labor is used for not only all kinds of skilled and unskilled manufacturing and agriculture production but also telemarketing and high-tech assembly (Browne, 2008).

Even though exploited prison labor for profit is a critical consideration that may further explain what lies beneath increased black male imprisonment, another noteworthy consideration is important to explore. This consideration is deeply embedded in the particular historical relationship between black men and white men and centers on black men's rejection of white men's power; this rejection challenged the legitimacy of white men's political, economic, and social supremacy and the structural arrangements created to maintain that power. This rejection must be figuratively as well as literally contained. In other words, the embodiment of black men challenges the hegemonic discourse of white manhood; it challenges the way white men do masculinity. This consideration may admittedly appear amorphous, nuanced in presentation, and my claim may be fraught with tensions, dilemmas, and important contradictions, especially in the current sociopolitical climate that embraces ideas, imagery, and experiences of a post-race and post-gendered society. Nonetheless, I believe that the peculiarities of this interlocking relationship between black men and white men—shaped by history—also lurk in the shadows surrounding the purposes about why black men in particular are increasingly filling America's prisons.

Broadly speaking, white men as a group have positioned themselves as powerful arbiters of history and civilization; therefore, their identities, experiences, and especially their political, economic, and militarized power construct a figurative as well as literal lens through which the "other" is expected to view the world. To justify white social and cultural dominance, myths are crafted that define the world in their images, which help to maintain that dominance. In that myth-making black men collectively symbolize a critical resource in their endeavors. The myths surrounding who black men are play critical roles in shaping the myths of who white men are in comparison, and images constructed from those myths signify different lived realities. To borrow from Toni Morrison's insightful critique of the white literary imagination, those images speak to a "denotative and connotative blackness" that black men have come to signify. For white men, to borrow further from Morrison's assessment, those images represent something different:

> Both a way of talking about and a way of policing matters of class, sexual license, repression, formations and exercises of power, and meditations on ethics and accountability. Through the simple expedient of demonizing and reifying the range of color on a palette . . . (it's) possible to say and not say, to inscribe and erase, to escape and engage, to act out and act on, to historicize and render timeless, it provides a way of contemplating chaos and civilization, desire and fear, and a mechanism for testing the problems and blessings of freedom. (Morrison, 1992, p. 7)

Figuratively, the myths, images, and their accompanying social and cultural narratives position black men and white men in an intricate and dynamic relationship that gives meaning to male bodies, identities, and experiences. Literally, however, those myths, images, and narratives structure very real realities and very real differences, where the tensions, dilemmas, and especially the conflicts between dominance and oppression intersect. At that intersection, Anthony Lemelle suggests that "crises centers" exist in the relationship between black men and white men, where "most black men have not accepted the value systems of middle-class, white-male culture, in spite of boldly creative efforts by social agents to inculcate them with the middle-class, white value systems" (Lemelle, 1995, p. vi).

For many black men, to accept "white-male culture" is to accept white male dominance as well, for they are seen as inexpiably linked. There are also those who outright reject that dominance, as seen in their refusal "to rear their children but continue to produce them." Also, it is seen in their refusal "to use the socially sanctioned process of education to increase their mobility, preferring instead criminal action and deviant productivity." Moreover, it is seen in the ways they have adopted "the perverse material values of the dominant culture and combined them with an equally strong commitment to an independent black culture, that is, bourgeois negritude" (Lemelle, 1995, p. vi). That refusal to conform to "white-male culture" blatantly challenges the social and cultural legitimacy of the order of things. By rejecting conformity black men became social and cultural deviants, and, accordingly in their refusal, they are subjected to harsh penalties.

Penalty and deviance converge behind the security walls of America's prisons, where racial and gender disparities have come to shape too many black men's experiences. For black men who are imprisoned, most have never been married, completed high school, or been employed full-time, but many have children. Many are incarcerated for nonviolent crimes, and many are repeat offenders. While in prison they are more often found guilty of breaking institutional rules, more likely to be assigned menial jobs, and more frequently held in prison longer than other inmates (Jackson, 1997). These general characteristics and trends, however, are devoid of a personhood: they do not tell us what imprisoned black men feel, think, and actually do as they live their daily lives confined behind the razor wire of prison walls, a confinement shaped by the omnipresence of race, gender, and violence. For this perspective, Jamie, Matt, and Richard offer telling perspectives, given their particular decisions and actions as they engaged guns, murder, and prison.

GUNS AND THINGS

As a young man, Jamie was extremely violent, but that violence was somewhat tempered by conventional aspirations. During his adolescence, he described himself as a "Frankenstein monster." Through a dual identity, he attempted to balance going to high school and aspiring to college with pursuing a "street life" of drugs, sexual conquests, and fast money and buying jewelry and expensive clothes. It was a delicate balancing act. After completing high school 1976, he enrolled in a local college in Minnesota. "It was a predominately white college located in a white neighborhood." On the day he went to enroll in classes, Jamie was informed by an administrator that going to "school costs money." But what she said next threw Jamie for a loop:

> She said, and I quote, "please don't commit any crimes to go to summer school." Maybe I was too young to get offended, but I knew something was wrong with that statement. As a matter of fact I believe she was a black woman. That kind of threw me for a loop. What is she saying about me? Why is she saying this to me? I'm not a criminal. I'm not a crook. I'm not robbing anybody. Why would she say that? At that stage in my life I didn't have the tools or the knowledge to interpret where she was coming from. I would learn later on how to interpret her comments and then get insulted by them. What she said stuck in my head. This is what people think of me.

Jamie's mother, ever-supportive of her only child, paid for his tuition. As a student, Jamie was interested in psychology. He said, "I was fascinated with people. But I was interested in psychology for the wrong reasons. If I could understand why you did what you did, then I could manipulate them. That was my basis, that's what motivated me to go to college." While attending his first year of college, Jamie continued to run the streets with guys from the projects. He described his peers as "corrupted and totally deviant. They were criminal. They would rob, steal, lie, cheat, and shoot people." Jamie claimed this was not a formal street gang; rather, these were just guys, "hustlers," whom he "hung out with" from the projects:

> They were guys in my age group that are acting like adults. They didn't pull me in to their group; I liked what was going on and became a willing partner. There was esteem in what we did. No one bothered us. We did basically what we wanted to do. You could walk down the street and there was no fear that someone would rob you and take your things. You had respect. You felt like a ghetto hero.

Hanging out with the guys from the projects, Jamie developed a "fascination with guns." For him, "guns were the ultimate power." But, "no one would give me a gun. Maybe they saw what lied underneath the surface? You know how people when they drink become another person. Well I'm the type of guy with a gun in my hand, I become another person. And you don't want to see that person. I'm totally aggressive." In reflecting on his fascination with guns, Jamie believed that he was trying to overcome something: "Maybe fear. I had a very strong fear of those streets, and even though I moved through them, I thought the gun would help me overcome that fear."

Jamie developed a new relationship with a guy who lived in his public housing complex. Although this guy was "very dangerous and unstable," "he was good to me, and he was good to our crew." Jamie was simply "fascinated" by him because "every time he had a gun he would shoot some-body. We would go somewhere, and it would not be odd for him to shoot somebody. It would never be an odd thing. This was normal behavior, given the circumstances, and you had to maintain your position." Jamie admitted, that at the time, "the only reason he was doing those things and I wasn't, was because I didn't have a gun." One time, his friend gave Jamie a gun to keep overnight:

> It was an old police 38, before they had glocks. I didn't take it out of the house. I'm playing with it in my room and I drop it and it . . . it falls, but it falls in a way that it hits the butt. I'm watching it in slow motion falling. The gun is fully loaded. It's falling on the butt of the handle. It drops and falls backwards. I'm watching and the barrel is pointing up at me. The first thought I have is I'm dead. I'm thinking, it's going to hit the trigger, the handle, and the gun is going to go off. But it didn't.

Jamie's fascination with his new friend, a fixation on guns, and the allure of street life gradually led to his involvement with armed robberies, where "you pull out a gun and take other people's stuff." This proved a turning point in Jamie's life, and he was now heading down a destructive path. In the circle of men that he was hanging out with, Jamie realized that "everybody is a bum and I was headed down that road." Prison for those men, as Jamie said, became "a rite of passage." Jamie recounted too many narratives of men he knew, at the time, who were convicted of crimes and had gone to prison. He was well aware of the consequences of armed robbery and the possibility of getting caught: "I was intelligent enough to see what could happen, but I was dumb enough not to care, and make the appropriate decision. So I did what everybody else was doing. I just didn't care," he said.

On the school front, Jamie was failing his college classes, even though he "saw education as very important. I would always take time to read some-thing." Yet that was not enough, and he "did poor the first semester." The second semester did not improve:

> I did even worse, and I dropped out. That's when I got into trouble. Even though I was conscious of the consequences of what I was doing, the long-term effects of that behavior did not become apparent to me until I left college. I didn't realize the full magnitude of the social, cul-tural, historical, and personal piece that went along with engaging crimi-nal behavior and the whole process that comes with it. I just didn't see it. Even though I was failing I knew I was in a place (school) where I was supposed to be in. I didn't necessarily want to be there, but I didn't nec-essarily want to leave. But I wasn't satisfied with my schooling because I was failing. I dropped out of school. I saw myself beneath that person

that I never wanted to be. I saw myself being a bum. I couldn't produce. My view of myself was based on my mother's expectations, and I'm not holding up my end.

After dropping out of college, the "monster" side of Jamie's personality began to take control, as street culture became the focus of his life. More and more he started to rely on "manipulation, learning the game, learning the con. I wanted to be the fast talker. This is what's going on in the world of the streets that I was in. I had a death wish. I was acting out and starting trouble." Increasingly, Jamie became "very self-destructive, and alcohol took over my life." He moved out of his mother's apartment in the projects. Jamie's life on his own was spiraling out of control, and even the guys with whom he was hanging out noticed his increasingly erratic but especially aggressive behavior. He said to them:

> You know what, fuck all of you. They saw what was in my face. They realized something was going on with me. It got so bad that they were scared of me because I became unpredictable, too irrational. I was depressed, and I didn't like where I was at. I had no one to talk to about it. There was no there for me; no counselor, no therapy. No one to say let me help you. I was carrying a gun. As a matter of fact I went from a sawed off shot gun to carrying a handgun. As a matter of fact I had a little ritual. When I took a bath, I would put a drink, a joint (marijuana), and my gun on a tray. And in the bath I would reach for all of them.

Unemployed, Jamie needed money: "I'm thinking economic now, purely economics." For him that meant more and more armed robbery: "you know, pulling out the gun, patting the guy down, and take whatever he has. I was primarily looking for money, jewelry, and drugs." Often Jamie had an accomplice when he robbed people, and they were bold predators: it did not seem to matter if it was day or night, on the streets or in an alley, or if they robbed men or women. Usually, they preyed on people in his neighborhood, and "it got so bad that we would rob someone and just walk away casually." Jamie and his fellow thieves did not, however, "rob establishments." As he said, "I didn't have the audacity for that because it was too much of a hassle." He liked robbing people: the "thrill of having power over somebody and the excitement in the immediacy of the moment." That destructive thrill and excitement, however, later turned into a nightmare with deadly consequences.

Similar to Jamie, Matt also became a thief. Leaving the Army and returning to Baltimore in 1975, he carried with him "about fifteen thousand dollar in my pocket" and the experience of a "hustler and player." But he wanted a different life. Upon returning Matt enrolled in a local college, got a job there, and paid for his tuition with army benefits. Early on, attending college for Matt became another game to be played, just another hustle. As he said, "school was like putting a predator . . . like putting a wolf in a hen house": "Within a matter of months, I went and copped some weed [marijuana]. I was selling weed on campus. I'm thinking shit, I got a population, and I'm going to get paid. I was moving real fast."

Matt was nineteen years old when he returned to Baltimore. He got an apartment in the black community where "you have killings, drugs, and gangs. You have nightclubs, but it's a nice spot that I move to." With his younger sister, he "started going to the clubs and dancing. We would sneak into clubs and dance in dancing contests. She was the one who taught me how to dance years before." Matt was becoming known in the club scene, and he decided to follow in his father's footsteps by becoming an event promoter. "I started promoting fashion shows and band stuff." And sometimes after the nightclubs closed Matt would hold after-hour parties in his apartment. He was indeed moving fast, and "girls liked me." But men wanted to be around Matt as well. "That doesn't mean they wanted to have sex with me. Men wanted to be like me; seen with me. It had to do with me just moving fast. It gave me status. It gave me power. It gave me power over men."

Hustling was now Matt's priority, and he failed his college classes. As he said, "I had all that other stuff going on, and after my first semester I was on academic probation. At the end of the spring semester, I'm like, see you later." He was once again a full-time hustler, and to make fast money Matt decided to turn his apartment "basically into after-hour joint." One night while a party was going on, Matt was tired and went to bed, but "gets up about five-thirty because I still hear music playing. There is this guy sitting on the couch that I don't know. His name is Jeff. He has a perm. Straight hair permed down to his shoulder. He fashion himself as a player, very unattractive guy, but he is dressed well. We get into a conversation." For Matt this initial meeting is important because "I'm starting to develop a crew in Baltimore and Jeff is apart of that crew." Shortly thereafter, Matt met the second member of his crew, Cadillac, who also "fashioned himself as a player." He introduced Matt "to the robbery game. I get into the stick up game. It became easy money. It's that simple."

Initially, Cadillac and Matt robbed "drop boxes" at shopping centers. They would wait in hiding until someone from a store went to deposit the day's earnings in a bank drop box, and then they robbed that person. Matt described what generally happened:

Cadillac was good at stealing cars. So he would steal the car we would use. Usually I drove. I was the get away guy. What we would do is go to a shopping center, shopping malls at night. We are sitting somewhere in the parking lot. All the stores would drop their night deposit into the drop box for the bank. We would wait until we saw a person. It was armed robbery. We were sticking people up at the deposit boxes. We would go into an area where there may be two or three malls within a mile and a half of each other. Hit this one then head across town and hit another one. Cadillac was big and all he had to do was say, "give me that motherfucking bag." It would be the luck of the draw. Sometimes we would bust it open and it would be $2,500.00 in there, and sometimes $5,000.00; and sometimes you bust the bag open and it was only $500.00. It all would depend.

Matt and Cadillac continued to commit armed robberies of night deposit boxes for about six months, and then things began to change. At first, Jeff was not involved in the robberies. Because Jeff was "basically staying" at Matt's apartment, "he wanted to join us because he sees the money coming in," and he does. Tensions gradually develop between them over ownership of the hustle, over who was in control of what was going on. Matt's crew had other problems as well, "opposition with these other cats." As a result, Matt "is strapped. I'm enforcing the law. Now I'm carrying pistols. Guns":

> I have a double shoulder holster, two pistols, one under my left arm and one under my right arm. I wore pistols twenty-four hours a day. I would sleep face down with my right hand or my left hand dangling on the floor with my pistol where I could grab it. I bought them at a gun store, and I had a seamstress that would make my suits. She hooked the holster up. When I stepped out of my house I was strapped. I'm getting a reputation in the city, and this is bad.

Matt's mother and stepfather, George, were still living in a predominately white community when he returned to Baltimore. Although he still hated George, occasionally Matt visited, and when he did he was "strapped." He described the effect:

> I would purposely take my coast off. I did it because of my stepfather. By doing so, I'm telling him I will kill you. My mother would say, "Boy what's wrong with you? Go upstairs and take those guns off. There are kids down here." So I do that. I had a conversation with my mother. She was afraid; she was scared for me. She didn't understand why I needed to carry them. Why I was carrying two of them. She said she didn't raise me to act like this. I was a good boy. I had a lot going for myself. In her mind, I went to the service, and I had a nice place to live. I still had a love/hate relationship with her because I still hadn't forgiven her for staying with this fool, George. So I quit wearing them in the house. I would take them off and leave them in the car when I visited.

Meanwhile, Matt continued to move fast, he continued to hustle, and as a result his crew of men was getting larger. They sold dope, primarily marijuana, and Cadillac was "stealing cars. He taught me how to steal cars."

But armed robbery continued to be the mainstay of the crew's activities, especially for Matt, Cadillac, and Jeff. During what appeared to be a routine robbery, Matt, for the first time, used his gun:

> We did a stick-up. I was in the back seat. Jeff was driving this time. I got out of the car with Cadillac to do it. We get in the car with the money. A car sees us, and it follows us down the highway. It's like the wild, Wild West because I shoot the back window out of the car. We're riding down the highway and I'm shooting out the back window at the car that is following us. Can I do some crazy shit or what? As I'm thinking about it I'm laughing because it was so stupid. As I'm shooting at this car, this is a three lane highway, an expressway, there are cars everywhere. By the grace of God, nobody got hit. We get off the expressway and duck inside some apartment buildings, and the car doesn't follow us. So we get out of the car and split up. This was the first time I had pulled the trigger in that way. It's not the first time I had pulled a gun. It was the first time I had pulled the trigger in relationship to sticking someone up.

This incident was a major turning point. Matt realized that he could in fact pull the trigger, if needed. For that robbery, Matt's crew got about five thousand dollars. But it was "fast money." The faster the money came in, the quicker Matt was spending it: "I don't know what I was spending it on. I was probably giving it away in clubs, for alcohol and shit; buying clothes and jewelry. The point is the more money I got, the more I needed. The more we stick-up, the more we had to stick-up." Armed robbery was now Matt's major source of income, and it was the central focus of his life. He offered an assessment: "You become dependent on robbing as a source of income. You wake up in the morning, you look at your bank roll, and it's getting low. Alright we are going to plan a stick-up for tomorrow night. Where are we going?" Similar to Jamie, Matt was headed down a path of destruction that too turned deadly.

Different from Jamie and Matt, Richard was not a thief. In 1976, he was in prison. Following his conviction for having assaulted his base commander in Germany, Richard was back in the United States serving a two-year sentence in federal prison. He thought that he could easily do "two years and move on with my life." But as he got off the yellow prison bus, which had transported him through the prison gates, Richard realized that his two-year stint in prison was going to be extremely difficult. When he and other prisoners were leaving the bus, with hands and legs shackled, the guards started "barking orders and using clubs: 'Get the hell off the bus.' They were just letting you know who the boss was right from the start. It was really cruel. When we got off the bus, we had to jog about a mile all the way in the rain to the area where the new people came into the prison for processing." Immediately, Richard started to worry about how he was going to survive imprisonment. While "stripped naked," a sergeant told the new inmates what was going to happen to them, and Richard never forgot his words: "He said this was his prison and 'I will kill you. You're in my prison now and I will make you disappear. Most of you guys will be faggots when you get upstairs. If the guys upstairs don't screw you, then we're going to screw you down here.' He said a whole lot of demeaning stuff, letting you know who was in control." Initially, military prisoners were separated from nonmilitary inmates. Before going upstairs to the general prison population, as a military prisoner, Richard remained downstairs in a "protective custody cell" for ninety days. During that period, he went through orientation: "They tell you their expectations. All the do's and don'ts, what to look out for as far as other inmates, and where the safe stations are in case you feel threatened or if someone is threatening you. In the next voice they're telling you that you have to protect yourself. A lot of fear is being instilled." And fear was, indeed, instilled into Richard. He was thinking: "kill or be killed. I need to get in the best shape of my life so that I could be able to protect myself. When I do get upstairs, I just have to survive. I more or less put myself in the frame of mind that I'm not going to let anyone do anything to me. The first wrong word, I just said, I'm in attack mode. That's how I approached it." When it was time for Richard to be moved upstairs, as he climbed the stairs he heard "catcalls" from other men, and his attention quickly turned to one man in particular:

> This big damn guy, probably about six feet, seven inches said "come here motherfucker." I said you're talking to me? He said "yeah, you." I dropped my duffle bag, and I just jumped on him. I started biting his ear off. The guards are hitting me with the sticks, and he is hitting me, but I'm not letting go of his ear. I'm still biting his ear off. The guards shoot me up with this stuff, and then they take me back downstairs. I'm in segregation. I'm downstairs for about a month before I have a hearing. They don't charge me or him with anything. They take me back upstairs to my cell that afternoon.

Following that initial violent incident, Richard was committed to taking care of himself by any means necessary to simply survive prison life. Shortly thereafter, while having dinner in mess hall, one of the guy's "buddies approached" Richard and said "you're dead. They had these big metal trays and I started beating this guy with the tray. I said take this back to him. The guards came over and asked what happened? The other inmates said nothing. His tray just fell on the floor. That's how inmates do it." Through physical violence, Richard gained respect from the other prisoners. He also gained respect from the guy whose ear he had bitten off. Richard learned that this guy had "murdered two people, his girlfriend and her lover. He tied both of them to a tree, put chains around their necks, and pulled their heads off. He was sentenced to 225 years to life. He was really scary." But after Richard bit his ear off and later hit his buddy in the head with a metal tray, the guy again approached Richard. This time, however, the contact between them was different. He said to Richard: "You know something man, you're alright. Then he shakes my hand and said 'if you have any problems, you say you're Raymond's cousin.'" For Richard this was a "really scary moment. I was almost ready to crap in my pants. But I still didn't let my guard down because I didn't believe that it was just over with."

Unlike most other inmates, Richard had money. Unbeknownst to anyone else, it was stored in a safety deposit box in a bank. He decided to hire an attorney, who could file an appeal on his behalf. As he awaited the appeal hearing, he settled into the daily routine of prison life. Richard was assigned to work in the laundry, pressing uniforms. He also developed a relationship with a black guy whose cell was next to his. That guy "was buying drugs from some Neo Nazis." One day, as he returned from his laundry job, "I saw all this blood. I'm asking everybody what happened. The only thing they said was that somebody got tossed. When I got upstairs, I see the guards by my friend's cell; they are cleaning the cell out. Because I knew what he was involved in I had a pretty good idea as to what happened to him. This probably happened about two months before my appeal hearing."

But this was by no means the only violence that Richard was aware of in prison. As a matter of fact, violence was ever-present, and sexual assault was a particularly common occurrence. Richard said, "I can't remember a day that went by that someone didn't get raped in prison. It happened so openly, usually in the shower, and the guards were aware of it. If you couldn't protect yourself as a man, you couldn't expect any help from anyone else. Guys had a really hard time, and it tore at my heart. In a way that was how they controlled what happened in prison, through the other inmates. A guard would say I have a problem with this inmate. Deal with him, and I'll do you a favor. That helped to keep the balance of power in prison where it needed to be."

After about six months, Richard's appeal hearing was scheduled. "The appeal judge realized that some mistakes were made during the trial, so he knocked a substantial amount of time off my sentence." Finally, Richard was free to leave prison. He recalled the exact moment he stepped through the prison gates as a free man: "It is in the springtime, and it's still morning. They open the gates, and I walk through the gates. I can hear this loud slam. I only heard it two times, once when I first got there, and then when I was leaving. It sounded like thunder clapping; that's how loud it sounded. I just dropped to my knees and thanked God for allowing me to make it through. I had seen a lot of things in those six-months, and somehow I had survived." But in leaving prison, Richard was not totally free of the Army. He was to be dishonorably discharged as part of his punishment, but upon release he had not received his formal discharge papers. Richard was required to report to an army base in his home state of New Jersey to await his papers. Six months in prison had not lessened Richard's anger or bitterness toward the Army; to the contrary, he did not know "how long it would take for my discharge to come through, but I knew that the military and red tape is something they do well." Again, Richard decided "to create as much havoc on that base" as he could in an attempt to force his discharge from the Army:

> I connected with some other guys that were waiting for bad discharges. We would rob trainees; sell drugs on base, anything and everything wrong that we could get into. We would give drugs out on credit and add interest on to that. People ended up owing us money. We would kick their asses. I had a hatred for white people and a serious hatred for the military. I refused to wear a uniform. I went AWOL [absence without leave]. I wanted to defy them. They caught me and my partner. We had drugs; heroin, cocaine, and some marijuana. They catch me with all these drugs. We get back to the base, and come to find out the military can't charge us with the drugs because we didn't get caught with the drugs on military jurisdiction. So there were no drug charges. But they got me on robbery charges on base. They try to court marshal me, but couldn't find a witness to testify against me. Their case is starting to diminish, and they offer me a deal. I said, yes let's do it. They said, "We're not going to waste anymore time on this guy. The streets are going to take care of him. Who he is now, he'll be the same person out there on the streets, and it will catch up with him eventually." I walked away from the Army the next morning with my discharge papers.

Murder and Things

Upon leaving the Army, Richard went immediately to Detroit to live with a woman whom he had developed an intimate relationship. They had met at a nightclub, while she was visiting relatives in New Jersey. She had a master's degree and was a "social worker at a state mental institution." In his description of her, Richard said that she was "a really nice young lady. A lot heavier as far as the women I would deal with at that time. She had three kids, a son and two daughters. She was probably about seven years older than me. She really had herself together. She didn't appear to have low self-esteem. She knew what she wanted. She was a go-getter, and I liked that about her. She was assertive and got the things she wanted in life." Richard felt that he "had landed in a pretty good situation. Things were going pretty well at that time." She paid the household bills, while Richard "sold weed, was drinking, gambled, and did a lot of partying." But he also got a legitimate job:

> I got a city job, working for the street department, as a sanitation person. They paid well, but not as well as she got paid. Plus I sold marijuana. I made pretty good money doing that. I didn't have to invest any money in household, because she had been doing that for years. Financially I was in a pretty comfortable situation. And she didn't know anything about my money in the safety deposit box at the bank. For me, it was like I'm going to spend what she got and make it work from there.

Richard felt "really lucky," and after about nine months together, his girlfriend asked him if he wanted to get married. He said "we might as well. We're together, I love the kids, and things are working out pretty well." But the real reason Richard agreed to marriage was because he "had fears that if I didn't agree she would end the relationship because she wanted more." And financially, he had a "pretty good situation" going for him. But shortly after the marriage, their relationship became increasingly "strained," and Richard responded with violence. Richard recalled the first incident when he physically assaulted her:

> We would go to dinner parties at her friends' house. People would always talk about what they did for a living. I found myself creating these profound names for the work I did. I was a sanitation worker, but would say that I was a custodial engineer. I made it sound like I was doing some heavy stuff, but nothing compared to what their qualifications were. I felt less than. I asked her, "Why do you bring me around these people. Do you do it to shame or embarrass me, or to make me feel less than, or to make yourself feel above me?" She would simply say, "I want you to be a part of my life in every way." I didn't feel that. I remember one time going to a dinner party, and I took her suggestion and tried the honest route. Her friends asked me what I did for a living, and I said, "I'm a sanitation worker; basically I'm a trash man." I overheard this conversation out on the terrace. They said, "can you believe she's married to a garbage man?" I blamed her for their overall attitude toward me or what they felt about me. Words were said. She said some words that I perceived to be very demeaning. She said, "That's what the hell you are, a trash man." I assaulted her because I just wanted her to shut up.

Following the first assault, Richard became "more and more physically abusive and verbally abusive." His intent was "to take control over her life. I was going to be in charge. That was the bottom line. No more voicing your opinion to me. I'm the damn man, and I'm in control." With ongoing phys-ical and verbal abuse, Richard achieved his objective: his aggressive behavior evoked fear, and as a result his wife "pretty much went along with the things I said and did." Although Richard exerted emotional and physical control over his wife, he was not in control over his own body, and around this period he became ill. He had major "colostomy surgery" and "went through a lot of physical pain" as a result.

No longer able to do the heavy lifting required of a garbage man, Richard drew upon some of the money he had stashed away in a safety deposit box to set up a drug business. He started selling drugs full-time and had several guys working for him. A younger brother of one of his dealers owed Richard money. When Richard demanded his money, the guy "got real belligerent and wanted to get physical with me. I had all these stitches in my stomach, and I couldn't fight nobody. This guy doesn't know who I am or the type of person I am especially dealing with violence." The next series of events altered Richard's life. Even though he could not physically fight someone, Richard could pull the trigger on a gun. Richard described what happened after the initial confrontation with the younger brother:

> This guy and his friends come riding down my block, and they're talking crazy. I go in the house, and I get my shotgun. I pumped it and aimed it at the car, and they speed off. They come back down the block an hour later, and I'm sitting on the porch. They showed pistols, and I had the shotgun so I fired at the vehicle. He's going to give me my money one way or another. A few months go by, I'm healing, and they're still driv-ing down my block talking crazy, but no one is making any moves. I see this guy in the bar one evening, and I say where's my money. He said, "We're going to get you." I said you going to pay me right now. I want my money right now. He lives right across the street from the bar. His crew is there and it's probably about six or seven of them, and I have my pistol in the car. We're talking crap to each other. The guy who owns the bar talks to me and says "just calm down he'll pay you." While he's talk-ing to me, they creep out of the bar.

This incident occurred during the summer. And when Richard left the bar, he returned home, and sat on the porch to watch his step-children play in the front yard. Again, this guy and his buddies "drive by in this convertible, and they are pointing guns. The kids are out there with me, and I push them in the house. I don't know if these guys are going to fire or what?" Richard immediately called a friend in New Jersey and said, "I need you to come here because I'm having some problems with these guys. The friend said, "I will be there tomorrow morning." But the guys did not wait until morning; again they drove past Richard's house, and "this time they shoot through the porch window." Richard decided that "I'm going to resolve this today":

> I go upstairs, and I get my weapon. I go down the street and knock on the door. The brother that owes me money opens the door. I said where is my money? When he reached . . . I don't know what he was going for, but I just reached in my pocket, grabbed my gun and started firing. I see someone coming downstairs, and I started shooting at them. Another brother is coming at me with a knife. So I shoot him, and he's bleeding really badly. So I leave. I'm coming down the stairs, and all of these people are getting off the bus. They saw the incident, and I just walked down the street to my house. I'm waiting for the police to come. I knew someone was going to call the police. That doesn't happen. Instead, the next day I get a message that we're going to resolve this like men in the park. Everyone is still alive at this point.

Anticipating the altercation, Richard sent his wife and the children to her brother's house for safe keeping. The friend from New Jersey arrived. Sometime during the next day, Richard heard that "one of the guys has passed away." Richard's friend told him "to pack up what I need and get in the car; we're getting out of here; and we leave." Later, he called his wife and she told Richard that "they burned the house down. She's talking really crazy." His wife also told him that, "the police keep coming to my job; they're looking for you; they said, you've killed somebody; and, his family is threatening us." To protect his wife and step-children Richard returned to Detroit to find the guys who burned his house down. He found them. "Nobody knows that we're coming, and we start shooting at the first people we see on the porch. I don't think we hit anyone. They started scattering and are shooting back at us; we're outnumbered." Richard and his friend left the scene unharmed. But knowing that he was wanted for murder by the Detroit police, Richard "just wanted to get away." Now he was on the run from the law.

Matt would also be wanted for murder, and like Richard he too fled. With his crew, Matt was planning more and more armed robberies. But Matt, Cadillac, and Jeff had decided to stop robbing night deposit boxes "because they (police) were waiting on our asses." Instead, with another guy added to the robbery crew, Alfred, they started robbing business establishments, particularly restaurants. Usually, they would wait until the restaurant closed and robbed the manager outside of the establishment, when he was getting into his car to leave. But Matt and his crew soon altered their strategy, and started entering the establishments as the managers were preparing to close for the night. As they entered a restaurant, Matt said:

I have the pistol and I'm telling them, give me your shit. These were dinner theatres. You go into one of these places, and you make them open the safe. You're doing it on a day like a Sunday evening. They are closing up and they probably got ten or fifteen thousand dollars in their safe from that Saturday. So we are deep into the stick up game now. And we would get away with that.

Matt and his crew did get away with a series of restaurant robberies, except for the fateful night when a stick-up went terribly wrong. On that occasion:

We wore masks to hide ourselves. We go into this particular place. Alfred got the tape, the ropes, and the knife to cut the tape. He was going to tie everybody up that was in there. Going in, it was expected that there would only be three people there, the manager, cook, and an older woman, who was the cashier. But when we get there, there are two people sitting at the bar: two white men and both of them weighing about two-fifty, and probably about six-four. When we get in, we go down on these people. Alfred is tying them up. Once they are tied up Jeff and I take the manager and the older woman down to the safe. Now we are talking stupid. Open the safe bitch or I'm going to kill you if you don't. Cock the gun and they are like . . . While all this is going on we hear someone holler: Help! Help! Jeff runs up the steps and runs back down to me saying "Alfred is fighting these two guys." He doesn't have his gun, but he has his knife. So he is fighting them with the knife. One of them has gotten loose, and they are fighting him, and he is stabbing them. So Jeff runs back down and tells me what is going on. So I go up to where he is. I stand there with my pistol pointed and my legs spread, so they stop. Alfred crawls between my legs and goes to the back door. Jeff is standing behind me. Both of those guys have been stabbed by Alfred. But they came toward us even though the guns were drawn. Bang. Bang. Bang. Shots are fired. I fired the shots. Several shots are fired.

Matt and his crew had locked the manager and the cashier in the downstairs office. Immediately following the shooting, Matt, Jeff, and Albert went to the glass door to leave, but it was locked. Matt "unconsciously hit the glass with the pistol and it shatters. I just walked right through it and they follow me." But when Matt shattered the glass door: "I cut my finger so I'm bleeding badly. There was blood on my clothes, it ends up being around the restaurant, and there is blood in the car." Fleeing the scene, they went to Alfred's house, where Matt "cleaned myself up. Took all the stuff, the clothes put them in a trash bag, rode down the alley, and put them in somebody's dumpster." At this point, Matt was ready to run.

Before Matt left Baltimore, he said: "I got all my cash and shit, went to my mother's, and gave her some money. And then split." He was headed to Prince George's County to stay with a woman with whom he had a relationship. While there he read in the paper about this robbery that took place in Baltimore:

> It says four people were hurt, one person killed, and one person in critical condition. So one of the guys dies and the other one is in the hospital. The older woman said her back was hurt when she fell or something. Somebody said they were hit by a glass that was thrown. So I'm like okay, now I'm panicking. What am I going to do? My first thought was I need to get away. Where do I know people? I don't want to go back to Chicago. Maybe I'll go to Atlanta because nobody knows me there. Then I was thinking about going back to California, then I said no because if they look for me they will trace my military records and come looking for me. What I did was stay in Prince George's County.

About a week later, Matt learned that an "all points bulletin" had been issued, and the police were looking for him. At the same time, he learned that Alfred had been arrested:

> The arrest was made by detectives because they began looking at potential suspects. They put his ass under the light, and Alfred knew that he didn't fire the shots, but he knew that he had stabbed the guys. This is Baltimore, Maryland, 1977. This is white victims and three black men. So they threatened Alfred, who had a past criminal record. So he agrees to testify. But I don't know this at the time, but I do know that a couple of days later another arrest is made, Jeff. One thing leads to another, and for some reason, I talked to my uncle, and he said, "deal with it." I turned myself in.

Jamie was also wanted for murder, but, unlike Matt, he did not surrender. Jamie and his crew continued to rob people in his neighborhood, at gun point. But he also started to pal around with a new guy, Simon, who had recently been released from prison. Jamie and Simon decided to rob a known drug dealer in the community and went to look for him at a pool hall, where he usually hung out. Jamie said, "I walked in the place with jewelry hanging all off of me—I have my gold watch, gold ring, and a gold bracelet." But Jamie also had a "handkerchief around my face and a hat cocked backwards. The only things you can see are some eyes of a mad man, a mad child."

When Jamie entered the pool hall with Simon, he was high on drugs. Jamie said that he "forgot all about we're supposed to be there trying to rob somebody. I wanted to act out. Dumb me, I'm there to rob somebody, and I'm just hanging out in the pool hall to be identified by someone. If we rob him, then everyone and their mothers are going to see us, and then we are going to jail. I'm not thinking right. I'm living literally in a drug induced moment." Not seeing the drug dealer in the pool hall, Jamie and Simon left. But as they were leaving, Simon suggested that they stop by the apartment building where the drug dealer lived, and they do just that:

> Low and behold the guy with his brother and another guy were coming out of the building. They are right there together. Simon asked them, "You guys seen Snake." That was my sign. I got the gun. I walked pass them, and now I can feel his eyes on the back of my neck. Simon and I leave, so now our backs are to the door. Then Simon says to me, "what happening?" I said, "Do you really want to do this man?" So I said. "Fuck it, man, come on." But I hear some noise behind my back. I didn't know if they had a gun or what? So I spun, and I saw them. As I'm spinning, I pull out the pistol, and I fire. Bang. The guy leaves his feet. The bullet hits him, and he literally leaves his feet. He hits the plexiglas door—he hits, drops down, gets up, and runs around the corner. Simon went to look for him. The other two guys ran. Simon came back, he had to take the gun out of my hand and put the gun away. We ran.

Immediately after the shooting, Jamie ran to his mother's house. He went to his old "room and cried. I said what the hell did I just do? I realized that I had shot him, and I didn't like it. And I didn't like myself. I'm angry with myself for what I did. You don't do something like that and just shake it off." The morning after, Jamie learned from a friend that the drug dealer was dead. And later he learned that "the word had gotten around in my neighborhood about what happened," from members of his old crew. Not knowing what to do, Jamie decided to stay put: "I stayed in the house and just drank." As he drank, he thought about the possibility of getting caught. Jamie knew that Simon was on parole, and if he got caught "he would eventually give me up because there's no honor among thieves."

The shooting occurred in December 1977. A month passed, and Jamie had not been arrested. But the murder was constantly on his mind. He believed that "it was just a matter of time before I got arrested. I was still drinking and smoking marijuana. Now it was just to numb me because the killing bothered me." Finally, Jamie told his mother what he had done. "I didn't want the cops running in and she not knowing what was going on," he said. But he also "wanted her help." Ever-protective of her only child, he said: "my mother wanted me to leave the area. I'm going to be honest, here. She wanted this to just go away." But his mother decided that they should seek the guidance of an attorney to determine whether or not Jamie should turn himself in to the police. "We went to the lawyer and said look let's turn myself in. He said, 'no don't do that, no one is looking for you.' This sounds good to me; he's the lawyer and knows what he's talking about."

Following the attorney's advice, Jamie decided to move on with his life. As he said, about a month after the killing, "the funny thing is, I'm back in school again and I got a job. I'm starting to look past the world of the projects." Yet, Jamie knew that he "was on borrowed time. In my heart of hearts, when I go to bed at night and when I wake up in the morning, I had this nagging feeling that prison is right around the corner." And five months after the murder, "There was a knock on the door. I get up to answer the door. I hear these deep voices. It's the cops. They handcuff me and take me out. They took me to the homicide division and handcuffed me to a desk. Now, I actually felt kind of relieved."

PRISON AND THINGS

After his arrest, Jamie was charged with murder, and his bail was set at $50,000. But his "mother didn't have the money so I went to jail" to await trial. Although Jamie had engaged in criminal activity, he had never gone to jail before; from hanging out with other guys from the projects, he knew that "going to jail was a rite of passage," for men in his neighborhood. Nonetheless, he was fearful because "I had heard about the things people do" in jail. Jamie recalled his first weeks in jail:

> A guy came up to me and said, "Take your sneakers off." I gave them to him out of fear. I get robbed. When I get back to my cell I said, "What the hell did you just do?" Two things bothered me about that incident. I didn't like feeling fear, and the guy was a punk. The problem with that incident is that I had to fight. By me giving my sneakers away, that was a sign of weakness. I'm back to my old self now. So I'm fighting guys. I'm thinking the sexual thing now. I pal up with guys I know from the streets, and some of them were snitches and low-rate cowards.

Jamie was angry about being afraid, and through that anger he found his "niche:" he found his "psychological safety niche, and my physical safety niche," by becoming one of the bad guys in jail. As a result, he "basically did what I wanted to do." Even though Jamie had found his "niche," he was by no means comfortable with the situation he was in:

> I had strong desires; desires to get the hell out of there and get back home. As the months pass you start to see . . . start to re-realize the life that you had. You reflect on your life. You say wow: my life really wasn't that bad. I've done some bad things, but pass those bad things there were some quiet moments with females in your life. Realizing where you messed up. You realize how people that you think would come and see you, don't come, and why would they want to come?

After nine months in jail, Jamie's trial was scheduled to begin. His mother had managed to hire a private white attorney for Jamie's defense. But "the only time I saw him was when I was in the courtroom; he never came to visit me in jail." As a result Jamie said, "I was not prepared for what was happening. There is always that hope of getting out. When will I be able to get out? Will I beat this at trial? You go to trial because you think you're going to beat it. Some way or another I thought that I was going to beat this. I needed to believe that this would all be over in about a week, and I would be back on the streets. Unbeknownst to me at the time was how dumb I was. How much of a fantasy world I was living in."

Jamie was right about the length of the trial; it did last a week. But he was wrong about the conclusion. During the trial, the two guys who were with the drug dealer the night Jamie shot him were key witnesses for the state, and Simon "pointed the finger at me" as well. Jamie said, "The whole process was uncomfortable: you have to sit there while someone points a finger at you, as they say you did something as horrible as take a life." At trial, Jamie was forced to face not only the reality the he had killed someone but also the consequences of having done so. He said, "You can duck, until you are judged for your actions. But trial was not make-believe; it was real. And taking someone's life is real, someone is not coming back, and you are held liable." Jamie did not testify on his own behalf at trial.

After the testimony and evidence were presented, the jury deliberated for "about four hours," and Jamie was found guilty. At his sentencing hearing, he recalled "saying to myself, I'm a first time offender; I was in college; I was working; I'm going to get five years." The judge, however, had a different opinion:

> I was found guilty of felony murder and killing during an attempted robbery. I got convicted of manslaughter in the first degree as a lesser included count of intentional murder, which meant that, although I meant to cause physical harm, I did not mean to kill the guy. And I got found guilty of the weapon charge. I got twenty-five to life for the felony murder, fifteen years for the manslaughter, and seven years for using a gun. I was speechless. I turned to my attorney, and I couldn't talk.

When Jamie was sentenced to "twenty-five years to life" in prison, he was only twenty years old. The nine months he spent in jail and the lessons he learned were now a useful resource for him, as he readied himself for long-term prison life. Jamie remained in jail for another month before he was transferred to a state prison in rural Minnesota. As he prepared for that transfer, Jamie said:

> I'm doing what you call jailhouse. I'm building up my cash flow to take with me. My cash flow is sneakers, towels, underwear, socks, cigarettes as

well as cookies, tang, and cakes. This is what drives the economy in prison. The more of that you have, the more you're seen as wealthy. Those things I just named are wealth in prison. When it was time for me to leave I had a dictionary, and the guards didn't believe the dictionary was mine. The other guard was amazed that I could write in cursive. These are things that stuck in my mind; the images that the guards had of us, as prisoners. I get on the bus to ride upstate. I'm shackled and hand-cuffed to another prisoner. Of course, it was face forward, and if you turn around, "we're going to kill you; we're going to beat you down."

During the eight-hour bus ride to prison, Jamie said that he had three things on his mind: "How am I going to get out of this? I don't want to do twenty-five years. But also pressing is what do I need to do to make sure I'm not victimized? I'm not going to be victimized. No one is going to victimize me. The other thing is how am I going to maintain my family ties? I'm thinking about my street family. I'm not really realizing the pain that my mother is feeling. That doesn't occur to me until much later. So I'm thinking about these three things."

Upon arriving at the state maximum security prison, Jamie found a mostly all-black world. "Just like in jail the majority of the inmates were black, and the bulk of the white prisoners kept to themselves." But the prison guards were a different story, Jamie said that "farmer John and his team were all rural white men. The ratio of who was here and who was in charge defi-nitely wasn't right."

During his first years of imprisonment, Jamie described his stay as similar to that of going to "gladiator school: violence ruled, and it was violent—violent—violent." In that culture of violence, Jamie was vigilant about pro-tecting himself, but he was growing increasingly resentful of the seemingly indiscriminate violence he participated in and witnessed. Jamie hated the fact that at times he had to tape thick magazines around his waist, which he "padded myself and have my knife, just in case something happened."

As the years past, Jamie matured, but in that maturity he refused to totally accept or adjust to the prison life. He realized that he was "in a world, but I'm not of that world." In other words, Jamie realized that, even though he was confined and surrounded by violence, he still could make choices about how he wanted to live his life, even in prison. He began to take a hard look at him-self and the circumstances that brought him to prison. Of the murder he said, "It's something that I should have never done. To this day I still carry it in my consciousness. I'm able to deal with it, but it's still there. I have to wear the fact that I took someone's life that will never fully grow into manhood." In taking stock of his life in prison, as he assessed his circumstances:

I'm seeing myself. I'm looking at myself in the context of where I'm at. I don't belong here. I don't want to die here. I don't want to be here. I hate being here. I'm around people that I don't like. Remember I have twenty-five years to life. I'm seeing guys come and go; guys that can't stay out in the streets. It's hard out there. I'm saying to myself, what do I have to do to get out of here and ensure that I don't come back? The first thing that I realize is that what I shouldn't do is commit a crime. I stopped running around doing knuckle headed stuff and being dumb. I have to disconnect and abandon associations. What are the things that I need to do to fit back into society? Now I was about my business. So I decided to play the academia game. I went to school.

A local community college had an educational program in the prison, and Jamie started taking college classes. Through his studies, he tried to figure out "what was happening to me: not only did I need to know what was happening, but how to interpret what was happening. What were those with intelligence saying about me in prison; I needed to find out." But, as Jamie observed, "the truth depends on who is telling the story." At first Jamie was pursuing education as a way of gaining increased knowledge. Through his studies, over the years, Jamie eventually earned four college diplomas: an associate, bachelor, and two master degrees. But as time went by, he was "seeing education as wealth, as a resource," for earning respect from the other inmates, in the absence of violence. Respect was an unanticipated consequence for his self-discipline and educational accomplishments. And Jamie began to notice:

> No one bothered you. No one took anything from you. No one lied to you. No one talked to you in any manner. It was not that those things didn't happen, but when they did, there were ways to address them. You didn't have to use violence: you didn't have to pull out a knife to solve a problem. Like listen, we don't have to do this, this way. You don't have to look at me as a threat. The bottom line is that no one was disrespecting me or taking advantage of me. I would come to realize that once you get pass a certain age and you're intelligent as well, guys respected that. That if you conducted yourself in a way that people respected you, then that's what it meant to be a man.

Over the years in prison, as he pursued education, Jamie developed a relationship with a white professor who taught at the prison. They eventually became close friends, and that friendship played a critical role in helping Jamie negotiate relationships outside of prison life. By now Jamie had been in prison for twenty-five years; he had spent more time inside prison than outside prison. He had a sentence of twenty-five years to life and did not believe that he would ever regain his freedom. He was eligible to go before the Parole Board, and Jamie knew that it was highly unlikely that he would get parole, especially on his first hearing:

> I didn't think that I was going home because the politics at that time was that you take your two-year hit, and maybe at your second hearing you hope that you can go home. So I went in there anticipating what was going to happen. I answered the questions, acknowledged responsibility for my actions, and I didn't blame any social factors, because the system doesn't want to hear that. I took sole responsibility for my actions and admitted that I was wrong. I talked about my achievements since being in prison, and about my future plans. There was a commissioner who was sympathetic to the incarcerated, and he thought that I could step outside of the institution and be productive. It takes about a week before you get word, but I was trying to get the guards to find out, the institutional snitches to find out, the runners to find out, and nobody could find out what the decision was. I think it was a Friday night, and I was getting nervous now because this was different. This was not following the usual pattern. The silence was unheard of because there're no secret in hell. So what happened, on the last count of the inmates in the dormitory, the security guard gave me a thumb up. So I went down and got the decision, and it said I'm going home.

All of a sudden Jamie had a different "mindset, what was important was not important anymore: it's not important if guys look at you crazy, it's not important to go to the commissary, it's not important to be involved in prison stuff." What was important was Jamie's life beyond prison; he was thinking about his "liberation from prison." He had a place to stay and a job waiting for him. Jamie was going to live with his friend, the white college professor, and work in his private business. Sixty days after he had been processed through the system Jamie was released from prison, but he was not completely liberated because he faced a lifetime of parole for his crime.

Upon release, Jamie went to live with the professor and his family in rural Minnesota. Prior to his release Jamie thought little about what it meant to live with a white family in an all-white environment. He said "any preconceived notions I had in prison were useless because I could never have perceived what I was walking into." The family welcomed Jamie and he lived "rent free, food free," and had his own room. "But the stipulation was that I do all the ground work." In addition to doing yard work at the house, Jamie was employed full-time in the professor's nonprofit family business. Jamie believed that he was a member of the family, and to him this meant that he had some leeway in making errors. But his perception of the situation quickly changed. Jamie was on parole and felt increasingly vulnerable because of it. Isolated and not knowing anyone in area, he soon realized that the professor and his family exerted too much control over his life: telling him what to do and how to do things. Trying "to get my feet under me as a liberated black man and as an adult," Jamie grew uncomfortable with his dependency on the professor's family. He began to see himself as their "black experiment." Their relationship deteriorated. They got into arguments, and "they let me know that I was not a part of their family." Not risking the possibility of being reported for a parole violation, after two years with the family, Jamie requested that his parole be transferred to Minneapolis.

Jamie had saved money and was able to find housing and live on his own, but he needed to be employed or risked parole violation. "I hide my background and dumb myself down" and got two jobs handling stock, one at a retail store and the other at a drug store. Eventually, Jamie got a professional job as an academic counselor helping former prisoners, and while working at that position he decided to attend school himself. Currently, Jamie is a doctoral student, he has settled into an intimate relationship with a woman, and they have a child. The social and cultural norms that Jamie once rejected as an adolescent are now important to him. Yet each day continues to challenge his attempts to negotiate in a world, where for most of his adult life he was marginalized and excluded. But Jamie does not allow himself to forget the fact that he took a life, and he accepts the responsibility, burden, and stigma that it has engendered. Jamie reflected on his life and the pain he has caused others as well as himself:

> When I took a life, at that time in my life I was depressed, angry, and saw myself up against a wall. I guess there was a lot of self-hating. I was nineteen and had just left high school, and I didn't like where I was in life. I saw myself becoming a bum on the streets. I took a hard look at my life as soon as I pulled that trigger. The first thing that I thought was what have I done? I went home that night and drank and cried myself to sleep. You don't ever forget that you've taken a life. You never have a sense of peace about what you've done. Christmas is hard for me because that's when it happened. I stay away from those places that bring back those memories. I'm always conscious of the fact that I took a life. I will be fifty years old, and half of my adult life has been formed in a total institution. My transition process is occurring as we speak, and will continue until I die. How do I come to terms with all of the errors that I've made? Once I forget that I've taken a life, then I'm going back to prison. I'm a guest in this world, and I'm learning the ways of the world. There so many things that I've done wrong even after prison, and I'm constantly working to make myself better. But most of my life has been trials and errors.

Richard probably agreed with Jamie's assessment that his decisions have led to a series of trials and errors, and if he could start over again he would negotiate a different life for himself. Like Jamie, Richard had also been wanted by the police for murder. But unlike Jamie, he went on the run. Fleeing Detroit, he hid in several cities before eventually ending up with his great uncle, a preacher in Mississippi; he did not tell his uncle that he was running from the police. Richard, however, settled into the routine of everyday life. He got a job as a laborer by assuming the identity of his cousin, who was in the military and stationed overseas at the time. After several months, he found unexpected company one day when returning from work:

> I pull up in front of the house and my uncle comes out and said, "Get out of the car. Don't be afraid, everything is going to be alright." I was like, "What are you talking about?" He said, "I know everything." He said, "Why didn't you tell me. I would have helped you get a lawyer." We were having that conversation, and I see these unmarked cars pull up. There was nowhere to run. They're the police, and I'm caught. They read me my rights and take me to the local jail. We go to this little court, and I sign these extradition papers. I'm glad it's over with. I can go ahead and face it now, and I don't have to run anymore. In my mind I'm thinking he deserved it. I just wanted to get it over with. I pretty much had the same feeling I had leaving Germany: I just wanted to get it done with so that I could move on with my life.

The police returned Richard to Detroit and soon thereafter he was arraigned on murder charges. He was "charged with first degree murder, reckless endangerment, and three counts of aggravated assault." Bail was denied, and he awaited trial in jail. Richard still had money locked away in a safety deposit box and again hired an attorney to represent him. Given the circumstances surrounding the murder, his lawyer developed a legal strategy based on self-defense. Meanwhile the district attorney handling Richard's case offered a plea bargain, a deal, of "twelve to twenty-five years," if he pleaded guilty to the crimes. Richard said, "That's not going to happen," so his attorney told the district attorney, "We're going to trial."

At trial, Richard's wife attended each day of the proceeding: "she supported me," he said. And the murdered victim's family also attended. But "the judge had to remove about eight of the guy's family members because of their threats toward me and the judge. They told her, we will kill you to get to him." Even though Richard's attorney presented a case of self-defense, there were no "witnesses to prove that." Consequently, Richard was convicted of "murder in the third degree" by an all-white jury and "sentenced to five to ten years" in a maximum security prison in rural Michigan.

Previously, Richard served a six-month sentence in federal prison and had experienced the violence that came with that confinement so he was not unfamiliar with the routine of prison life. But when he walked into state prison, he immediately found that "my life is in danger." Another prisoner sent word that "he wants me dead for killing his cousin." Knowing that this was a serious threat against his life, Richard needed to protect himself. Drawing upon his past gang affiliation, he aligned himself with a prison gang for protection. There were attempts on his life: "fights would break out, and they tried to stab me. My partners would stab them." But, then, a well-known drug dealer that Richard had known from the streets of Detroit arrived at the prison, and "a lot of people respected him. When he came through and found out I was there and having problems, he went straight to the source of the problem. He just let this guy know that I was his cousin. And if anything happened to me, he knew where his family was on the streets, and they would also be invited to the party." As a result of that threat, the attempts on Richard's life ceased.

Richard became heavily involved in the prison gang and its major activities, drugs and violence. As he said: "I'm seeing a lot of mayhem and violence everyday. I saw this guy get his eye knocked out with a mop over some crazy drug stuff. I saw stabbings. And I remember when I saw this guy get burnt alive right in his cell." As he went through the routine of prison life, Richard continued to be angry and defiant and refused "to take orders," particularly from the white prison guards. For a violation, he was placed in solidarity confinement where he "spent about six months in the hole." Isolated from other inmates and confined to his cell for long periods of time, Richard began to take stock of his life; he began to reflect on the things that had led him to being caged.

Shortly after Richard was released from "the hole one weekend I was called to the visiting room and my mother and brother were there." This was the first time in years that Richard had seen any family members. Richard described this visit:

> It was like a family reunion. I literally cried. I hadn't seen my mother in quite a while. I hadn't seen my little brother since he was probably two years old. I knew that my mother couldn't afford to come and visit me from New Jersey. The greatest gift that she gave me during that visit was she told me I would survive and what I needed to do to survive while being there. She told me how hard it was for her to survive when she was in prison with women trying to gnaw at her, and trying to get her involved into activities she just didn't believe in. She knew the same things were happening in men prisons, probably even more so. My mother is a very religious person, a Jehovah's Witness. And she directed

me to understand that despite anything else I'm a man, and I'm one of God's children, that I needed to find myself to begin to enjoy who I truly am. She told me that "I know that you blame me for a large part of your life. I understand a lot of the pain that you went through. I didn't see it all right then, some of the decisions that I made that affected your life." This was the biggest gift she gave me that first and last visit.

Richard heard his mother's words and took seriously what she said, but he "didn't know how to begin to process what she was saying." Following that visit, Richard committed himself to "finding out who I am." That commitment was a major turning point in his life. At that time he "didn't know what it was going to take" in order to turn his life around. His search for self began with questions: "I always believed that there was a God, but I wondered why he treated me so bad? What did I do to deserve this from you God, if I am truly one of your children? Or, is it the fact that it is me that is doing this stuff? And had you been trying to give me directions and some answers all along?" To find answers, Richard turned to religion. First, he began to talk with a Catholic priest, who visited the prison on a regular basis "about the God's word." Next, still seeking answers, he turned to his cellmate who "was studying divinity through a correspondence course at that time." Then Richard decided to take the correspondence course himself to try and find answers.

Studying the bible had a calming effect on Richard. He said: "I began to see that a lot of the stories in the bible were about me. I could find myself in the book of Proverbs so easily. That was kind of scary. I could really see all the wrongs that I had done, and why I did them, and why I continued to do them." Gradually, Richard was changing. "The first noticeable piece was that I could talk to God openly about how I felt. I didn't have a concern about what you or the next person thought, the only thing that mattered was what I was feeling about myself. I never felt like that before, it was always about what others thought about me." Not only was Richard changing how he thought about himself, but he was also changing his behavior: "I'm not defiant anymore while in prison."

As part of that change, Richard started to "work in the cannery making twelve cents and hour." But he also entered prison programs "that are going to help me when I get out of prison." He participated in the anger management and chemical dependency programs. In those self-help programs, Richard began a process of seeking to "forgive myself, for the pain and harm I have caused others." Richard also sought the forgiveness of others:

I'm writing to my mother and siblings asking for forgiveness, for the things I've done. I put my family in situations that could have jeopardized their lives because of the choices that I made and the things that I was doing. They forgave me, and in fact they have always forgiven me. I started writing to my wife. I'm doing more writing than she is. She's running out of words. She hasn't found forgiveness yet, and she can't believe I have made these changes in my life. There are still a lot of fears and a lot of trust issues.

But Richard's greatest struggle in that process of forgiveness was coming to terms with the fact that he had actually killed another person; he had taken a human life. He said "now reality is right before me, and I realize the damage that I have done":

It was hard for me to forgive myself. I can never change what I did. In fact I can't even go back to apologize. I asked myself the question, how do I get past this? When I committed murder, I didn't realize at that time that I was taking a father away from his children, a son from his parents, and a brother from a brother. I didn't realize that. I asked God for forgiveness. And the reality that came to me is that, if I truly made changes in my life, and if I don't repeat those things of the past, then I can forgive myself. That's how it began for me. Once I made it through that hurdle of forgiving myself for the murder it would become easier for me.

Yet amid the self-directed changes occurring in Richard's life, old feelings and old ways of doing things were ever-present, and he was constantly challenged by them. After being in prison for "almost nine years," in preparation for his release, Richard earned "a furlough home one weekend to spend some time with my wife and kids." When it was time to return to prison: "I allowed my old behavior to say man, you might as well bring some drugs back and make some money; you know you only make twelve-cents an hour" working in the prison cannery. In that moment of temptation, he decided to swallow twenty or thirty balloons of cocaine and heroin. And my buddy and I are going to make some money. I bring most of the balloons up, but one won't come up, and it bursts inside of me. I take a urine test and it comes back dirty. It's a violation. So I couldn't see the parole board for another two years. I have this damn attitude, and I slump again. I'm going through changes. I shake it off, and I come back to the religious piece again."

Richard sought solace in religion, and he explored with his cellmate the possibility of opening "some big church" after they were both released from prison. As they both continued to take correspondence courses in divinity in anticipation of obtaining a college degree, they spent long hours studying and interpreting bible scriptures together. Richard realized that they had different views and understanding about the word of God. During one particular discussion, when Richard and his cellmate were studying scriptures and envisioning the development of their church, Richard realized something new and important about himself:

> There were some scriptures where we talked about false prophets, and what would happen to them on the day the Lord came. We had been talking about speaking the word of God, and that we were going to get paid for doing it. I remember reading the scripture, going to bed that night, and not being able to go to sleep. I was thinking about all the things my mother had told me. And I was like, I can't do this. I woke my roommate up, and I said we can't do this. There is no way that we're going to open a church because we're going to suffer when God come. We are talking about getting paid for helping people, and this is no different from pimping and hustling. I just couldn't do it. I said, I've crossed a lot of people in my life but I was not going to cross God. I know that there is a God; there is not a doubt in my mind. I knew that I wasn't going to cross the line with God.

In his desire to be a better person, Richard realized "that day I found out that I did have a conscience. And it enabled me to say, I don't have to be a follower. I have choices in my life; I have options too. For the first time I could see clearly."

Finally, after eleven years of imprisonment, Richard was released. He returned to Detroit to try and start anew with his wife and step-children. He was no longer consumed with anger and embittered; not only was he older, but he also had a new and hopeful outlook on life. Richard had changed, and arriving in Detroit he found that his wife had changed as well. She now assumed authority over the household. But Richard "still wanted to be in control, and she wasn't having that in any form or fashion. If anything looks like control on my part I was confronted; she wasn't going to take any crap off of me." Tension developed in their relationship; that tension was exacerbated by the fact that Richard was on parole. Richard was feeling vulnerable by both his wife's behavior toward him and the need to comply with restrictions as part of his conditional release from prison. He described this period and especially the tension with his wife:

> She knew I was on parole. She knew my parole officer, and they had had private discussions. She was just waiting for me to fuck up. There was pressure on me. I had a certain amount of time to find a job. My wife probably could've helped me with some employment opportunities, but she didn't. I wasn't working. She had made up in her mind that this wasn't going to work. I knew that it wasn't going to work too. But I didn't have anywhere else to go at the time. I needed money. And I still have this money. But I didn't want anyone to know about it. I couldn't leave out

of the state or I would violate my parole. I don't have anybody that I could trust to go and get my money for me. An option was I could run and get my money, but I would probably get caught and be sent back to jail for six months. I didn't want to go back to jail.

Richard responded to this dilemma by doing nothing. Having the social stigma of a former prisoner, he became increasingly discouraged by his inability to find job and stopped looking. Instead, he sat around the house. One day, when his wife returned from work, she found Richard and a friend talking in the living room. Distrustful and tired of Richard's idleness, she provoked him by threatening his sense of manhood. What happened next was:

> She said, "You deal with men now? You're a faggot now?" I said, "What did you say?" I asked her because I didn't want to get violent with her. She wants to provoke me. She said, "You probably were screwing men while you were in jail, and probably before you went to jail." I said, "You know something you need to sit your old ass down." She said, "What did you say to me?" Then she picks up the phone and calls my parole officer. She tells him, "I'm feeling threatened by him." He comes with three police cars. They didn't ask any questions. They just snatched me up, handcuffed me, and threw me on the floor. He said, "Your ass is going to jail."

Although he went to jail, Richard did not return to prison. There was no proof that he had threatened his wife: "no bruises or witnesses to that effect." But he was not released from jail until he could find a new place to live. Richard called his uncle, and he agreed that Richard could live with him. Richard's parole was transferred to New Jersey. After he got off parole, he was still unable to find steady employment. Gradually Richard drifted back to what was familiar to him: "I started selling and using drugs again. With a partner I opened up a barber shop. There was gambling, parties, and we would have ladies dancing. We just hustled and made money that was the purpose behind the shop." One night as he sat in a neighborhood bar that he occasionally sold drugs out of, an older black "gentleman" who Richard did not know bluntly said to him:

> "You know something young man I've been watching you, and you deserve better than this." He said that I was a drug dealer destroying the neighborhood and that I was contributing to people losing their lives. I didn't see how he figured that I deserved better. I really didn't understand what he was saying or what he meant by saying that to me. I didn't threaten him. I just told him if he had been watching me, then he knows who I am, and he better be careful what he said to me. I just told him to go about his business, old man. But while I was driving home, I was trying to figure out what he meant by "I deserve better."

The old man's words haunted Richard and "that night I made some decisions about my life." As soon as he got home:

> I called my partner and told him I can't do this anymore. He said, "What are you talking about? Are you crazy? We're making all this money. We're living the life." I said, "I quit." I proceeded to flush the drugs that I had down the toilet. I realized also at that time that I was addicted to drugs again. I would smoke cocaine with marijuana, sniff heroin, and take about thirty shots of Hennessey in a day. I had a lot of vices and a lot of addictions at that time. The next day I went into drug treatment. I said I want to stop using drugs; I need help.

When he went into drug treatment, Richard was forty-one years old. He has been "clean and sober" now for almost fifteen years. He reflected on his life:

> I believe that in order for me to become the person that I am today, it's a cliché, but I had to experience all of those things. When I look back over my life, I always knew throughout my life that my purpose was somewhere else. I just couldn't find it. I couldn't see it, feel it, or smell it, but I always knew I had a purpose. Now, in my life what it means to be a man is to understand why life is so important. And I know that this is kind of broad, but it is important to understand why my life is important, not just for me but for those I love. I no longer have reasons to squander my life. My purpose here is to serve other people. For all those years, I thought my life was about me. I have become, I believe, one of the best people to serve others that I have known, and I've been a few places. I don't know anyone who is truly into serving mankind as much as I am. I live for it and I breathe for it. That is the gift that I believe the creator gave me. There's nothing like seeing the joy and happiness on someone's face because of your contribution. I don't need a pat on the back.

Today, Richard is a committed husband, father, and grandfather. He also works as a drug treatment counselor and educator. As in the past, he continues to actively participate in the shaping of his life experience. But different from the past, violence is no longer a meaningful part of Richard's experience. Violence is no longer a critical part of what it means for him to be a man or of how he sees himself as a man, even as he continues to interact within and against the racial and gender constraints that shape his life. Richard has rearticulated the meaning of black manhood for himself, by embracing an understanding that deliberately shuns the need to exert power, exercise control, and eschew dominance over others. That rearticulation has not only enabled Richard to transform his self-hatred but to also see others as himself. This, in turn, has given him the ability to love himself as well as "the ability to love other people regardless of who they are."

Twenty-one-year old Matt has not come to this place in his life; he has not developed the ability to see others as himself. When he walked into a Baltimore police precinct with his mother, uncle, and attorney at his side, Matt was arrested for murder. Surrendering to authorities, Matt was "thinking that I'm not guilty of murder," and he walked through the front doors of the police station with "an arrogance and cockiness" that suggested that he was "going to beat this rap." After Matt was processed, after he was fingerprinted and his mug shot taken, he was placed in "the bullpen" to await arraignment, to be legally charged with murder. He spent the night in the bullpen, the holding cell, where he said:

> You have to picture this place. It's dirty, it's nasty, and it stinks. People have been pissing on the floor. People come in there with all types of diseases. They have cysts from shooting dope. It's real nasty. It's real depressing; it's loud; it's difficult to really go to sleep because its twenty-four hours of noise, lights, slamming cell doors, people coming in all throughout the night being put into this place. What you got are people sitting up talking about who they are and what they did; doing a lot of fronting and a lot of lying. You can tell who is seasoned because they are quiet; they're minding their own business. They're the people that can be a threat. Immediately, I knew it was the survival of the fittest.

The next morning, with his attorney present, Matt was arraigned. He was officially charged with "first degree murder, felony murder, and all this stuff. It was about twenty charges altogether." Based on those charges, Matt was denied bail and reprimanded to the county jail to await trial. As he was hand-cuffed and chained to other prisoners to be transported to jail, Matt said: "It was stressful. Everybody is scared. You can see it in their eyes. It's so thick you can cut it with a knife. You don't know what's getting ready to happen." When he arrived at the county jail, he said:

> I was body searched, then they give you clothing, jailhouse clothes because they take everything you have away. They give you a plastic bucket with a top. It has a roll of toilet paper, towel, some soap, tooth-paste, toothbrush, a bible, and a sheet for your mattress. And then they give you a mattress. They take you upstairs. When you get there, now everybody starts looking alike. Your individual identity is taken from you; your dress, your style, your flavor is taken away. Now you are just a bunch of cats in orange suits. It's a whole new different set of rules that you have to play by. At that moment when you're all sitting around in those oranges suits, you're stripped of your identity, and this is when the predators and the victims come to the surface.

Challenging his own sense of humanity, in this "very barbaric environment,"
Matt was determined that he would not become a victim. Within the jailhouse environment where all prisoners wore bright orange uniforms that
masked their individuality, Matt had an identity viewed as somewhat different by other inmates; he was not there because he was a sexual pervert, a petty
thief, or drug dealer, but because "I got a murder case, and that gives me status in the joint." In this all-male environment, he was extremely conscious of
how he presented himself to the other inmates. He said, "I don't want to
show fear, to be afraid. So, I'm relying on the fact that I'm here for murder.
The gangster in me comes to surface because I have to be a predator to survive. I know they're looking, but there is something in my eyes that tells
them don't fuck with me."

Initially, Matt was placed in a dormitory with other inmates on cell
block B. He described this particular cell block:

> When you walk through the door there were about forty-five people in
> this area. You have four or five picnic tables, steel picnic tables that are
> welded to the concrete floor. You have a TV in the back, so people are
> looking at the television. Then you go to the right and you have a bunch
> of double bunks. When you walk through the door you have two open
> showers. There's this catwalk that goes all around the cell block so the
> guards could walk between the wall and the bars to observe you, or
> throw tear gas or whatever they want to do. You go in and you see guys
> who have been in there for six, twelve months. The people in here are
> from eighteen to thirty years old. Street hustlers, robbers, petty thieves,
> dope dealers, sex offenders, parole violators, you name it. They're pred-
> ators and victims. A lot of these people know each other because they
> have been in and out of the system.

Matt also knew someone; his codefendant Jeff was also in the county jail. He
told Matt that "Alfred had been arrested, he agreed to testify for the state, and
he has identified Jeff and me." But that was the last conversation Matt had
with Jeff. Shortly, thereafter, Matt heard a guard say, "Get your bed, bucket
of shit and get to the door." Matt was being transferred to another cell block
that had only individual cells; this section was reserved for those charged with
murder. Placed in a single cell, Matt found "a little table welded to the wall,
a little sink with only cold water, and a little toilet. It was concrete with bars,
sliding doors, everything is just steel and concrete." For seventeen months,
"this little cell is home." And Matt settled into the daily routine of jailhouse
life. He said:

> You get up about five o'clock in the morning because you will hear the
> hole. The door on the hole in the wall where food comes in will sound

real loud. And somebody would holler food in the hole. Breakfast varied. Generally you would get powdered eggs. One day you might get powdered eggs, a couple pieces of bread, and some oatmeal. You would get gravy a couple days out of the week. A lot of people liked county jail gravy and it might have sausage in it. You might get some juice, watered down, but you would drink it because you needed the vitamin C. Guys would give people three or four cigarettes for their breakfast tray. You had about an hour to eat. Then after that they started the court call, which meant anyone who is on the court docket for that day, you head out. People would generally go back to sleep until lunch, which was around eleven. After lunch people start to move around. They are looking at television; people start doing their exercises; people start gambling; people are talking; they are doing whatever. You get visits a couple of times during the week. They hit the horn for dinner. And after dinner you watch television, play cards, or whatever.

One routine that Matt was ever-mindful of was taking a shower because it posed potential risk to his personal safety. There was no privacy. "The shower was in this area that was about three times the size of a cell. It was also where they would lock people up when they didn't have enough space. When there was an overflow, they would put you in there, and people would sleep on the floor. So you want to take a shower, and people are sitting here looking at TV, and you're over there taking a shower." In the beginning it was "awkward" for Matt to take a shower because he did not know what to expect. He assumed a "don't fuck with me posture," a manly posture, as a way of sending a message to other inmates. Naked, what Matt did was simply:

> Grabbed a towel, throw it over my shoulder, go in the water, come out, dry off, and go about my business. That's how I demonstrated my manhood, plus I was fit. I would fight butt naked where I'm at. But you notice men are looking at you; men are lusting at you. I remember times coming out of the shower and I'm drying off, and I turn around and you have people with this crazy look on their face, like I'm a piece of meat. Those were the realities of the situation.

More than being sexually assaulted while in the shower, Matt's greatest fear while in jail was not "what someone might do to me. I was more afraid of what someone might make me do to them. I knew that the time was going to come when people would begin to try me. I'm trying to navigate the waters here because I don't want to go to lock-up. And I don't want to mess up my record because I'm trying to go home. So how do I deal with this?" Matt wanted desperately to go home so initially he "mainly stayed inside his cell." In his little cell Matt mostly "read anything that I could get my hands on" and slept for long periods. But he needed drugs to help him sleep, and there were plenty of drugs circulating in jail: inmates would sell their prescription medication, and drugs were brought in "by the trustees, family members who visited." Depressed, Matt easily obtained drugs that allowed him to sleep for long periods.

But, gradually, Matt began to interact with other inmates. He learned how to play poker. In so doing, "eventually I started running the poker game, which means if you got the game, you're the power on the block, because you have the money." Controlling the poker game as the "house," Matt collected 10 percent of each hand played. As a result, there came a point when Matt also controlled the commissary—potato chips, Twinkies, Hostess Cupcakes, Tang, cigarettes, and the like—which was not only important currency in jail but also used for placing bets in the poker game. "Now that I have all this commissary, I start to run the store. I have all of this excess stuff and you have to sell it to get real money," he said. Again Matt is a player in a game of his own choosing: controlling the poker game on his cell block was a hustle, but it was not the only hustle he participated in while in jail. Matt started writing letters for other prisoners. He said: "I was surprised at the number of people that just couldn't write: so I would write letters to judges, letters to their attorneys, and letters to their girlfriends." As Matt made money for each letter that he wrote and each item he sold from his store, he began to understand that "it's the smart man who rules and not the physically strong." This understanding proved to be important resource for him during his imprisonment.

As his trial date approached Matt was also beginning to realize that his attorney's preparation for his murder defense was not going as smoothly as he had anticipated. In fact, given the state's evidence against him, Matt's attorney was encouraging him to enter a guilty plea: "He's telling me to plead guilty. I don't want to plead guilty. I want to go to trial, and it's getting very stressful," Matt said. In preparation for the trial, Matt's uncle bought him a suit: "a black suit and tie, with a white shirt." But in contrast to Matt's presentation, on the first day of trial, his attorney's "comes in there dressed in a lime green suit. His hair is down to his shoulders and whipped up like Super Fly. He's very flamboyant. He's challenging the dress code of the courtroom. All he had to do was put a hat on and step into a nightclub later on. He's a hustler and a player on the streets, and he's my attorney!"

At trial, Matt's defense was that he "wasn't involved in the robbery and murder at all," that he was not guilty of any crimes. To mask his feelings about what was going on during the hearing Matt kept busy at the defense table by taking copious notes on the proceedings. For Matt the proceeding had a "surreal" quality, and to make sense of what was going on, again he used a game metaphor to explain what was happening: "it's just another game that's bound by rules." Matt realized that he was both a central and a subordinate player in this legal game. He described some of the highlights of the two-week trial:

> We went through the whole process, people being called as witnesses and a lot of forensic evidence. They call Alfred to the stand, and he says that he was there and that I was there. But he didn't know who pulled the trigger. He couldn't say if it was me or if it was Jeff. He didn't admit that he had done any of the stabbing, of course. The autopsy report said it didn't know if the cause of death was from the stab wounds around the heart or the gunshot wounds. They had gruesome pictures of the person that was killed—stab wounds and bullet holes.

Amidst the testimony of witnesses and forensic evidence, Matt believed that the proof against him was weak. He began to think that "just maybe I'm not going to be found not guilty of murder." However, as he noticed the faces of the victim's family, Matt "could see the hurt in the women's faces and the hurt in my mother's face. I'm sitting there and we're exchanging glances; I would turn, and the families would look back at me." Their faces said something quite different, and he began to weaken under the possibility that he just might be found guilty and convicted of murder.

The time came for Matt to take the witness stand in his own defense, but once more he said, "It's just a game." Matt was on the witness stand "for about ten minutes." During that time his attorney simply asked him if he had committed the murder, and the "prosecutor really didn't ask me much." Following his testimony, the prosecutor and defense offered closing arguments and then rested their cases. As the jury deliberated, Matt was not hopeful. He saw the trial as a losing game where the rules were rigged against him:

> The law and criminal procedure is a farce. When I say a farce I'm saying the conclusions are preordained by the very process. Depending on where you are in the pecking order you're going to come out on top or on the bottom. So much is preordained before you even step into the court room. Being a black man in Baltimore in 1977, accused of killing a white guy and another white guy getting hurt, it's the realization of who I was and where I was slowing creeping up on me in that courtroom. When the jury was deliberating I sat there and I wrote a letter to my mother and said I was getting ready to be found guilty. I was trying to prepare her to deal with what was about to happen. I was trying to comfort myself to help myself deal with it. Then someone said the jury is in.

Before the jurors appeared, Matt gave the letter to his attorney and prepared himself to hear the verdict:

> Count one, guilty of felony murder. Count two, guilty of murder in the first degree. And so on. I hear my mother crying. I go through this daze where I hear and I don't hear, where I see and I don't see. I'm sick in my stomach. I'm nervous. I have control of myself, but I don't have control of my feelings. I'm sick. I'm stressed. They take me back to the cell block. Everybody asks what's up? I said I'm guilty. I go to my bunk and lay down, and I go to sleep. I probably stay in bed for the next couple of days. At a certain point I came out of that. I got a visit from my attorney, and he said "we're appealing," and all that stuff. I'm adjusting to fact that I'm going to prison. So I'm in a different mindset now. I'm starting to transition myself out of the county jail, and this is like a couple of weeks. I go back to court for sentencing. They sentence me to two terms of life, and at that time it meant without parole. The judge didn't say life with the possibility of parole. So in the state of Maryland that meant life with-out parole and the only thing you can do is get clemency. So I get sen-tenced to two terms of life in prison, at twenty-one years old.

Sentenced to life, Matt remained in jail for about a month before he was transferred to a state prison in rural Maryland. With his conviction, Matt knew that he was now "a member of a unique club, men sentenced to terms of life in prison." While still in jail, he began to anticipate what was going to happen to him when he went to prison and tried to prepare himself for that life:

> I'm getting all the green money I can. So I'm starting to stash. They had given us toothpaste and I had opened up the toothpaste and I had taken money and rolled it up real small and wrapped it up in plastic and stuck the money inside the toothpaste tube. I already had a couple of hundred dollars coming in, so now I'm just getting all the money I can and all the cigarettes I can. I wanted cash, if I had money I could get things done. It is important to remember that most of the men in the county jail know each other. There were guys giving me this information. There were guys telling me who to look out for and who to hook up with. I was get-ting ready. I was making weapons, toothbrushes with razors. Pencils, I kept pencils that were very, very sharp. Getting ready meant having money, getting armed, and just getting ready mentally to do this thing.

Matt did not know exactly when he was going to be transferred to state prison so he could do nothing more than wait. Then "one day it happens. I get up, I get my shit, and I'm ready to go. I'm shackled, both at the feet and at the wrist. And it's a little bitty box that looks like a cassette tape and it goes over the handcuffs. I'm shackled at the wrist, handcuffed, and shackled at the feet, and they put me in a van with several other people, and we start this three and a half hour ride from Baltimore to the state prison. It's a solemn time."

Upon arriving at prison, Matt was immediately introduced and became a part of a select group of prisoners, the Lifer's Organization. He said "the Lifer's became like a surrogate family to me":

> I had big brothers, little brothers, all of that. We played poker together. They were like mentors for me. That's where my boots were put on. I was raised by guys that had seven and eight life sentences. The head of the Ku Klux Klan, Big Mack, raised me. When I got to the Lifer's Organization I began typing. I've been in the Lifer's Organization for three or four months, and I began helping people with their cases. I have a different type of power now. This source of power is real. I have the ability to help you get out of prison. The Lifer's Organization put together this paralegal training program. You could get a certificate for that, and I went through that. I became a legal clerk. I'm being exposed to the law. I'm going into the law library. I'm writing up basic petitions for time reduction or whatever it is. The whole time I'm still kind of in a daze, but I recognize myself. I understand that I'm in control of certain things. I have a certain amount of agency in that I can choose to do or not to do things.

While working in the Lifer's office, Matt chose to "sell weed. That gave me status; that gave me power. But it was false status and power, and I gave away a lot more than I sold." Matt also chose to enroll in a vocational training program where "the professors would come from outside and you could get a technical certificate in things like electronic, auto mechanics, and auto body. I got into electronics. I got into it because I could get money. I found out that I could get a check from the VA (Veteran Administration) if I went to school from being in the service. It was a lot of money in prison, and I could buy this stuff. A lot of money meant there were a lot of drugs flowing." All of Matt's prison activities kept him on the move and quite busy. This was important because it allowed him to conceal his feelings, even from himself:

> I still don't want to believe I'm in prison with a life sentence. I'm always thinking I'm going to get out. I did what I had to do. What I did is I shut off certain emotions. Those emotions that could hurt became dormant because I didn't allow them to live. If it was an emotion that might make me sad, might make you cry, you destroy them. I shut myself off to those emotions. Things that are important to people in society—their daily, monthly, yearly rituals—were removed from the rituals in prison. So those rituals lose their meaning; they lose the effect. A lot of the emotional involvements in those rituals were gone. You don't respond the

way they expect you to respond on birthdays, anniversary, mother's day . . . you're not around the family on thanksgiving and Christmas. You're not a part of that ritual. You're removed from it. You stop identifying with it. It helps to keep the stress off of me.

In addition to the Lifer's Organization, Matt gradually became involved with members of the Gangster Disciples, with Folks in prison. In the early 1980s, he noticed that the "gang presence was increasing" in prison: "All of a sudden you hear that the Aryan Brotherhood is in the joint. There were always the Ku Klux Klan and motorcycle gangs, white guys with bandanas, Hell's Angels types. Now gangs are beginning to fight." So Matt decided to hang out with Folks as he watched their prison membership gradually increase. He had "currency" or status among the gang members. Matt's prison currency was derived from the fact that he was active in the Lifer's Organization, a legal clerk, selling weed, and going to school. But, important, Matt had money. He said, "I was getting like three hundred dollars a month in prison, and that's a lot of money. I had money which meant I had power. And people were beginning to see me as the leader of the Gangster Disciples." As the leader, Matt was drawn into the violence between the different gangs:

> Prison is becoming much more violent on many levels. The Gangster Disciples were the ones that were always into some dumb shit because the members were younger. Being empowered as Folks, they would just walk up and smack somebody, or walk up and take something, or just walk up and intimidate somebody. Then everybody else would have these attitudes toward Folks because of the behavior of one or two people. That caused a lot of problems. There were a lot of times where I had to wear body armor. The way you make body armor was you would keep national geographic or any thick magazine like Life or Ebony. What you do is you put on a t-shirt, and you take those magazines and wrap them around your body. Then you put another t-shirt on and you have body armor.

Even though Matt did not shy away from violence, as the leader, he tried to be a peacemaker, especially between the Gangster Disciples and the Black Disciples, who on the streets were at war with one another; that conflict had spilled over into prison. Matt was particularly interested in protecting some of the younger Folks from sexual predators, even from some of his own Gangster Disciples. In this all-male environment, manhood was highly determined by how an inmate was positioned in the prison hierarchy and this, in turn, determined the degree of physical, personal, and social respect an inmate received. Within that hierarchy younger prisoners were especially vulnerable, but they were not the only ones who were open to attack. Matt discussed the social pecking order among inmates:

Respect or the lack of respect is linked to the roles guys played. For example, the guy who gets a lot of visits from women is a player. So he's respected. It doesn't matter what these women look like. He's a player and he's respected. Respect comes in different ways: if he's a gang member; if he's intellectual and has the ability to sit down and write something up; and, if you're a great basketball player. If you're a bitch, whore, or slut these are degraded men. They are disrespected. Within that disrespect you have commissary: punks, fags, you have the gay person, and you have the queen. The queen is the person who is probably the transvestite on the streets. Sometimes they come in and they still have the effects of the hormones and they're treated like a real woman. Then you have the commissary punks who are just engaging in homosexual behavior because they want to get cigarettes. He's not gay, he didn't come in gay, but he's allowing these men to have sex with him, sodomize him for cookies. And then you have that person that has a real messed up nasty crime that involves children and women. You do that to a child, you that to a woman, it's not a lack of respect; it's a huge amount of disrespect. You might get knocked down and wake-up and somebody is urinating on you.

The prison administration started to take note of Matt's leadership skills, as he tried to negotiate between the different gangs and protect younger gang members from sexual assault. As he said, "the administration knows what's going on in prison. And they knew, no matter what else I was doing, I could keep the peace." The administration gave Matt a job as a clerk: "you ordered supplies, which meant I always had office supplies because I had a desk, typewriter, and I had access to the phone so I could call around. I could call the hospital and check on someone's pass. I could call and see if someone's visitor had arrived. I had access to legitimate resources as well as the illegitimate market. It also allowed me to stash stuff because I was a clerk and if the guards shook me down they didn't mess with me. If you were strong you could run things. If you weren't strong, then somebody else ran things through you." Matt was good at his job and was transferred to the position of Grievance Committee clerk: "I processed grievances when it was filed by prisoners, set-up the initial hearing where the person would come and state their case, and typed up the findings. That was basically what it was."

In that position, Matt aggressively pursued two interests: he started to take a more involved role in working on his own legal case, and he enrolled in an academic program with a local college that held classes on site at the prison. During the appeal process, Matt's "attorney was disbarred for life by the state Supreme Court a couple of days after my direct appeal was denied." But working with another lawyer on appeal, the State Supreme Court "took one life sentence off of me. So I now only have one." And as his lawyer filed another appeal "claiming ineffective assistance of counsel, there wasn't a lot for me to do" so Matt "started taking classes at the University."

In addition to college classes, Matt was also "doing all of this other stuff," namely, "I had people bring me drugs":

> I had these cops hooked up. I had this one cop, Martinez, specifically moving shit. They knew that I didn't do anything but smoke weed. They also knew I was credible. I had a thousand dollars just for giving access. That's the kind of money I was making in the joint. I was the man with the drugs. I'm still working with the Lifer's Organization. We smoked weed and worked on legal stuff to help get people out of prison. One day I go back to the cell house, and it's quiet as hell. I'm like what's up? Willie the president of the Lifer's Organization had escaped. He had been sentenced to seven life sentences. What happened was this white sergeant and Martinez were escorting him to a hospital. The sergeant goes into a restaurant and when he comes out Willie is sitting there and he has a gun on Martinez. The state police told Martinez that they knew he had something to do with this because somehow a gun got into the car. They didn't feel that the white guy, part of the family, had anything to do with it. The only way they could see that he got a gun was for Martinez to give it to him. They told him he could resign if he told them everything that he was doing. So he told them everything, and he gave me up.

What happened next was fateful in Matt's efforts to transform his life. Martinez told the prison administration that he had assisted Matt in the prison drug trade:

> I go to lockup and charged with trafficking. I stayed in lockup for ninety days. The second day I was in lockup, I was sitting on the bed. This is a small eleven by six cell. I could sit on my bed and put my feet on the wall. Unconsciously I jumped up. I ran to the cell doors and shake the bars. When I shook the bars, it was like I shook myself. What is this? I have to get control of myself. It was an unconscious action, me responding to being in a cage. It's important for you to understand that prior to me going to lockup I was one of the people that who was out of my cell the most because of my jobs. Now I'm on lockup. I was in my cell on average of twenty-three hours a day. I would take a shower then go back to my cell. On lockup, you get whatever you get. You are denied access to commissary as a part of punishment. At the time I was doing a criminal law course through correspondence. So during those ninety days that I was on lockup I finished the course. That was an experience being on lockup like that. It gave me the lockup perspective. It's worse than jail.

Lockup had a profound impact on how Matt saw himself, and he intentionally changed his behavior: "I began to act differently. I told the other guard that was bringing me dope, motherfucker you can't bring me dope because if you get busted, you're going to tell on me, and I ain't going back to lockup." Also, after Willie escaped from prison, Matt became vice president of the Lifer's Organization. The president of the organization, Matt said, "wasn't sharp enough to get out of a situation without causing problems. So I took charge. I became the enforcer more or less. I made him do things. I called the shots." And one of the shots that he called was convincing other inmates to keep the peace, especially among themselves: "I used to bring the leadership of the brotherhood, Vice Lords, Kings, Ku Klux Klan, and black militant groups into the Lifer's Organization office and shut the door. "A lot of it was rooted around the fact that the different groups were all competing for the same source of money, which means dope money. I'm convincing them we need to keep the peace; they needed to control their own people because it wasn't good for business."

The prison administration was watching closely what Matt was saying and doing with his leadership and influence in the Lifer's Organization. And in "the best interest of the institution," he was transferred to another prison. After ten years of prison, Matt now found himself in "B cell house which was the doghouse at the state reformatory." It was the most violent environment that Matt had encountered since his incarceration. He said, "Life there was different; the racism that was there was huge; and, prisoners being killed and prisoners killing guards." Matt recalled inmates' riots: "White guards beat up black prisoners on lock up and those black prisoners' cousins, brothers, or Folks heard about it. And they just took the guards and beat them up. What people were doing to guards, taping them to chairs, pushing them up and down the cell blocks, and pissing and shitting on them. I went into that environment." In the violence of that environment, Matt took advantage of the limited opportunities available and immediately enrolled in a college extension program where he actively pursued a college degree. Because of his behavior, Matt was moved to the "honors dorm." But given his gang affiliation with Folk Nation and statute as a leader in the Lifer's Organization, Matt continued to be an integral part of the prison culture, even at the state reformatory. Using his influence, he attempted to lessen the violence by "using my head," by organizing activities especially for members of Folks. "I put together baseball teams, basketball teams, coached, and played." But, at the time, prisoners around the country were increasingly frustrated over the more restricted conditions that were placed on their confinement, restrictions imposed under the Reagan administration of the 1980s.

During protest at a "super maximum facility" in Maryland, Matt said "one guy cut his finger off and sent it to Amnesty International to complain

about the conditions in the facility." Word spread among the prison population about that inmate's action "so we decided to do our thing at the reformatory. What we did was everybody got to rec (recreation) and we just
walked the wall. With walking the wall people are hollering, screaming, and
clapping because they don't expect us to do it because we are the honor
dorm. We scared the administration because it was white, black, Muslim,
Christian, gay, straight, you name it; everybody was there," Matt said. As a
result of the inmates' protest, the entire reformatory was placed on lockdown.
"They put us in our cells and didn't let us out. It was recorded as one of the
longest lockdowns in the history of U.S. prisons": "We were on lockdown
for nine months. No visits. The media was not allowed in. It was considered
a major issue. We were considered by the Maryland State Department of
Corrections as problem people." After lockdown, again Matt was transferred
to another facility, but this time to a less violent and less restricted prison,
the Institutional Correctional Complex (ICC). At this transitional facility,
inmates were required to work as a way of developing useful skills and/or
participate in educational programs that prepared them for leaving prison.
When Matt arrived he "already had my bachelor degree, so I started coaching
the debate team there and I'm working in the law library." Even though day-
to-day life was a bit easier for Matt at ICC, he still hated the fact that he was
in prison and "didn't do stupid shit" because "I always knew I was going
home." But in that knowledge, Matt also knew that he had a life sentence
hanging over his head, and his appeal had been rejected by the court. He had
hired another attorney, but meantime Matt met a young white female attorney at ICC, and Melody decided "she wants to help even though this other
attorney has the money."

Rather than continue to rely on a formal appeal process in the courts,
Melody decided to employ a new strategy—one that asked the prosecutor in
the initial case to support Matt's petition for release based on his years of good
works and accomplishments in prison. At the time, Matt was helping to set up
a workshop aimed at younger inmates, and "all these people who said they
were going to come in and help did." The workshop was a major success for
the institution, and "all of a sudden I get some evidence to suggest that I was
not the person responsible for the death of the person who died in the case.
Whether that's true or not that's what the evidence suggests." With all of this
in hand, Melody went to the prosecutor seeking support for Matt's release
from prison. On reflection, Matt believed that the reason for Melody's success in getting him released from prison was not because the people involved
"cared a damn" about him, but they cared about her. Matt said:

> They didn't want to say No to her. Melody is a pretty white girl. She's
> petite, blonde, blue-eyed, and she is what I called a white man's dream.

A lot of white guys like smaller women. Her father was one of the heads of the Ku Klux Klan. She grew up with money; a privileged white girl. She used her sexuality. She went into the prosecutor's office and crossed her legs. The only thing he could see was her knees, and that's all it took. And she talked to the victim's family, his wife and his sons. Melody worked to get me out of the joint.

The prosecutor agreed to support Matt's petition to the court for immediate release, but after his upcoming election. The prosecutor lost that election. But "the incoming prosecutor agreed that I should be released." With that support and the support of the victim's family, the court agreed to release Matt. After "seventeen years, ten months, and ten days" Matt walked out of prison. Shortly thereafter, he walked into a college classroom determined to continue his pursuit of education. Eventually, Matt obtained a doctoral degree, and he is now a college professor. He reflected on the role of and the importance of education in his process of transformation while in prison:

> The type of education that I'm talking about doesn't produce marketable skills. Education was important because it allowed me to keep my mind sharp. It kept my mind alive. I was challenging myself. I read; I wrote. I read the newspaper to stay current about what was going on in world. Education was important because it gave me the skills necessary to write: to be able to take a pen and put words on paper. That's what kept me sharp. I have articles that I wrote while I was in prison. Education provided me a vehicle through which I could express myself. Expressing myself provided me a means where I could feel a sense of control. It provided a means by which I could continue to grow. Education gave me a sense of structure; I lived my life on a semester basis around the academic year. Education provided me a vehicle to excel. I saw my growth. It made me feel worthwhile. Education made the possible, possible.

CONCLUSION

The ways Jamie, Richard, and Matt portrayed their sense of masculinity as young black men became inexplicably linked to violence. That violence led to destructive ends, which resulted in each taking an irreplaceable human life; each man spent a considerable period of their adult lives caged for their actions. As they went about defining for themselves what it means to be young black men that definition gradually began to take on the functional embodiment of the criminal-black-male image—an image that imposed a particular cultural and social reality on their lives. Their decisions and actions were made both within and against the boundaries of that reality. In their own ways, each knew what was socially and culturally expected of them.

In their attempts to adhere to those expectations Richard and Matt went to the Army, and Jamie and Matt enrolled in college, but for different reasons those attempts at conformity were all unsuccessful. And, if not in the military or in school, they were expected to be gainfully employed in some kind of legitimate work. Following their own paths, each stepped further and further outside of the boundaries of that particular expectation and embraced criminal activities as a way of life.

Jamie, Richard, and Matt actively participated in the making of their experiences. Engaging the world of men they faced the tensions, dilemmas, contradictions of their lives: they were simultaneously positioned as victimizer and victim, exploiter and exploited, as well as that of predator and prey. As young black men, they sought the privileges of masculinity: power, control, and dominance over not only their own lives but also the lives of others. Those privileges, however, were pursued from a social and cultural marginal position, from a position of criminality, to which violence was a critical resource. Their exceedingly destructive and painful narratives are only individual consequences of what happens when the real becomes inseparable from the criminal-black-male image; at the intersection on the real and the criminal severe punishment is levied and containment is socially imposed.

As convicted criminals, Jamie, Richard, and Matt entered the maximum security world of imprisonment. That world challenged not only their sense of manhood but also, and more important, their sense of humanity as well. Prison is a seemingly abnormal world unto itself: men are corralled and warehoused; they are denied basic privacy; uniforms strip them of their individual identity; they are placed under close surveillance; movements are regimented and restricted; distinction between consent and coercion are blurred; conformity is demanded; and violence is expected. Arguably, these undeniable oppressive qualities are a tremendous price to pay for challenging the norms of hegemonic masculinity. In the absence of conformity to the working and structures of hegemonic masculinity, rigid controls are imposed on deviant behavior. That said, ironically, within and against those controls, inmates themselves reproduce a way of being inside of prison walls that affirm cultural patterns and social practices of hegemonic masculinity norms, even during their debasement and banishment from society,

Prison masculinity is predicated on power, control, and dominance, prevalent within the all-male prison subculture of inmates. A hierarchy is evidenced in the performance of prison masculinity, and violence plays a critical role. "*Men* occupy the dominant position in a social hierarchy of masculinities maintained through the subjugation of the feminine. *Men* have the greatest authority and power among male prisoners. In essence, *men* rule the joint. They establish values and norms for the entire prison population. They are political leaders, gang members, or organizers of the market economies within prisons, including the drug trade, sex trade, protection rackets, and contraband smuggling" (Miller, 2006, p. 158). When Jamie, Richard, and Matt entered prison as convicted murders, they occupied the status of *men*, which in itself garnered a degree of privilege.

Yet, even as they actively participated in the routine of prison culture each, in his own way, gradually began to understand the oppressive nature of that culture and his complicity in the system. In their maturity, they actively sought to carve out a space that allowed self-reflection upon the harm they caused to both themselves and others. In prison they had time and opportunity to reflect on their lives. Matt articulated the importance of that self-reflective process and its meaning to his life:

> In prison you may have the time and opportunity, but then it takes the courage to actually look at yourself in all the ugliness, and all the pain that comes with that ugliness; the pain you created for other people, and your own pain. To look at that pain with the realization that I wasn't a good son, a good father, I wasn't a good community member, and that I was just something other than. To have the courage to acknowledge that pain and look at that pain straight in the face and say okay this is what it was, but this is what I'm going to do. That was me: I reflected, I acknowledged, I took the bull by the horn and made things happen. Today I can say to you there's not much that I ask for. And I'm not asking not to be a black man; that I wake-up in the morning and be a white man, and have the privilege position assigned to white men, and everything would be perfect. I'm a black man and I like being a black man. But it brings with it the possibility that I could die tomorrow at the hands of the police.

Self-reflection aided by education and the courage to take a step toward change allowed Jamie, Richard, and Matt to forgive and find the humanity within themselves. The process of forgiving themselves for the human destruction they caused enabled them to renegotiate what it means to be a man. In their current lives, they have stepped beyond the controlling image of the criminal-black-male, even though they continue to face the scarring stigma of having committed murder and served time for their crimes. Each has adopted a manhood stance against oppressive power, control, and dominance, as they now pursue paths that prioritize not only their own but also the human potential of others, amidst circumstances limiting that possibility. The significance of education has become all important for Jamie, Richard, and Matt in that pursuit. In fact, education has also become instrumental in the transformation of the lives of the other men.

CHAPTER 5

Manhood Rearticulated

DURING THE 1960s, as governor Ronald Reagan vowed to end student protests erupting on college campuses throughout the University of California system. Following his order to "clean up the mess at Berkeley," the National Guard with bayonets drawn occupied the campus for seventeen days. Reagan's hard lined approach drew national attention that not only helped to positioned him as a future presidential candidate, but also set the tone and tenor of his administration. As President, in the 1980s, Ronald Reagan played a critical role in shifting the political landscape to the conservative right, which resulted in a restructuring of both international and domestic relations.

On foreign policy, Reagan rejected Jimmy Carter's proactive stance on human rights to the seemingly neglect of the Cold War. Carter was viewed as soft on communism, and from a conservative perspective his human rights policies compromised America's bold and tough international identity. Reagan sought to restore America's statute as the preeminent political, economic, and military power in the world. His administration readily embraced the Cold War tensions and adopted a "zero option" foreign policy toward the Soviet Union. Asserting a hard lined approach, even in the midst of a severe economic recession with high unemployment, his administration increased the Department of Defense budget and launched a nuclear arms buildup program in order to mount a strategic offensive against what Reagan considered to be the main "evil in the modern world," the worldwide spread of communism. Under his administration, again the Cold War framed the United States' approach to international affairs.

Reagan was intent on using America's resources to halt communist excursion in the world. Under what was called the "Reagan doctrine," the United States provided aide to Afghanistan in the war against the Soviet Union invasion into that country. In South and Central America, the United States actively undermined the Cuban backed Sandinista government of Nicaragua and armed Marxist-Leninist insurgents in Chile, El Salvador and other neighboring countries. And to stop the spread of communism in the Caribbean, in 1983 the United States invaded the tiny island nation of Grenada.

In addition to perceived communist threats penetrating the Western Hemisphere, the Reagan administration took note of a more radical form of Islamic fundamentalism appearing on the world stage. Targeting Western intrusion into Middle Eastern affairs, fundamentalist groups used terror as a potent weapon to articulate their interests and demands. Israel invaded Lebanon. In 1983, 241 marines stationed in Beirut, Lebanon as part of a peace-keeping mission between the two countries were killed by a suicide truck bomber. Iran and Iraq were at war. TWA flight 153 was hijacked by terrorists, and 39 Americans were taken hostage. Publicly vowing to never give in to terrorists' demands, secretly the Reagan administration through Israeli representatives sold arms to Iran in an attempt to free the hostages held by Iranian backed terrorists. Nonetheless, in accordance with his "zero option" stance toward communism, Reagan adopted another important foreign policy, the National Security Decision Directive 138, designed to aggressively response to what was deeded as state sponsored terrorism.

On domestic policy, Ronald Reagan continued his hard lined approach. Mounting an aggressive assault against the liberal welfare state while attempting to reinvigorate a stagnate economy; the administration's economic policies emphasized unrestrained market competition, which thereby limited government oversight and enforcement. Widely known as supply-side economic or Reaganomics, his polices called for lower federal taxes, increased savings, greater investments, and stronger work incentives. To induce a favorable business climate, to put America back on the road to prosperity, the burden of Reagan's economic recovery policies was placed on the backs of the poor. Although his economic policies were not race-specific that burden, however was disproportionately borne by poor African Americans.

Determined to dismantle the liberal social welfare state, the Reagan administration quickly moved to end or reduce social programs specifically aimed at the poor and slashed the budgets of Medicaid, Medicare, and Food Stamps; terminated the Comprehensive Employment and Training Act (CETA); and placed stringent eligibility requirements on Aid to Family with Dependent Children (AFDC). Draconian budgets cuts and modifications were accompanied by conservative ideas that blamed the poor for their poverty. Supporting the drastic cutbacks, conservatives argued forcefully that the poor existed in a "culture of poverty:" that poverty was somehow rooted in their values and way of life, which was perpetuated from one generation to the next, regardless of governmental intervention; and that the poor dependency on social welfare programs harmed and inhibited self-reliance and therefore, such programs must be abandoned. The main target of this ideological assault with it pragmatic implications were poor blacks, especially those living in the inner-cities or "urban ghettoes." To justify their claim of unworthiness, conservatives pointed to the high rates of crime, teen pregnancy, unemployment, and female headed households among blacks at the time. In spite of the devastating effects his policies reeked on black life, particularly on the poor, in a seemingly cynical gesture designed to show that he was tough but compassionate, Reagan signed legislation making Martin Luther King's birthday a national holiday.

For many, but especially for conservatives, Reagan's policies were heralded as major accomplishments and he was seen as a genuine American hero. His "get tough" approach to foreign and domestic policies helped to rearticulate Western hegemonic power. Abroad, Reagan's hard lined stance against communism eventually led to the fall of the Berlin Wall and the collapse of the Soviet State. At home, his fiscal and social conservatism shifted the discourse on the liberal welfare state by redefining the meaning of poverty and that of race relations, whereby poor blacks in particular were blamed for their own direr condition. But for all of Reagan's seemingly foreign and domestic policy heroism yet another, but rarely unspoken, benefit was derived from his particular brand of aggressive leadership. Arguably, Reagan's heroics renewed a sense of Western masculine pride, for he embodied the meaning of white male power, control and dominance upon which both conservative and liberal white men could often agree. For many men, regardless of their particular political interests or allegiances, Reagan symbolized the personification of the quintessential man's man. As President George W. Bush noted in his eulogy of the man:

> President Reagan was optimistic about the great promise of economic reform, and he acted to restore the reward and spirit of enterprise. He was optimistic that a strong America could advance the peace, and he acted to build the strength that mission required. He was optimistic that liberty would thrive wherever it was planted, and he acted to defend liberty wherever it was threatened. . . . As he showed what a President should be, he also showed us what a man should be (Bush, 2004).

During the early 1980s, in the midst of the "Reagan Revolution" and the "New Right" ascendancy to power, a new black politics was also making its presence known on the political landscape. It appeared as conservative economic policies reeked havoc on black life. At that time, nationally the median income of black families was only fifty-seven percent of that of white families. The unemployment rate for blacks was almost twice that of whites, and for young blacks it was a staggering forty-percent, as manufacturing in urban areas all but dried up. The economic disparities between black and white Americans during the 1980s were indeed profound. But Reagan's budget cuts were especially devastating for poor blacks: one in five blacks received AFDC, thirty percent received Food Stamps, twenty-five percent received Medicaid, and as many as 300,000 blacks held jobs under CETA. And with cutbacks in low-income housing programs, where almost fifty-percent of public housing residents were black, Americans began to witness unprecedented numbers of homeless families living on the streets and in homeless shelter across the country. As a result of Reagan's economic policies children—particularly black children—constituted the largest poverty class in America.

Black elected officials, but especially community activists, were outrage over Reagan's domestic policies. Nowhere was that outrage more prophetic than in the city of Chicago. There the "economic struggles were transformed into a political movement;" that movement resulted in several noteworthy protests which held important national implications in shifting the political landscape away from the conservative right (Alkalimat & Gills, 1989).

Initially, a coalition of black community leaders organized a citywide fight against the closing of the Cook County Hospital—a public hospital that treated 250,000 inpatients annually—utilized by poor blacks and working class for primary health care. Following that struggle, mass protests were organized against the Chicago School Board; organizers sought greater black participation in policy-making and structural improvements in the conditions of the public schools, where black students constituted more than sixty-percent of population. With increased anger over political patronage, graft, and violence that helped to reduce public housing to a substandard living environment, tenants organized around housing conditions and the right to manage their own complex. Blacks were more than ninety-percent of the public housing residents and sixty-percent of the families were headed by women. In their struggle to assert greater tenant control, residents engaged in a series of protests against the Chicago Housing Authority. And, activist groups such as POWER and the Illinois Coalition Against Reagan (I-CARE), were organized in response to the fourteen-percent black unemployment rate and cutbacks in health care, daycare, education, and public assistance that effected an estimated 800,000 people in Chicago. They mounted a series of political challenges around basic economic rights. Of particular note was the massive voter registration drive that they undertook in the fall of 1982.

The success of those struggles rested upon a progressive approach that not only opened up new areas for political protests, but also new structures of black leadership. The social and economic crisis spurred on by the "Reagan Revolution" ignited political movements in black communities around the country. And, again in 1982, black civil rights leaders, most notably Reverend Joseph Lowery head of SCLC and Coretta Scott King, issued a call for another march on Washington. But in Chicago, black organized resentment, anger, and frustration led to a different political strategy; one that focused on mobilizing grassroots electoral power. A citywide Task Force for Black Political Empowerment, which consisted of fifty community organizations, was established to challenge the powerful Democratic political machine in the city. As the standard-bearer for this new black political mobilization, the Task Force selected Harold Washington to run for mayor during 1983 fall election. Manning Marable noted that Washington's campaign represented a major turning point in black politics in America. It differed from other black electoral campaigns in several regards:

> Firstly, it represented the culmination of a series of Black social reform movements for socio-economic and political equality which had finally assumed a bourgeois democratic electoral form. . . . Secondly, the focus of the mobilization was against the most entrenched and corrupt municipal political organization in twentieth-century America, the Cook County Democratic machine. This movement was disciplined and coordinated across class lines: the ballot had become a weapon for the Afro-American masses to attack institutional racism and political patronage. . . . Thirdly, the struggle against the Democratic machine highlighted in unambiguous terms the central theme of Black political culture, the historic division within the petty bourgeoisie between the accommodationists and the reformers. The former practiced clientage politics as a subsidiary of the Democratic machine, while the latter attempted to advocate programmes that represented the material and political interests of the Black working class. Only when the reformist tendency acquired a mass constituency, drawing upon the resources of Black activists, revolutionary nationalists, and trade unionists to their left, could such a campaign triumph over both the Democratic machine and its Black apologists. Finally, the Washington effort of 1983 illustrated not only the racial divisions within the American working class, but the inherent instability of social class forces that the Democratic Party comprises (Marable, 1985, pp. 192–193).

Consequently, as a result of this new black politics, in the fall of 1983 Harold Washington was elected as the first black mayor of Chicago. Taking note of the successful coalition form among blacks, Latinos, and liberal whites, and the strategically important grassroots organizing efforts, the Democratic National Committee viewed Washington's election as a major pushback against Reagan's economic policies and the first step toward defeating the Republican Party in the 1984 presidential election. Mass voter registration and participation, especially among poor blacks, was thought by many to hold the key to that election. It laid the political foundation necessarily for Jesse Jackson, a young advisor to Martin Luther King and the founder of Operation PUSH, to run as a viable candidate for the 1984 Democratic presidential nomination. It also laid the foundation for another young African American man to mount an unexpected and improbably, yet audacious presidential challenge. From a distance—as a young community organizer on the South Side of Chicago—Barack Hussein Obama watched and took careful notes of the possibilities of this new black politics.

During the late 1970s and early 1980s, the men interviewed also took note of the new black politics that swirled around them. But unlike Richard, Jamie, and Matt whose path in life had led to incarceration during this period, the other men proceeded along different paths in their struggle to understand themselves and their relationship to the world, in this age of Reaganism. Yet, what linked the men's divergent experiences to that of Richard, Jamie, and Matt was the importance of critical self-reflection, for which education played a major role in transforming their lives.

The pursuit of knowledge, of actively engaging an intellectual process in the confines of imprisonment, not only broaden their self-understanding but, importantly, enabled them to reflect upon and assumed responsibility for their predicament and lives, as inmates. With a critical lens, Richard, Jamie, and Matt in their own particular ways examined their past decisions and actions as black men. In taking stock of their life circumstances that informed assessment opened up a new space of reality, which enabled them to see themselves and engage the world differently, even in a prison environment. That critical reflection provided the necessary means to create space within and against their own personal histories to claim their humanity; to move beyond their complicity in reproducing the disfiguring racial and gender stereotype of the criminal-black-male, by embodying that image.

Through critical reflection aided by education Richard, Jamie, and Matt came to an awareness of self that rejected such mimicking and the violence it engendered. Even though they could not fully escape the image imposed on them by white society, they could however, redefine for themselves what it means to be a black men locked behind prison walls. For them, the pursuit of knowledge was empowering and the critical consciousness derived therein laid the foundation for their transformation: they walked away from prison, but from their old lives as well, committed to never returning.

Even though the other men's particular pursuit of knowledge differed from that of Richard, Jamie and Matt, it also held for them the key to articulating what it means to be black-and-male in America. Following high school most went to college, more often in a predominately white educational setting where they had to prove that they possessed the ability to learn. They understood that no amount of education would allow them to step completely outside of the trapping of the rigid racial and gender stereotypes reserved for black men. Yet they were determined to follow their own particular paths, and education offered a shallow buffer against the power of imposing images and a degree of legitimacy attesting to their capability, if not to others at least to themselves. Their will to learn guided them toward clarity of purpose, and as they matured their increased curiosity about themselves and world provided a foundation that allowed them to claim their humanity.

THE WILL TO LEARN

Thomas attended a predominately white community college in California, where he engaged the black power movement as a student/activist. Torn between the black nationalist's politics of Us and the more socialist's stance of the Black Panther Party, he decided to focus his activism on strengthening the Black Student Union in attempts to make the college more responsive to the academic needs and interests of black students. But feeling a need to connect to African culture and spirituality, Thomas adopted the Yoruba religious tradition. Yet, even with his active political involvement and participation in the Yoruba faith community, Thomas felt "isolated and a little alienated," in California, so he decided to dropout of college and return to Chicago.

When he returned, Thomas did not know exactly what he was going to do, but he did know that whatever it was, it involved working in the black community. Rather than moving back home with his mother and younger brothers and to the more racially diverse community in which he had grown up, Thomas stayed with friends in the black community. After he got a job as a counselor working with young people at a street academy, which he described as one of the first charter schools in Chicago, he lived in an apartment that the program owned. In addition to his work at the academy, Thomas began to get involved in community issues. He said, "I got involved with this group on the South Side. Any issue that came up on the South Side that had to do with poor folks, we were in it. Politically, I was jumping from issue to issue, nonstop. I'm making relationships in the community with other folks who sort of thinks like I do." After leaving California, all Thomas wanted to do when he returned to Chicago was "work in the black community," and by joining this coalition of activists he did just that. He said "the coalition worked on every issue":

> Health care and we're doing the gangs stuff, and then we would be doing that for a while and then something else would happen while that's going on. We got the park cleaned up. We helped organize in public housing. We fought to raise the minimum wage issue nine years before anybody else dealt with it. We organized laborers. Ten building in my neighborhood went co-op. I had a key role in all of that. I wanted the community to stay black and stay black-owned as much as it could. I could look out of my window and see the trees I helped get planted when there were no trees. All of that was significant for me because I never accepted the proposition that black folks were failures. That was really important to me.

By the early 1980s, people in the community took note of his activism and started to view Thomas as a leader, as a person who could get things done. He recalled "one time walking on a block and some kids, who I used to give a hard time to, where sitting outside and the street light was out. I was walking by and one of the girls said, 'oh, speak to him; that's the guy who can get the light fixed; he'll get it straightened out.' But I didn't want to be bothered. And I looked at that broken light for a week. The light got fixed, but I didn't have anything done. But people associated getting it fixed with me because I did a lot of stuff in the community." Yet Thomas was resistant to the idea that he was a community leader: "I'm just throwing out some ideas and just doing what I want to do." But regardless of how he viewed himself, others saw him as a leader. He said:

> Newsweek interviewed me. I had an article in Newsweek as a community leader. But I was really clear about what leadership is and I didn't seek it. I didn't seek at least the traditional notion of what leadership is in the community. I didn't want to be the spokesman. I can play all kinds of roles. I can just do all the work and let somebody else be the spokesman. I don't need to be up front. I'll do whatever is necessary; I prefer to just be a worker. I like to be a worker and show other folks how they're supposed to work. That's how I saw myself. I never saw myself as holding the power. I really saw myself as sharing the power that folks had already. They got it. Now whether they know how to use it or not, is another thing. But I'm not interested in holding power. I'm only interested in using it to get some things accomplished, but in the end it's the people's power.

Thomas' passion was politics—black political empowerment—and he devoted his skills, time, and energy to that endeavor. In other words, it was the overarching priority in his life. It not only defined how he saw himself, but it also allowed him to mask personal feelings, especially when it came to intimate relationships with women and dealing with family matters. On reflection he said: "Politics kept me going. I kept myself so involved in issues that I don't feel I'm drifting, but I am very unhappy during this period of my life."

After returning to Chicago, Thomas resumed an intimate relationship with an old girlfriend Katherine, whom he described as a beautiful girl—"light skinned with long hair"—that he "really loved." But he had always had a lingering sense of insecurity about their relationship, precisely because of the way she looked. Katherine's physical features created tensions in their relationship, and it started when her mother told Thomas upon meeting him that: "I was to dark, and that I was not good enough for her daughter." But after they renewed their relationship another tension gradually developed between them; Katherine wanted to get married. Even though he loved her, Thomas was not prepared to make compromises to his political life; he was not ready to make marriage and children a priority. Because of this, the relationship ended, badly. He became "clinically depressed and had very low self-esteem because the relationship failed. I didn't know how to get out of that, so I continued my political work. I was so involved because I didn't want to be with myself. I didn't want to be alone with me."

But Thomas did not want to be with his family either. As he said, "I built my life around relationships outside of my family." His active political life and the relationships developed therein were a "substitute family" that allowed him to put emotional distance between himself and his mother and stepbrothers. When he returned to Chicago, Thomas said: "I really wasn't dealing with my family. My mother was one area in my life where I considered myself utterly vulnerable. I did not like the feeling. I felt my emotions were being used by her. So because I didn't like the feelings I had when I was around her, I stayed away. Essentially, when I left my mother's house for college, I was gone for good! I lived my whole life outside of her house." Resultantly, Thomas seldom visited his mother or saw his younger brothers. But, then, one day his mother called and said: "your brother has disappeared." He searched for his brother, but no one had seen or heard from him in two days. Finally, Thomas and his mother went to the local police precinct for help in trying to locate him. While there:

> The white cops are acting all nasty to us. I'm pissed off because I am in the situation where I have to ask these white cops for help. They say he didn't disappear; he's in jail. He did this and that. My mother is completely humiliated. And I didn't like being in this situation.

Thomas younger brother was "a junkie" addicted to heroin. He was in jail the main jail downtown, and Thomas bailed him out: "I was making jive money and I didn't have a lot of money, but I got him out of jail. And we were driving back and he's talking about being a gangster and a criminal." Thomas could not relate to the conversation. This was not the brother he remembered. His brother had changed. As far as he was concerned, "my brother had always been smarter than me and he had been a writer." But now Thomas' brother appeared to be a different person. Even so, Thomas was familiar with the unpredictable behavior of junkies and was concerned, because his brother was living with his mother. He tried to discuss his brother's addiction with his mother and to convince her to put him out, but she refused to listen to Thomas' warning:

> I told my mother to kick him out. She said, "what are you, crazy?" I said he is talking about being a gangster and a criminal, and you need to kick him out. He needs to find out what that's about. I told her that as long as he lives with you that stuff is going to come back to you. She said, "no

this is my son; you don't understand." She didn't do that. So there were a series of incidents. The most serious was when some people came to the house with guns and held her (mother) hostage. This girl said he (brother) had stolen four or five thousand dollars worth of drugs from this guy. So they came looking for him. They held her hostage for a couple of hours. She was lucky. When they left, she called my other brother, he's a cop now. He is going crazy; "I'm going to kill these niggers." I talked him out of it and nothing happened.

Finally convinced of the potential danger his addiction posed, Thomas' mother sent him to Florida to live with her brother. This incident and the painful break-up with Katherine created enormous stress, for which Thomas' political activities no longer offered an effective outlet; he became even more depressed and "unhappy" with his life. During that period, he said, "I probably went through about five different personality shifts in my personal life." Those shifts in demeanor were aided by Thomas' use of cocaine. For six years, "between 1980 and 86," Thomas said:

> I'm sniffing cocaine; not a lot a first. I got a new job and I'm trying to learn that. I don't have any close intimate relationships. I busy and on the move. I'm playing paddle ball and I'm spending a lot of time in the park. The political thing is still there and the desire to see things better for the people. But my nightlife tends to take over a lot where I'm not doing anything. I'm just hanging out and getting high. I progressively become more and more unhappy with my life, especially after dark. When I'm at home I don't like being home. I find when I'm home I'm getting high. I'm confused. I'm not seeing the person I think I am. The deeper I get into cocaine the more unhappy I am. This goes on for awhile. I run into a few folks I know and immediately I realized that I feel embarrassed about seeing them, while they are very happy to see me. I can't figure out why they are happy to see me. I had sworn off of the politics; I wasn't going to do that for awhile. I felt burnt out. I felt ashamed. How did this happen? It wasn't the people it was me. I felt ashamed and I don't know quite when it happened, but at some point I do just wake up and say this is not what I want to do. I was clear that I was unhappy with myself. The coke wasn't satisfying me anymore. I was unhappy and I was in debt. I didn't know why I was getting high. I said this is not you. You need to get straight. I wanted to reinvent myself. And at that point I just stopped getting high. Yeah, I stopped cold turkey.

Thomas did reinvent himself, it was a gradual process, and again his unrelenting political passion played a critical role in helping to renew his sense of self. In that process, he reconnected to his political mentor: who "always showed me how a victory wasn't necessarily a victory; that the struggle itself could be an important lesson, in and of itself." He also reconnected to his passion for politics when he started working for a social justice organization that was sponsored by a local church.

Through that organization Thomas had the opportunity to fulfill a dream, to go to African. His mentor encouraged him to attend a conference in Ghana, because he was "into that African stuff." Following the conference Thomas had the opportunity to travel to several African countries and experience the day-to-day lives of the people there. He refused, however, to go to Uganda with his traveling companions because as he said, "Idi Amin was a dictator; he's killing his own people. I'm not going there! I don't support stuff that's wrong and I don't care what the color is, I don't do it. Every thing black ain't right. I don't support it. So I can't go to Uganda." But he did go to Mozambique where he donated blood, and was proud of the fact that "I can really say that my blood flowed through the veins of revolutionary fighters in Africa."

That trip had a profound impact on how Thomas viewed the world and how he saw himself within it. He "soaked up the whole experience," and came back to the states even more determined to appreciate his African heritage. Although in the past he had occasionally worn African garb, it now became his everyday attire, and with it a renewed sense of pride. As he said, "I was proud to be a black man," and for Thomas that meant having "honor, integrity and a sense of responsibility to yourself and others." He believed that those qualities allowed him "to do what I wanted to do and to learn what I wanted to learn." But in his political journey, Thomas encountered lessons that he did not necessarily want to learn because they brought him face-to-face with the ugly side of black poverty.

He accepted a job as a property manager for city-owned housing: "that was the era when the city was taking property from landlords for serious code violations that were substandard, and site managers were the people who were managing the property." He detested the deplorable conditions of the buildings and the general hazards associated with the job, when he said:

> The buildings were really substandard; in the summer time they were hot and they didn't have heat in the winter. The apartments were in such bad shape and the cost of repairing them was prohibitive, so we would usually relocate the tenants into a building that was supposedly a little better and close up the old ones. Almost all of the property on the South Side was in bad shape and I had a hand in closing them. It was really like a plantation job. My first experience in the job was putting notices under the doors of a building, and a guy ran after me with a butcher knife. The notice was alerting the tenants that the building was under consolidation

and that we would be closing the building and relocating them. I used to carry a little gun. I'm not really violent, but I'm sort of real clear, and you got to hold your ground. I was prepared to use it if I had to.

As part of his job, Thomas moved into one of the city-owned building as site manager. He welcomed the opportunity because as he said, "I'm rooted in black folks' lives. I want to be around black folks. I want to dedicate my life to bettering our conditions, and that was my service. That's what I always wanted to do." But a conflict quickly arose, "we had a drug problem in the building and they were selling in the hallways, so I started trying to do something about that." There were some vacant apartments that drug dealers had taken over, and Thomas evicted them. In so doing, he won the respect of other tenants, especially from the senior citizens who lived there. But it appeared that he had also won the animus from some young black men living there. Thomas found that he had a particularly hard time relating to them because "there was this whole life style going on that I couldn't get my finger on; I didn't know what it was about." On reflection, he said:

> Young folks don't talk about integrity and principles. They don't talk about doing something for somebody. They talk about doing something for themselves and how they can get over. They don't know God, they don't know a thing, and that's scary to me. To them life's a game; it's all a game. It's the class thing unfortunately, but it seems to cross class lines, I think. Uneducated and poor, that's a bad combination. They're only materialistic in a country that's materialistic. They got no notion about work; how you get it; you steal it. So there's no connect. It's very difficult for young black males in this society. It's hard to connect with them because I'm talking about work, responsibility, unity, and they're talking about how can I get mine. Not how can I make this better and we all can get something? The values used to be teaching your son he's got to go to school; he's got to get a job; he's supposed to take care of his kids. There was a set of values transferred to the children. But what is being transferred to young males is completely warped. School is important. Responsibility is important. Work is important. And taking care of yourself is important. That's your foundation. I say those things made you a man, which have never actually really changed. When you talk to white men they say the same thing: be responsible, you work, you take care of the family. All over the world men say this. It's not a mystery. You go to Africa, what do men do? They have a real specific role. You go to China, what do men do? Men have a role in all societies. It may change depending on how complicated the society is, but basically you work, you take care of family, take care of the tribe, take care of the neighborhood, you mentor and interact with the young men and at some point train them on

how to be the same way. Although I don't have children and don't see myself as a father figure, I do see myself as a black man who tries to present a positive image to them.

Even though he found it difficult to relate to values of the young men in the building, the senior citizens loved him. Through that interaction Thomas became more than just a site manager for the building, he became a tenant organizer. He organized the tenant association for the building and "the seniors were the backbone" of that effort. They elected Thomas as the president of the association and he readily embraced this role. Given the poverty conditions of many of the tenants, who were mostly elderly or single mothers, he tried "to address some of the social issues. So I started going to the police precinct council meetings. I even joined a democratic club. I started going to the churches to try and see what they can do."

Under Thomas' leadership the tenants became more politicized; they went on a rent strike to get the city of Chicago to improve their housing conditions. But, clearly, there was a problem; Thomas was not only the president of the tenant association but a city employee as well. "And the agency that I'm working for started getting hints that I was working for them and I'm leading a rent strike against them. I knew I had a problem. I had to extricate myself from that situation." But, before he could remove himself, the FBI arrested Thomas. At that time, Thomas was loosely affiliated with a black nationalist's organization, whose leadership had been charged with conspiracy against the United States. To avoid arrest some of the leaders had gone on the run. Of the group, Thomas said that "they were organizing, but what got them into trouble was they had a lot of anti-American and anti-cop rhetoric; you know, fuck the pigs stuff."

When the FBI was rounding up members from the group, they claimed that Thomas had provided "a number of safe houses," for some of the members. Although the FBI released Thomas, he was issued a subpoena to testify before a grand jury about his involvement. He decided to comply, because he "was not prepared to be in jail for a whole year," and he had obligations with the tenant association.

Meanwhile the city attorneys found out that Thomas was indeed the president of the association when he "represented the tenants in court." The tenant association loss its case, but importantly the city fired Thomas and decided to close the building. Thomas was devastated by the results, because:

> I've always considered myself very successful at politics. I couldn't conceive of me failing at something political, at all. I was willing to do anything if I thought it was about principle, I was prepared to do it. I clearly made some serious errors in judgments that ended up costing me. The arrest was a failure. Not relating to the kids in the building was a failure.

Being forced out of the building—it wasn't because I wanted to leave, I had no choice—was a failure to me. I hadn't internalized how to accept failure or how to change failure into a victory. I just felt ashamed that I had not been able to finish the job. When I moved to the building I had this grand vision. We can do all of these things here, we can develop this stuff, and we could change the whole area. It was devastating. I had a lot of emotion invested in the people and my vision. I was not in any way prepared to if fail. It was a sense of betrayal. I couldn't figure out, how did this happen? I was not able to carry this vision out and not be able to change the dynamics that's going on here, by the force of my will. I simply could not understand how I failed!

Thomas had lived with the tenants in the building for eight years and "a big piece of my identity was invested there." He felt a drifted, but this time rather than turning to drugs to numb his deep "unhappiness," Thomas returned to what had sustained him in the past, his spirituality: "It was the thing that saved me from going completely crazy, because I'm a spiritual person."

Thomas had not attended church services since childhood, and although he had worked with a social justice organization that was church affiliated, for Thomas that involvement was political rather than spiritual. But feeling a need to be "around a bunch of healthy people," he decided to renew his contact with the organization, and this time his primary motivation was largely spiritual in nature. Thomas started to attend church on a regular basis: "it was a black Presbyterian church," and rather than wearing the usually suit and tie, "I'm wearing my African stuff." Through his reconnection, Thomas realized that he had a spiritual reverence for the black church and the important political role it played in society, especially in the area of social justice. He wholeheartedly embraced its legacy as an active member. He said:

> I think the black church mirrors society. Once you lose your sense of who you are as a people it's real difficult to function. America keeps on being what America is, a capitalist society. It's materialistically dominated; it's not a spiritual place. It's not necessarily a place that's going to hold up certain values. Church for black people traditionally had been the place to get that stuff held up. I really truly believe that it is important how you act and how you treat others. I believe in God. I'm convinced that he has had a plan for me, even when I don't want to do something I end up playing a role that I don't ask to play. Spirituality gives me calmness and a sense of peace, but it's still a struggle, and that's the challenge.

Now, as he reflected back over his many years of activism, Thomas believed that he has almost come full circle in his life. And in that circle he said, "I realized that my politics and my spirituality have always been rooted in the church." Currently, as he ponders the possibility of retirement from his current job of eleven years as a property manager for several dwellings, Thomas continues along a path that blend his spirituality with that of active political engagement; it continues to give him meaning as a black man; and he continues to embrace a commitment to making life, in whatever ways he can, better for the black community.

Yet Thomas' political and spiritual commitment has never extended to a personal commitment to marriage and children. That commitment has never extended to establishing a conventional family life. As he said, "I don't know at what point in my life that I realized I could not commit myself to a woman that could lead to marriage and children. My politics is about black families and nation building, and I know there seemed to be a contradiction and a conflict with that. But I think early on I probably built up some emotional defenses against being hurt by women. I know I did. So I'm a bachelor and committed to being one for life." Even so, Thomas emphasized that "having a healthy relationship with black women is very important to me. I respect them entirely."

That being said, it was the respect of black men however that Thomas seemed to cherish. But not all black men, as he said: "I have always made sure that I had the respect of black men of honor; men who have principles, accomplishments, and integrity who were trying to do the right thing. I've always wanted respect from those kinds of men and I believed that I've gotten it, absolutely."

LEARNING TO LOVE

Following his brother's advice, John decided to leave segregated Albany, Georgia in 1965, and move to the less racially restricted city of New York. Immediately upon arriving to the city John was introduced to a whole new world and "it was really a cultural shock." He lived in Harlem with his brother's family. There, for the first time, he "saw tenement houses and all kinds of people. I had never seen Spanish people before, and I thought they were so beautiful and colorful." For John, New York "was the most beautiful dirty place you ever wanted to be in. It was dirty, but it was just beautiful. I saw buildings, clothes were out on the line, and people were on the fire escape and sitting on stoops." Drawn to the excitement of the city, John went about the business of making it his home.

With a bachelor degree in business administration, John took any job that he could find. As in childhood, he believed that there was no honest work beneath him, a belief he continued to embrace as an adult. He worked a series of low pay menial jobs, but while working as an usher at a movie theater the manager discovered that John was good with numbers. One day when he went into the manager's office for something, the manager said, "John do you know how to use an adding machine? I said yes. He had this list of two digit numbers. He started calling out these numbers and I just added them up in my head. He said, no I want you to add them up on the adding machine, I said okay. He gave me the numbers and I added them up. He said you got the numbers rights. He said to me, how long are you expecting to be an usher? He said did you ever think about being an assistant manger?" John became the assistant manger at the movie theater. This was his first, but by no means his last professional job, and from that position he would gradually build a career based on his math abilities.

Soon thereafter, John met Rosetta. He thought that she was absolutely beautiful, very dark skinned with straight black hair, and six-months later they were married. He married Rosetta "because I told her that I would. One thing that means more to me than anything else is my word. I was taught from an early age that that's all that we have, that's all that we own. What is the measure of a man? His character is tied in with his word. Short of me dying, I'm going to keep my word to you. And I promised Rosetta that I would marry her. And at the time I couldn't see any reason not to, so I did it." One reason not to marry Rosetta was because he did not love her. As he said: "I liked her a lot. But I don't know if I was in love with her. That's something that I always struggled with."

John's ambivalence toward love was deeply rooted in his past. He believed that ever since his mother died, there was no one else who had truly loved him, and, in turn, he committed himself to never loving anyone again. He said:

> I think I really wanted to get married because I really didn't want to love anybody. Since I was young, when my mother died, I said I would never love anybody again. I respected Rosetta a great deal and I would give anything and do anything in the world for her, but I didn't know how to put myself out there for her. My concept of love is really a man being supportive, responsible for the woman I'm with, and protecting her. That's my concept of love. I married Rosetta because I told her that I would.

However, with the birth of Sara, his first child, John's concept of love changed in profound ways. Unabashedly, he adored the child and Sara loved him. To support his family, "because the man was responsible for his family," John worked two full-time jobs, one was with a department store and the other at a beer brewery, and Rosetta stayed at home to care for Sara. Even though John did not have a lot of free time in his busy schedule, he always found time for little Sara. Early on, as he said:

> I used to work nights and when I came home in the morning she would be dressed and sitting by the door. We had to go to the park. Rain or

shine, she would be sitting there ready to go. We would spend an hour or so in the park. It didn't matter how cold it was, she just needed to be in the park with me. It was like a ritual. And she wanted to go everywhere I went. When I went into my old neighborhood, Sara had to be with me, so I would see the guys and they would say, "why you bring your daughter?" I said, because I wanted to bring her. I loved her the way I believed that my mother loved me. This little child who can't do anything for herself and everything that she gets, and everything that she has, I knew I had to get it for her.

Through Sara, John learned how to love another person, and eight years later with the birth of his second daughter Bonita, his ability to love someone else other than himself only grew. By the 1970s, John had firmly made New York City his home and had settled into a conventional way of life, where marriage and children were a clear priority and a man's responsibility. He returned to school to learn computer programming: "it was different types of programming like fortran and cobol, you had to do a lot of writing of programs and I learned how to do that. We're talking about the old 1400 computer where you had to slide the punch card through the computers. It was exciting because no one was doing it at the time and it was on the cutting edge of everything." During this period, John continued to be the sole provider of his family as he worked two full-time jobs, but even with a busy schedule he found time to be politically active in his community.

Having grown up under racial segregation in Albany, Georgia John believed that "voting would make a change, it would make a difference" in black people's lives. So he joined a local democratic club "to help get black people elected to office." Drawing on past experience, he said: "when I grew up in Georgia, black folks had to pay a poll tax to vote. So I always understood why it was important to vote. I understood the power of the vote. So I worked real hard trying to get people register and trying to get people to vote." But John political involvement was largely limited to voter registration drives because as he said, "I worked and had a family to take care of."

Meanwhile, after fourteen years, John's marriage began to unravel. Throughout his married life, he usually worked two full-time jobs, but over the years Rosetta grew increasingly jealous because she believed that John was seeing other women. Consequently, "the difficulty in our marriage came with the jealousy. Rosetta was an expert at that." And there came a point in their marriage when her "jealousy became unbearable," for John. He said:

I had two full-time jobs that seemed like forever. The money was great. I could provide for my family. My daughters had everything and it allowed my wife to stay home with the kids. That was important to me. After my second child the jealousies became unbearable. I was working nights and the supervisor was a good friend. Rosetta used to call my job at night. She had gone to sleep and would wake up to call me. She would tell my supervisor "I know that he's not there, that he's with a woman." He would say, "he has been here all night." My wife has never ever caught me with another woman. I didn't even talk to women. I had a commitment to one woman. I really didn't play around, and if I did I would've said so. But that's just not something that I would do. I think Rosetta was so jealous because of the way she looked. Rosetta was very dark. She was beautiful, but I mean very dark. In her family there's light and dark, but nobody as dark as Rosetta. I think that her family used to make fun of her because she was real dark. I said, let me tell you something you're black and you're going to always be black and nothing you say is going to change that, so get over it. We didn't fight but we had arguments over her jealousy.

It appeared that Rosetta became almost obsessive with her jealousy. John recalled one time when "she was so upset that I'm fooling around on her that she said she was going to kill herself. We were living on the sixth floor and she would always threaten to jump out of the window. In the beginning I would say baby why are you doing this? But one day I simply had had enough and I pushed her. I just nudged her, and she panicked and said I was trying to kill her. That was the end of that drama." But it was not the end of Rosetta's jealousy. From John's perspective Rosetta played emotional games with him. On several occasions, he would come home from work and find Rosetta, the children, and their clothes gone. She had gone to her mother's home in Detroit without telling him. John said that Rosetta knew that "I would come and get her." But there came a time "when she had just picked up and went to her mother's" and emotionally drained John had simply had enough of Rosetta's behavior:

> I told her, Rosetta you know something the next time you do this test of me, I will never take you back. And about six months later she did it. We had had an argument about nothing, about her jealousy. So she decided that she was going to go to her mother's. She called me up about two-days later and said, "I'm coming home." I said, nope you can't come back here. You don't have a home here anymore. I said, you took your clothes and I will never accept you back, never. I loved my kids but I wouldn't accept her back. That hurt me, that bothered me a lot, but I just couldn't accept her back. I wasn't going to play that game anymore. I was never going to do that again. I remember that my father used to tell me that my word and my pride would kill me. But I meant my word. It was my pride but I was going to keep my word. I told her she would never do that to me again. I can't tell you how much that hurt me.

Even though John was deeply hurt by the breakup of his marriage, he did not shed a tear over it. He said, "I didn't cry; I don't know about crying; I hadn't had anything to hurt me bad enough to cry over, other than when my mother died." But John did feel however a sense of "extreme loneliness." And to cope with that loneliness, he turned to spirituality, rather than to "alcohol and drugs." He said: "because my father drank, I knew that I would never get drunk," as a way of coping with his problems. Instead John "coped by reading the bible" and meditated. Yet "it took me years to learn how to cope with the loneliness and not having my children."

Rosetta would not give John a divorce, but he continued to provide financial support for his children, as he moved on with his life. He started dating again. John said, "I never thought of myself as a handsome guy, but I thought that I had skills. I could get any woman I wanted." But he also started to develop friendships with other men: "Rosetta didn't even want me to have men friends." Those relationships developed largely through his jobs and they were mostly white, because his work environments were mostly white. John said that "I think the people that have helped me the most in my life and have done things for me where white men." But his friendships with white men were not uncomplicated relationships. For instance, "I had a friend that said he just never saw me as black. And we had issues with that. I told him you can't see me any other way. You have to see me as black. If you don't see me as black, then you can't see me as a friend, because that's what I am."

John continued to work two full-time jobs, and during his daytime job he received periodic promotions. He was promoted from a computer operator, "to a lead operator, to a shift supervisor, shift manager, and then data center manager in fourteen years." Describing his professional work experience up until that point, John said:

> Everyone that I worked with was white and everyone that I worked for was white. I was good at what I did; I was good at my job. I didn't play or laugh or joke around. I got promoted basically because of being professional, really doing my job, being good at my job, and willing to learn new things. I started as an operator, but I was always looking to go further and do something different within the realm of computers and management. I never felt different. I've always felt that I was better than them. I really always felt that. I don't remember anyone ever treating me black. You know when people are prejudice to you, and how they talk about you, and talk to you. No one ever talked down to me. But I know I could've gone further and higher than I did had I been white.

Even though he had advanced in his profession, John realized that he had hit an invisible ceiling because of his race. That he had advanced as far as he was going to within the company. He said that "you have to be exceptional for them to promote you. That type of prejudice is always there. You can't prove it, but it's always there. It makes you angry, but you can't stop and say I'm not going to do anything. You still do your best because it was about me. My job was never about anybody else; it was about me being my best."

During the 1980s, John decided to find a new job, and was hired as a manager by a local college to upgrade their business technology department. "At this time, I became involved with Beatrice," a friend who lived upstairs in the same apartment complex. He said, "Beatrice was a pretty girl. I always had pretty women. I don't know why but I'm just attracted to pretty women. Beatrice was a light skinned Puerto Rican. After eleven years, Rosetta "was angry, I mean really angry," but she finally gave John a divorce. John and Beatrice "went from being real close friends to me having somebody permanent in my life." He married Beatrice. And with that marriage, once again John settled into a conventional way of life, where family and the responsibilities thereof were the primary focus of his attention. Beatrice agreed that John's two daughters could live with them: and "they liked her and got along well. They even called her mom." And shortly thereafter, John and Beatrice had their first child, a girl, Elizabeth. "This little chubby face beautiful little girl; we bonded right away, and spent a lot of time together." And six years later, John and Elizabeth had another child, a daughter named Peggy, who "looked a lot like my mother and grandmother, light with hazel eyes, and everything."

John continued to work two full-time jobs as Beatrice "stayed home and took care of the girls. That's what she wanted to do; she wanted to take care of our daughters." But within the conventions of family life there were cultural differences between John and Beatrice that created tensions in their marriage. John described Beatrice as a "server:"

> I come home dinner is ready, the bath water is ready, and she wants to take my clothes off. I didn't really understand it in the beginning. I'm not really taking into consideration her culture. Everything in the house was her job. That was always a problem with her. The kids were independent and they wouldn't let her serve them. She wouldn't let them do anything. Serve, serve, serve; it drove me crazy; absolutely crazy. We argued a lot about that. We really started to argue when she wanted to fix me dinner and I wasn't eating. She got angry, real angry. She would curse me out. She was mad because I wouldn't eat her food and she would say, "I bet you're eating some bitch's food." I didn't like confrontation. So I moved out of the bedroom to the second floor because I just didn't want anything to do with her anymore.

Even though he moved to another part of the house the tensions between John and Beatrice escalated. "It really got to be bad and she really changed a lot. She was always complaining." Although they continued to live together under the same roof, John tried to avoid his wife, but it was difficult to do because he still interacted with his children on a daily basis. But in one of their confrontations Beatrice "hit me and I hit her back." This was the first time that John had ever struck a woman, his wife, and he was deeply disturbed by his actions. At that point, John realized his marriage had ended. He told Beatrice that he "was going to court to get the kids."

The tensions between John and Beatrice had created such distrust in their relationship that John started to lock his bedroom door, secured with nails, before he left for work:

> About two weeks before we broke up, she broke into my room. She told my daughter that she had to go in there because she didn't know if I was dead or what. She hadn't seen me in a couple of days. That was a lie. She took the nails out, opened the door, and went in there. She went through drawers, pockets, and everything. When she left out she had to nail the door shut. She hit her hand and broke a finger. When I found out, I said fine. I just made sure the door was secure. I told her I've had it, I'm going to court and I'm taking my kids.

Immediately, John filed a court petition for sole custody of his two daughters. He said:

> We got to court and I'm telling the judge I want to keep my daughters. The judge talked to my daughters and they told him how much they loved their mother, but wherever their father went is where they wanted to go. The judge asked Beatrice how she hurt her finger. She told the judge I had broken her finger. The judge was really pissed with me. I said that's not true. He said the lady has a broke finger, why would she stand up here and lie if that's not true. I said she tried to close my bedroom door and hit her own finger. He said John "this is the most asinine thing I've ever heard." I said ask my daughter, she was there. Then Beatrice said "I don't want you questioning my child; I don't want my child to go through trauma." But the judge talked to Elizabeth and she told him what happened. He gave the children to me and that's how I got my daughters. I got custody.

John's two older daughters were now away at college, but the two younger ones were at home. To take care of them, John decided to quit one of his jobs in order to be at home on a more regular basis. But, shortly thereafter John "was laid off. This was the first time I was ever not working. I was laid off from the college." This proved to be a difficult period in John's life: "the hard times were I just couldn't get a job no matter where I went. I went to get a job parking cars and they said I was over qualified. They wouldn't hire me.

I had resumes everywhere. I couldn't get a job for two years and four months." For John, on reflection said, this period "tested my faith and belief in God." But with "odd and end jobs," he managed to hold his household together during his unemployment. Even though John "couldn't get a steady job, I got temporary jobs when I needed them. I just got stuff. If I had to tell you how I made ends meet during that time, I have no idea. I was just blessed. You know when people say miracles happen in your life. My kids didn't know how bad it was. They never missed a meal. I just had a great faith that things were going to work out for me, and I never waiver from that. Finally I got the job that God wanted me to have."

John got a job at a large community health care clinic setting up its computer networking system. "I worked with them to do that and I think it took me about seven or eight months to get it up and running. Everybody was happy with it." Indeed, unexpectedly, John was promoted as manager over the clinic's grant programs. What this meant was that his department was responsible for submitting funding proposals and monitoring how those funds were used for the purposes in which they were received. During the mid-eighties, one of the major funding areas that John pursued and was responsible for was the clinic's new HIV and AIDS initiatives. HIV and AIDS—a disease that was spread through the sharing of body fluid, which attacks the immune system—were spreading throughout the black community. The clinic established anonymous testing sites and later used mobile "vans that went out and did testing and counseling" in the community. John's department was responsible monitoring and making sure that the clinic was in compliance with the provisions of those grants.

John found his work at the clinic extremely rewarding. Indirectly, he was helping people that he cared about in real ways and he was also learning in the process. He went to seminars, workshops, and "started talking to a lot of people," as he tried to understand and educate himself on black health related issues, and especially the effects of HIV and AIDS. At the clinic, John became the first "director of special events," where he used preventive education as a foundation and actively engaged young people in the process of HIV and AIDS prevention, as he also addressed other health issues of black health. He said:

> We targeted a lot of young people at a time when nobody was paying attention to them. We explained to them that it was not just a homosexual disease. That if you didn't practice safe sex you could get it. People really got to understand what it was. We gave away thousands and thousands of condoms to people. We broadened our efforts to address other diseases. We went to smoking, asthma, and T.B. and hepatitis was probably the worst. We used to do special events and we had to do more counseling.

Meanwhile, John's two younger daughters had graduated from high school and like his older children, they were living independent lives. And in those lives they began to present John with grandchildren, "five grandsons and two granddaughters." But never having boys of his own, John began adopting sons in Africa. He said, "I have fifteen adopted sons in Tanzania." While working at the clinic, he met a priest that was trying to raise money to build a teaching hospital in Tanzania, and John got involved in that effort. There was a need to bring doctors from Tanzania to the United States to undergo additional training, and they needed places to stay while doing so. What happened, John said:

> I asked everybody I knew to take a doctor. And I knew a lot of people. But no one would take one; they didn't want to disrupt their lives. So I committed to taking in three doctors every four months for two years, and I did it. So they were like sons. I had to teach them how to go to the Laundromat, how to go to the store, how to travel in the city and all of that. I got involved because it was one doctor for every twenty-five thousand people in Tanzania. Even worse there was one dentist for every three hundred thousand people. So these are my sons. They're waiting for me to come to Tanzania.

John continued to have a close relationship with his adopted sons, and they write to each other on a regular basis. And he has developed others meaningful relationships that continue to connect him with the African continent, as he work through an international organization to help build housing for Africans. In large part, John's efforts are guided by his religious faith. As he said, "I understand my spirituality. I understand my faith and belief in God. And I understand where my power comes from." He has always drawn upon his faith, and in his commitment became an ordained minister. At sixty-five years of age, he has "never thought about retiring," because he cherish his active involvement in life. In the daily act of living, John continues to draw upon his faith, but also rely on the companionship of other men to keep him "strong," as he moves on with his life. As an active member of a group called the Disciples, he said:

> There're about twenty-five of us. We teach and talk to young black men about how important it is to be a son; to be a brother. We help families during those hard times when they have very little. It's also a brotherhood. We protect one another. There is nothing that I wouldn't do for a brother. Maybe all he needs is someone to be respectful to him. I enjoy the laughter with them and the things we do together. Black men are my life force because they are my brothers. None of us can stand alone. If we can't find black family men to stand with, then we are separated from life. There's a lot of brotherhood in black men getting together. Personally I think that is really important.

LEARNING TO NURTURE

After his father tried to murder his mother and his own suicide, Daniel at eighteen years of age assumed responsibility for his family, during a moment of crisis. Added to the pressure of caring for his mother and two younger brothers, Daniel found out that Angela, his high school girlfriend was pregnant with his child. But his father's destructive behavior took an enormous toll on Daniel as well as the effort to try and put the pieces of his family's life back together again following his death. Daniel was simply not prepared to take on the added emotional and paternal responsibility for a child.

This was in 1978, and for Daniel it "was an amazing and traumatic" period in his life. While his mother was recuperating in the hospital, Daniel packed up his younger brothers and moved them to Michigan where he was enrolled in school. "I have stuff to take care of. I have to handle this money, get this house, get mom back here, and I have to get back in school." Daniel busied himself with finding a place for his family to live. With insurance money, "one of the first things I do is buy a house," and then Daniel returned to Indianapolis to get his mother: "she has to take it easy, but she is doing fine. She is also being reflective, writing and journaling a lot, and really trying to force us to talk about what happened, and not wanting us to hate my father."

After his family was settled, Daniel returned to school to pursue a degree in engineering. But not only has the circumstances surrounding his life changed, he has changed as well. Daniel had always thought of himself as a scholar/athlete, but playing football no longer held his interest because he realized that physically he could not complete with more skilled and larger college players: "I'm not good anymore in some regards, which is an interesting thing for me and I have to accept this. These guys are great and I'm good, but this is not a big deal. Sports and athletics were no longer going be a part of how I defined myself." Even his intellectual interest in engineering began to wane, and he started taking college courses outside of the discipline. He said, "I'm really beginning to have a connection to the intellectual history of being black:"

> I'm in this new world and I'm changing. I'm beginning to think about the world and analyze history. I'm thinking about my parents, my father, and what it means to be black is a continuing theme around my development. I think I had always taken being black for granted. Even though I had read a lot, I had not read very much black writing. Engineering is all math and science, but my black friends were all liberal arts majors, and reading different things. I knew who Dubois was but I hadn't read his stuff. I read at that time the Soul of Black Folks. So this is what I'm doing. I started reading and started having these heavy discussions. Intellectually I have expanded. I'm aware of Africa in a cultural way and I connect to these people as black people.

Daniel's mother realized that intellectually he was changing and noted the importance of that change by presenting him with a gift: "she got this book, The Crisis of the Black Intellectual and was like this is for you, and wrote a note to me." Also, in her own persuasive way, his mother tried to get him to acknowledge his unexpressed anger toward his father and also the fact that he had a child in the world. He said, "my mother was very adamant and very aggressive in pursuing conversations over the next four or five years." With regard to his father, she helped Daniel to:

> Understand that he couldn't be any different than he was. He was always a little afraid. It's the way racism expressed itself in a sixty-year-old black man. I really do see the fear and insecurity, and how that played out in my father. He never had the ability to accept people who cared about him. It ruined him because he thought that being a man was a certain thing. He had short man disease in a big way. I think he was really unhappy for many years. What I took from him was the inability to be extremely close to people in long-term relations. The inability to really connect to people, I saw that for a long time in myself. That was a definite part of my personality. It's something that is created. It's not a natural response. It's what you do to feel safe. I was motivated by negative emotions.

His mother also recognized the difficulty Daniel had in establishing meaningful relationships with others outside of family, she was not going to allow him to become disconnected from his child, and she "stepped in." They "talked a lot about Angela and the baby. She specifically asked me what I was thinking, what my plans were, and what I was going to do." Even though Daniel was keenly aware of what was expected of him, he said: "I have issues with doing exactly the right thing. I'm not feeling the love; I'm not overwhelmed, or proud to be a father. None of that is going on with me. I feel that this is a mistake and a blemish. I'm just not happy about it. As far as I'm concerned Angela and I are done." But as far as his mother was concerned the baby was Daniel's responsibility and he could not simply walk away. She thought of Angela and the baby as part of their family, although they were still living in Indianapolis. From a distance and with his mother's insistence, Daniel too gradually began to embrace his child. However, he had made clear decisions regarding his relationship with Angela:

> We're not getting married. I loved the baby and the baby is family, but I'm not having a relationship with Angela. We are not going to play house, and you can not come and visit. I will come and see the baby and you. I will send a check every month. I'm interested in other things. I'm done. I'm clear about that. I wasn't torn. It wasn't in my heart. I was really clear in terms of who I was and where I wanted to go. This wasn't the relationship that was going to help me get to where I want to be.

Over the years, Daniel continued to provide financial support for his child and on occasions he would visit and she would come to see him, but they did not develop an especially close father/daughter relationship. Instead, Daniel continued to move on with his life. As one of "the few black students in the Institute of Technology," he got "straight A's" in his classes and graduated with a degree in engineering. But he was not necessarily interested in pursuing engineering as a profession. He got a job at a company in Michigan making thirty-thousand dollars a year: "it's all about consumer products and it's more interesting to me because it is less technology and more marketing and consumer driven." Even though he did not want to work purely as an engineer, Daniel was active in engineering professional circles which introduced him to a broad network of people from around the country, particularly other black engineers. During the 1980s, "life is great" for Daniel:

> I'm independent. I'm an adult now. I'm single with money, a car, really having a cool life with black folks, and becoming a part of middle-class blackdom. I'm living really high. I have a network of friends all over the country. I can go to New York, Miami, and have a place to stay and hang out. They are all engineers and everybody is doing great and they are accomplished. This is really a great and peaceful time for me.

Also during this period, Daniel had a series of "amazing" relationships with women, but "the relationships ultimately comes to a point where you are either going to get married or something else is going to happen." At that point, Daniel was not interested in marriage. Furthermore, although he had developed an interest in marketing and advertisement, he was no longer interested in working in consumer production, making and testing products. He decided to return to school and pursue a master degree in business administration, because "I like marketing stuff." While in college he got a job "managing and developing" health clubs for a major company. He made "like 100k,"and decided to quit college because "the fitness industry is booming." As a result, Daniel said: "I'm really loving life. In my universe I am the man, there's a lot going on and it's a great time. I feel good about life. I think I have a good life. I'm successful as I would define that, and successful as most people would define that in America. My family loves me and they are all doing well."

Yet Daniel was single and "all my friends were saying dude you're never getting married." Around that time, he "had a good friend from India," who tried to arrange a marriage for Daniel. "So I'm going through this whole process and it's pretty amazing. I would get a photo and we had a lot of debates about it." Having difficulties in selecting a bride, finally his friend told him, "Americans don't get it. Marriage is not an emotional act. Marriage is economic. You guys break up with people because you don't like the way a person eats. That's stupid; that's not what marriage is." Daniel told his mother that he was contemplating an arranged marriage and she laughed at him. But later, "I really found someone and really fell in love." Daniel's mother introduced him to Marlene. They dated for about two years and then "I asked her to marry me."

Marriage and subsequent fatherhood were major turning points in Daniel's life, for he believed they brought him fully into manhood. He was highly conscious of what was required of him in those new relationships; Daniel had to "connect emotionally" in ways that, heretofore, had been difficult for him. But he "looked forward to being connected" to his wife and later his son, and "committed himself to nurturing" both. In speaking of his marriage, Daniel said:

> I'm alright as a husband. I still retreat into myself and impose isolation sometime. But it is very comfortable for me. I'm a good husband in that we share every aspect of the house. I'm better at it than she is. I'm better at cooking, so I cook everyday, and do much of the domestic stuff. I'm committed to creating an environment that allows her to fulfill her aspirations. I don't want her to give up her dreams for me or our family. For a while, in the early stages in our marriage, there were elders that we would go to and talk with when there were tensions. We developed strategies to reduce our conflicts. I don't like fighting, let's do something different. We worked on specific strategies that we could agree on about how we were going to fight, how we were going to disagree. It's the creation of a new kind of relationship, one that is longstanding. We're a good team, and she's interesting and compelling. We agreed on how we see the world. It's not built around breadwinning, being in control of the family, and the center of the household. It's a partnership.

On fatherhood, Daniel said:

> I feel I am a really good father. My son coming into the world increased my capacity to be loving and nurturing. He clearly increased my absolute capacity to love and be expressive. I like being a parent. He is two and he is bright, excited, polite, and simply amazing. We come here ready to love and ready to receive love. When children are not that way, then you know something is wrong. I love my son and he has made me a better person.

Reflecting on his own life as a husband and father, Daniel believed that "a man does not become a man until he is at least forty years old." For him, it is at that point "when a man can say I really love you and mean it." With this perspective, Daniel said:

> I see manhood as the ability to create what is really inside your head about yourself. We are protectors, but not in the sense of keeping someone from

physical harm. What I realize now is that it is about providing the emotional foundation for others. If I protect my wife and child's emotional wellbeing and create a safe space emotionally for them to thrive, then they will be all right when they have to go out and fight their own fights.

Learning to Move On

As a young man, more than a scholar, Bobby saw himself as a pure athlete and his passion was football. Bobby's daily life had been consumed with anything and everything concerning football. The game provided him with a sense of absolute enjoyment. It also provided a sense of freedom that enabled him to express his manhood. But with a knee injury that sense of enjoyment and freedom abruptly ended. He graduated from high school and wanted to play college ball. His chances, however of doing so were quite limited, because his coach had "blackballed" him in the eyes of football recruiters. Yet determined to play again on his surgically repaired knee, Bobby was accepted at a major college in Pennsylvania, but as a student, and not as a scholarship player for the football team.

Upon entering college, Bobby found "this whole new world" to which he was unaccustomed and unfamiliar: "I had to register for classes. The line for registration was half a day long; I'm not exaggerating. By the time I got to the window there were only classes that nobody else wanted to take. Oh, it was horrible! After he arrived on campus, the doctor told Bobby that he had to wait a year before trying out for football because his knee was not completely healed. But he went to practice everyday and watched the other players. By watching them, he felt that he could compete with the other players, he said: "I was still absolutely confident that I could play. I knew I had what it took. I knew the positions. I had the skills. I waited and watched."

As he waited and watched, a friend on the team who was a starter told Bobby that if he was not one of "scholarship guys," he would probably not get a chance to play even if he was more talented; "the alumni are going to say we're paying for these guys to go to school and play ball." Given the situation, the most that Bobby could hope for or expect was to be a walk-on member of the practice team, but he would be at an increased risk of injury. Bobby realized that possibility and said, "that's the end of my football career:"

> I watched them and I assessed the fact that I could be hurt and it's not worth me taking the chance. I realized that football was no longer a part of my life. It took a while. For years I refused to watch football because I was so passionate about playing. But I still felt that I could play. I just didn't act on it because other things became more important.

Bobby was never going to play college football. But he wanted to "prove to everybody that I could be successful," so he turned his attention to his studies. Bobby wanted to be a doctor. In adjusting to college life as a student, he decided to join a fraternity, Phi Beta Sigma. At a fraternity party he met Susan, and "we became a couple." What attracted Bobby to Susan was his "need to be her protector." Early in their relationship, Susan told Bobby that "she had been really hurt, really badly the year before" they met. And this "bothered" Bobby: "It bothered me so much that we got even closer." She told Bobby "the story about how she was hurt." What happened, he said, "this group of guys hurt her. I don't like the word rape; I don't like the connotation. She was hurt pretty bad and they repeatedly hurt her. I got angry to the point where I wanted to kill somebody, in particular this group of guys. I felt like I was living through what she experienced, and now she's hurting, and I needed to take care of her. I knew that it was going to affect her entire life and our relationship too." But shortly after they met Susan became pregnant:

> Her family was in great emotional turmoil, especially her mom because that was her only child having a baby. Then my mother was hugely disappointed: "you got a girl pregnant. You're not going to bring her home and take care of her." My mother made it clear to me. But I brought her there anyway, and my mother said to me in front of everybody, "you're going to get out of this house by the time I come home from work. I don't care if you have to sleep in the car." And she meant that. My mother turned me out when I came home with Susan, who was pregnant. This was 1980, and I couldn't believe that she did that. We had to sleep in the car.

Bobby's mother meant what she said, and even though they "went upstairs and washed and changed" while his mother was at worked, for about a week they slept the car. He found an apartment and later a job at a truck stop, yet Bobby struggled to make ends meet. His relationship with Susan grew increasingly strained while she was pregnant because of what had happened to her and he thought that she needed professional help, but Bobby could not afford it. As he said:

> She's not really prepared emotionally to understand what she's even feeling. It was a constant battle even when I'm trying to be positive. I really can't understand what she's going through. She really can't understand what she's going through. She really needs some help. She's got this mother who knows about everything that happened, but acts like it never happened; and she treats her like it never happened. And when she's hard on her, she's making the situation even worse on her. Then when she gets pregnant she makes her feel like she's a bad woman for being pregnant. There were so many bad things connected to that experience.

Bobby considered marrying Susan. But he had serious reservations and resisted, because "she was always what most people would term as depressed; laying in dark rooms by herself, not really having any friends, and just kind of woe is me all the time." Kitt was born and shortly thereafter Susan became pregnant again, "but she had a miscarriage early in her pregnancy. As a result, Bobby said "she grew even more dark" in her personality, and the emotional and financial pressures of the relationship grew unbearable. Bobby wanted to get out of the relationship. He decided "to go back to school," and so he "left her there in North Carolina" to fend for herself and the baby. Bobby abandoned his family. He said: "this was my first experience with letting down people that are close to me because I can't keep up my end of the agreement."

When Bobby left North Carolina in 1982, his daughter Kitt was only two years old, and they "didn't really reunite again until she was seventeen." He returned to college, but "that didn't go well because I wasn't focused." He dropped out of school and got a job; while working he took computer classes, because he "wanted to find a career that I could take care of myself and potentially excel at it." Over the years, with some training he pursued a career in business working on computers. He also pursued a series of relationships with women. For him the more troubling aspect of Bobby's life has been his relationships with women. On reflection he said: "my relationships with women tended to stem from me wanting from them what I didn't get from my mother; and that was nurturing. He believed that the lack of nurturing has "led to a lack of trust," and his relationships have failed as a result.

From Bobby's perspective, the lack of trust was what destroyed his marriage. But he did not describe his marriage or relationship with his children. He only said: "I've been married now for over fifteen years, and we've been separated, and we have three children." But the precise nature of that distrust which led to his separation was unclear because Bobby had difficulty in articulating what happened, so the content was unrevealed. Vaguely, he only said:

> I got hurt. I got hurt emotionally by this woman I married to the point where I was devastated. I got put in jail by this woman making accusations about this man that she married and had three children with. The accusations were completely false. They were false to a point that it took nine months before she backed away from them. She refused to admit she was trying to hurt me because she thought I had hurt her. I lost 30 pounds over the nine months. I went through emotional duress that I didn't understand. I felt myself change physically, emotionally, and mentally. It was like I was at the top of a hill sliding and could not stop myself. I lost everything—took my children away, my house away, lost my car, lost my income, and lost my business. I was at the bottom.

Gradually, Bobby has tried to rebuild his life, "however, there still a lot of pain." The first pain, Bobby said, "is the separation from my wife and my children. Something I never wanted to happen again, since it happened with Susan and my daughter Kitt; the second pain was my mother, who had never really been sick, and then dying; and, the third pain was another woman, which I haven't talked about, which emotionally destroyed me because I allowed myself to fall in love and give a relationship that I wanted another chance, just to be really hurt again." In picking up the pieces of his life, with assistance from a professional counselor, gradually Bobby is learning how to go on with life.

LEARNING TO START OVER

Because of the bullying and violence Robert received at his public school in New York City, his mother decided to send him to a private more integrated Lutheran school, during junior high school. Later he attended a parochial high school of the same denomination. But when he entered that school it was predominately white, with only sixteen black students out of a student body of six-hundred, and a largely white faculty. Even though the school was desegregated, it was not in Robert's estimation truly integrated. He said: "it was like we were tolerated. There may have been pockets of acceptance or openness, but integration was not the intention." Of his high school experience, Robert said: "It was like looking through a window. You can see everything that is happening, but there's a barrier between you being inside and the reality that you're on the outside." And for the few black students attending, "we had to be exemplary, by proving that we weren't less than," he said.

In high school, Robert saw himself as a student/athlete and "played football and was exceptional in wrestling too." Based on his athletic ability, he hoped to get an athletic scholarship to Iowa, his dream college that had a nationally ranked wrestling program. But Robert "wasn't an exceptional student; I was an average student." And, upon graduation from high school, he did not receive the coveted athletic scholarship to Iowa. Although disappointed, his mother encouraged him to apply to a local college and he did. Accepted, Robert "was the first in my family to go to college," and his mother's dream had also come true. With a sense of appreciation, he said, "I felt I was doing something she really approved of, I felt validated by her, and I felt she was proud of me."

Robert readily took to the college environment: he liked the mentoring he received from black faculty, the classes, and the free tuition. But in many ways, he said the college "really felt like a sophisticated high school on some level because it was basically in a city school." At the time, however, it was what Robert needed. As he said, "I didn't know how to be a student and that's what I was trying to accomplish. I needed to improve more, to be responsive and attentive to my academic expectations." But Robert also felt a need to wrestle, because "wrestling was part of my identity and I didn't know how to let it go yet."

The school did not have a wrestling program, so in order to stay in shape, Robert went to a junior college to train because "my goal was to go to Iowa and get a letter. I was interested in pursing the dream of being a varsity wrestler at Iowa." In that pursuit he talked to the wrestling coach at Iowa. Given his success as a high school wrestler, the coach was also interested in him, and "made efforts to make sure I got in." He was accepted. With his earlier experience of attending mostly white schools, Bobby felt prepared for Iowa and "relished the idea of being a student there." But more than anything else, he "wanted to earn a letter for my jacket."

Robert thoroughly enjoyed his status on campus as a student/athlete. He said, "I'm having a blast in school generally speaking and I'm feeling comfortable." Not only did he earn a letter in wrestling, but good grades as well. As an athlete, he had always been particularly conscious about taking care of his body and staying in shape: "I took the idea of not abusing my body through drugs, alcohol and smoking very seriously, and I didn't do it." At Iowa Robert was especially pleased with how he looked, because women were taking note. When he entered Iowa, Robert quickly "made the transition from being a virgin to not being a virgin." He said:

> I started to experiment with sex. I started serial dating. I didn't know anything about sex. As a boy, I didn't know that my testicles were my testicles. I thought they were my kidneys, for a long time. Women knew I was an athlete and told me I had a nice body. Women would say things to me like they had a dream about me, or they were thinking about me when they were masturbating. One time I found a woman in my bed naked. I'm going for it. I wasn't a responsible person. A lot of times, in those days, I sort of expected women to take responsibility (for contraception). I thought everything was going to be okay. I kind of trusted them.

Robert dated black women, but had interracial relationships as well. Previously, he had dated a Chicana and a Panamanian, but he developed a serious relationship with Betty, who was white and on the gymnastic team: "she was beautiful, nice, and sweet," he said. However, several black women on campus took exception to that relationship, and told Robert so in no uncertain terms:

> They came to my dorm room, knocked on my door and asked me why I was dating this woman. I was kind of baffled. They may have been

interested, but they were not going to tell me what to do. I felt like they were intruding on my privacy. I think they felt like I gave up my ghetto pass because I was dating a white woman. I still went to black events. I tried to include her; she came into my world just as much as I went into her world.

Robert was in love with Betty and "introduced her to my family. She was a bit hesitant and I didn't understand that. I got really angry about that." In turn, Betty "introduced me to her brother and father and one of her sisters. But she didn't want to introduce me to her mother." She had good reasons for not doing so: "her mother didn't like black people." Nonetheless, Robert enjoyed Betty's company and "she tried to be a part of my world," and even though "I was kind of exposed to her world, I didn't have access to her world," he said. However, he had access to Betty and during their relationship she got pregnant. Although it would have been difficult to assume responsibility for a wife and child at that point in his life, Robert "loved her and wanted to marry her." But Betty:

> Decided to have an abortion and I wanted the child. I did not want her to have the abortion. Her feelings were she didn't want a life with limits. That was telling and it kind of hurt. I felt sad and on some level I felt relieved. I felt relieved of the responsibility. It would have been an embarrassment. I understand that having an abortion was her choice. But I could not articulate to her my emotions, my feelings. I couldn't tell her that I wanted the baby; a child I thought resulted from a loving relationship. At the very least it was a child that would have been loved. Maybe it would've experienced two different environments. But she was a good enough person that I don't think she would have gotten in the way of the child valuing being an African American, and a child that grew up in her environment too. If it had a meant I had to get out of school and get a job to try to support them I was willing to do it. I felt powerless in the situation. I felt like I wasn't a decision maker in this situation. It's the woman's body.

The abortion was a deeply emotional experience, for which Robert has rarely discussed: "I don't like to talk about it, because I have felt ashamed about it all of my life. I felt ashamed because I didn't have a roadmap to manhood; someone to talk to me about what it meant to be a man in a relationship," he said. Following the abortion, his relationship with Betty grew distant, until finally it ended. Robert said that he "was so emotionally vested in the relationship that when it ended, I was devastated. I didn't know what to do." He started "searching for affection, for some tenderness. I was pretty needy. And, I was kind of a slut honestly." After a series of brief and unsatisfying relationships with women, Robert imposed "a kind of moratorium on relationship for about six years, as I tried to figure out how to get my head straight about this."

Meanwhile, Robert was losing interest in wrestling; it was no longer a priority after his failed relationship with Betty and especially after he had achieved a letter, he said "I was really done and I started losing my desire to wrestle." So he began to focus on his studies, but he was not exactly sure what to major in, and graduation was approaching. The summer before his senior year, Robert remained in Iowa and was working in a men's clothing store when:

> An old black man came in and asked me what I was doing. I said I'm a student. He said "what's your major?" I said "I'm not sure; I've changed it several times." He said, "why?" I said "I was trying to figure out what I wanted to do. I'm unclear." He told me to write down what I wanted to do on a piece of paper and where I wanted to be in ten years. Then in two or three weeks take a look at what I wrote. He said, "identify the things you want to do that gives you pleasure, even if you didn't get paid for it." I did that and it made me reflect on the things that I was doing.

One of the things that gave Robert pleasure was volunteering with "disabled kids; kids that had physical retardations not mental retardations. I worked with them on kinesiology. That was most interesting to me." From that experience, Robert decided that what he really wanted to do with his life was to help people. "I felt like it was rewarding to me if I could reduce someone's suffering in some way," he said. He attributed the conversation "with this old black man" as defining and consequently, leading to his decision to major in social work. And, although he was one among a few black male students majoring in social work, "I felt like I had made the right decision for me."

He was an athlete majoring in a mostly female dominant academic discipline, but Robert had no problems adjusting to the environment and readily embraced the mentoring offered by women professors in the social work department. He graduated with a sense of accomplishment and it "helped to reduce my sense of feeling that I wasn't so smart when I was kid." As the first person in the family to graduate from college, his accomplishment was shared by his mother and his large family. The only regret that lingered was the fact that his father was not there to share in the experience as well. He died when Robert was fifteen years old.

Overall college was a positive experience, and Robert wanted to continue on with his education; he "wanted to go to graduate school," but did not have money to do so. So he worked a series of jobs, including one at the college where he worked in "maintenance cleaning the grounds. That was real humbling for me and not what I expected." But determined to go back to school, finally he did, in Oregon where again Robert pursued his interest in social work. The college "was kind of small compared to Iowa and it didn't have a lot of social life for me. I went for two years," graduated, and moved back to New York. Again, Robert wanted to continue on with his education. He pursued a Ph.D., but not in social work, this time in a maternal and child health program at Connecticut where he got a scholarship in 1984.

Working at a field placement as part of his graduate program, Robert encountered a situation that would have a lasting effect on him personally, and shape his academic and later his professional life. There was a man caring for an infant child and four other young children because the mother had simply disappeared. "There was no explanation for why this woman just up and left," and this bothered Robert deeply. He said: "when I investigated, I found out the reason why she left was basically to escape from him because he had been brutalizing her. She left the infant and the children in hopes that he wouldn't follow her." Prior to that incident, Robert said he believed that "women's behavior influenced men's behavior" toward them; that women somehow caused men to react in violent ways toward them; that belief, however, started to erode as he attempted "to make sense" of what had happened earlier to the missing woman. He started volunteering at a battered women's shelter, where he held group discussions with men abusing women: what crystallized for him was that "if they weren't physically abusive, clearly they were mentally abusive" as well to women. What he learned from that experience, Robert said was that:

> Men never have conversations about healthy relationship. But there is an assumption that men are supposed to be behaving in healthy ways; to know what's allowable and what's not allowable. I'm not saying that any woman is perfect. I'm not saying that women don't cause conflicts in relationships, I don't believe that, but I understand the privileges that men do have: I'm clear men have more and that women don't. I see it in the experiences that women have and I see men deny it. The shelter and the groups taught me a lot about domestic violence.

Robert took what he learned about men and violence in the field back to the classroom. He began to study the literature and developed strong disagreements based on his field experience. For example, he said, "the literature talked about men's violence in the family, as if that was the only place that they could learn how to be violent." In his assessment he said:

> I didn't believe that because I heard men talk about the fact that in their homes they didn't have an abusive father, but they managed to be violent anyway. They didn't learn it in the family environment. They learned it in a non-family environment. I started asking questions about that and found out that a lot of the men who were violent ended up learning

violence in other places; in schools, in peer relationships, and in neighborhoods. I think I was trying to find out a way to truncate that behavior. I think I was learning different ways to think about how men could undo what we have been so predisposed to do; to do violence.

In his search for answers to the problem of men and violence, Robert did research in the area that turned into his dissertation, and upon completion, he graduated having obtained his Ph.D. in 1985. Robert decided that he wanted to stay in academia, and got a job teaching at a small mid-western college, where he met his wife Adriana, who was a black Puerto Rican and a graduate student. Early in their relationship he realized that his work with violent men, had forced him to reflect on his own life, and particularly on what was essential for a healthy relationship with Adriana. For him, he believed that the key was simply respecting the value of her life, as he respected and valued his own. He said, for instance:

> Adriana was a virgin until we got married. I didn't want to push her to lose her virginity. For some reason if I wasn't the person, I could not give her virginity back to her if she wanted to give it to the person she married. I had to value that. We cuddled, kissed, petted, and all that stuff. We were together usually on the weekends, where I might crash over at her place or she crashed over at mine. Her mother was petty conservative and insistent, she was in Puerto Rico, and would call to check up on Adriana to see what was going on. I was respectful of that.

Robert dated Adriana for three years before they got married. After they were married, having children became important to their relationship. However, they had a difficult time conceiving: "we had, I think, seven or eight ectopic pregnancies, but we were committed and wanted to have children. It was hard to see her in the hospital bed and go through some of the things she went through with all the tubes and knowing that she had an ectopic pregnancy, and also knowing that it reduced the risk of being able to have children," he said. But finally they were able to have a successful pregnancy outcome, and Charlie was born. Robert described the birth of his only child as "the best thing that happened."

Robert has continued to embrace the importance of education, not only in his academic life as a scholar/activist in his on-going work to get black men to reflect on the damage that violence play in shaping their relationships with others; but also in his personal life as he try to "teach Charlie how to be a man, by defining manhood in the broadest of terms." In offering reflections as teacher, and the lessons he want to pass on to his son, Robert said:

> When I was in school, we had this saying, if you can't get along then get it on. It was a saying that encouraged you to fight. I'm trying to teach

Charlie how to negotiate those situations differently. Foolishness like
fighting doesn't get you anywhere. There are times when you do have to
stand up and be assertive; but you have to use different skills, and not
your fist. If someone attacks you physically you have to use your fist and
get them off of you. But Charlie has to figure out what stuff mean; that's
thinking it through; that's taking a different approach to situations. My
father was not a rough man. He was a very gentle man, but he was very
clear about letting his feeling be known. Charlie is not a hard person and
like my father I think he will have a broadening definition of what manhood means. As a father, I see myself as a guide for him along his path in
life; as a guide to understanding his own manhood. If you only see the
world in a certain way then you are predisposed to act in a certain ways,
and that's not good enough. It's important to think and undo the things
that we have come to believe are essential to who we are as men.

CONCLUSION

For each of the men, there were defining moments in their lives when
they were forced to reconsider their actions and decisions, because denial of
the critical lessons learned through experience would only inhibit rather than
strengthen their ability to grow beyond limitations. Through experience they
were forced to reflect upon what it means to be black-and-male in America,
and each came to different conclusions based upon the particular context of
their social and culture lives. They offered their own version of black manhood that was form both within and against dominant expectations, where
they adhered to and rejected an imposed masculine script, in attempts to realize their full humanity. Their experiences were in many ways most ordinary,
while at the same time they were not, and this in turn created tensions, dilemmas, and contradictions for how they saw themselves.

Thomas adopted a manhood stance that was informed by his political
world view. He devoted much of his life attempting with others to advance a
political agenda that embraced strategies of social and economic justice for
the black community. Integral to his activism were beliefs about black men's
responsibilities. As defined by him, those responsibilities—adherence to
honor, principles, and accomplishments—were not far removed from the
more established expectations for all men where, consequently, he embraced
a positivistic view that extolled the centrality of men in black life; even
though his experiences suggested that he strongly valued the importance of
black women in that life. Nonetheless, as he embraced a more established
view of masculinity, that view was rearticulated when it came to his personal
life. Thomas consciously decided to live outside of the boundaries of conventionality by rejecting established responsibilities for a wife and children.

John, however, readily embraced the essential core of that convention by marrying twice and having four children. The notion of family responsibility was a priority as he adhered to established expectations for what it means to be a man—central to that meaning was being a good provider for one's family. Consequently, the significance of work became a major component of John's identity as a man. But the failure of his marriages forced him, even as he continued to conform to convention, to rearticulate his sense of manhood: he insisted upon being the custodial parent by raising his four daughters as a single male. It was John's children who taught him how to truly love another human being. And that love opened up possibilities for forming new and meaningful relationships outside of his immediate family of daughters.

Daniel, unlike John had difficulty establishing emotional bonds and long-term relationships with others, who were outside of his immediate family. This even extended to his first born child. Having grown up in a conventional family environment and his father's destructive path in that environment, he eschewed conventionality, and it impacted his relationship with others, particularly women. Prior to marriage, Daniel had never lived with any women, except for his mother with whom he had an extremely close relation. Although she in her own way nurtured Daniel, nurturing was not something that was automatic for him; he had to learn its meaning, and it took time for him to do so. Daniel was in his forties when he got married, and even though he adopted a conventional family structure, he did not however adopt a more conventional approach to family life based on established male expectations and a gendered division of labor. Within established conventions, Daniel rearticulated the meaning of manhood: one that was not predicated on "breadwinning and control," but rather one that was committed to an emotional foundation, where nurturing lay at the heart of his ability to support and protect his family.

Bobby was committed to the rules of conventionality, especially when it came to his passion, football: a game that defined his needs, interests, and aspirations. Because his identity was so thoroughly linked to that of an athlete and playing by the rules of game, when he was forced to walk away it was difficult for him to adjust to life beyond that of football. What it meant to be supportive and protective of others in the context of conventionality changed, along with his notions of manhood. Within and against the conventions of family life, Bobby abandoned his girlfriend and infant child. And later in marriage, he walked away for reasons that were not entirely clear from his interpretation of what happened, but resulted in his abandoning the norms of conventional family life as well. Bobby continued his struggle to rearticulate the meaning of manhood, outside of the boundaries of football and in the absence of conventional family life.

Robert has sought to broaden the definition of manhood. Similar to Bobby, his identity was linked to athletic performance. Dissimilar, however his identity was also linked to that of being a serious student. By questioning the norms of conventionality and what it means to be a man within them, this opened up the potential for Robert to challenge his own sense of manhood. That questioning was seen in his work with men who are violent, but also in his work with women who are, more often than not, victims of that violence. Within conventional structures Robert has given himself permission to respect and value the needs, interests and aspirations of others, and with that understanding has attempted to rearticulate what it means to be a husband and father in his family life.

Conclusion

THE MEN WERE BORN during or in the immediate aftermath of World War II. In the postwar world that lay before them, they lived through enormous social and cultural transformations. Lingering on or just beneath the surface those changes announced the complex interplay of race and gender. In many notable historical moments men's decisions and actions offered competing visions of humanity: one advanced the hopes and dreams for peace, justice, and freedom around the world, and the other undermined and compromised the value of human life on a global scale. In the decisions and actions that shape the course of human events, violence was an important resource upon which men draw.

In and around historical events and the ensuing international changes, the men of this book proceeded to live their lives. At times they were drawn directly into larger historical moments of change and conflicts, despite their positioning at the margins or exclusions of those changes. More often than not, when momentous events swirled around them, they were seemingly oblivious to historical linkages that impacted their daily lives. Regardless, the men's lives were by no means detached from the larger historical debates and responses that shape human relations. History reflects the cumulative decisions and actions of all human beings. The men's smaller narratives in comparison were intricately linked to the larger historical accounting of what happened in human events. Fundamental to that accounting was the role that race, gender, and violence played in shaping the contours of human life, for which the men's lives offered no particular exception.

In the ever-unfolding process of becoming, each man traveled along his own arduous path, as his life was created and recreated by circumstance for which he had little control. Despite this, each actively participated in the making of his own personal histories. The men asserted agency, and their decisions and actions vividly revealed the tensions, dilemmas, and contradictions embedded in their experiences. In the complex coexistence between agency and structural arrangements, the decisions the men made and the actions taken occurred under conditions that shaped the choices, options, and opportunities available to them. Their experiences revealed what happened when decisions and actions were in conflict with the arrangements under which they lived their lives. Their experiences revealed some consequences that emerge from such conflict and the human costs often engendered as a result.

Those consequences told us why race, gender, and violence matter. They matter simply because they provide the very foundation of human relationships. Race, gender, and violence encode a set of social norms and cultural values that structure everyday lives in ways that simultaneously validate and diminish opportunities for human flourishing. Those influences of the human condition, as the men's interpretations and experiences suggested, were not absolute determinants of their life chances. Neither were the men simple victims of oppression, nor did they exercise complete control over their lives. Rather, I show how they could transform their lives even within and against rigid structures of inequality and injustice. Those transformations were notable to the shaping of their self-images, interactions with others, and what they came to value.

Even as their decisions and actions led to seemingly predictable outcomes, it was important that predictability did not strip away their sense of humanity, where they could easily have become a social category that rendered them just another black male type with a simplified reality. As the complexities of their lives revealed themselves through childhood experiences and later during adulthood, I have marveled at their strengths while regretting their fallibilities. Regardless of the emotions their experiences evoked, the full embodiment of the men's humanity was on display: the good, bad, and ugliness of who they presented as both individuals and as a group.

Events in their narratives may have challenged or threatened our ability to fully acknowledge the men's human worth. If so, we must ask ourselves, what about their lives led them to the thoughts and actions they took? In other words, why did they make certain decisions and act in certain ways in the context of the choices, options, and opportunities available or unavailable to them in given situations? Of course, reasons abound to justify their thoughts and actions. But ever present, whether on the surface or just beneath, a partial answer for understanding their decisions and actions rested on how each theorized the importance of race and gender in their lives. In turn, the racial and gendered experiences provided an important frame of reference for understanding how they saw themselves and how they engaged the world as a result.

The scope of their experiences, the enormous similarities, and the important differences that existed made it extremely difficult to package the men's lives into a tightly bound black male box and place a neat bow upon its wrapping. At times their experiences suggested that they performed from a script.

They became "interchangeable with the uncanny, deeply unsettling, projections" of stereotypic imagery demanded by social and cultural normative behavior: whether they adhered to behavioral norms and values that were either viewed as acceptable or deemed unacceptable in nature or both. Acknowledging this does not, however, negate the complex realities of their lives. Rather, it was simply impossible for the men to somehow step outside the social and cultural context of their lives.

Because of that impossibility, the men's experiences suggested that they rearticulate the cultural and social meaning given to their lives to maintain their own sense of self-worth in the process of living. As their multidimensional lives unfolded they negotiated the different social and cultural spaces available to them. As children they were sons, brothers, students, and athletes. As young men those identities were layered with those of fathers, husbands, students, soldiers, and employees. Overlaying those complex identities were ideas regarding race and gender that shaped how they interpreted and performed in those roles. The complexities of their lives suggested that, even as they performed socially and culturally acceptable roles, unacceptable roles also became defining features of their lived experiences. Furthermore, in situations where they either abided by the rules of the game or totally disregarded them, some form of violence often accompanied their experiences.

As the men attempted to interpret and make sense of the world, critical to their understanding of the black male self was the role of violence in shaping that meaning. Whether limited only to childhood or consistent throughout adulthood, physical, personal, and social violence—in one form or another—became powerful features of the men's understanding of self. Nothing innate made them more or less genetically predisposed as victims or victimizers; rather, violence and its meaning were learned. That process of learning provided an additional layer of understanding to what it meant to be black-and-male in the performance of manhood. Based on their experiences some learned to eschew violence, even though they could not fully escape it or avoid its impact on their lives. Others learned to embrace the value of violence as an important resource in their decisions and actions, before they eventually rejected its significance to defining who they were as men.

All of the men, in their own ways, learned the importance of violence and the meaning it held for their particular lives. None more so than those whose deeply disturbing decisions led them down a destructive path where their actions resulted in the taking of human life. Here, it is emphatically important to note that the working of race and gender relations accompanied by violence, no matter how oppressive, do not provide any adequate justification or rationale for all self-directed decisions and actions. This is especially true in the case of the men who killed. Clearly, they made abhorrent decisions; no excuses were acceptable for their actions, and none were given.

Yet it is important to understand why the men thought and acted in the ways they did. Race and gender relations deeply rooted in structural social and cultural arrangements of both marginalization and exclusion do shape life choices, options, and opportunities, or the lack thereof, and cannot be easily dismissed depending upon good or bad decisions and actions of individuals. To do so would grossly distort the realities of the men's lives by dismissing how they were positioned in the world and how as individuals they interpreted and responded to the ways their particular reality was constructed.

The men's reflective journey has now brought them to a place in their lives where they have accepted their past: they know that they cannot change the past, but they also know that they can draw upon the lessons of the past as important references for how to proceed into the future. They are comfortable with who they have become, especially in their identities as black men. Matt accepted this reality and its ramifications:

> I am a black man. This has less to do with manhood or masculinity, but more to do with my morals and principles. Being a black man for me means standing up for what's right no matter what. I don't see my manhood; I see my humanity. I don't have to do masculinity that allows my manhood to be more visible. I now have ways that allows me to say that to the world. It means being a good father. It means being a good husband. It means being a good friend. It means being good to me and not putting up with bullshit. But it doesn't mean being mean, or arrogant, or evil. I'm in that stage of life where I know what it means to be a victim. I know what it means to be put in a position where it feels like if you don't tow the line people will take your life away. I can never forget that I'm still a black male, an urban African American black male, and what it means. But I'm more than just that; being a human being is important.

In their acceptance of who they were and who they have become, the men have embraced their strengths as well as their weaknesses while confronting the on-going tensions, dilemmas, and contradictions that exist between the two. They have offered their narratives, but I presented their stories as neither entirely unique nor as emblematic of the experiences of all African American men. The men's personal stories varied in many significant ways, but they were nevertheless linked to one another by a broader social history where the critical threads of race and gender were often knotted together by the presence of physical, personal, or social violence.

Those threads and that knotting linked the men's understanding of who they were as individuals to who they were as black men. That identity, formed within and against the broader context of history, shaped how they saw and thought about themselves and significantly how they gazed upon, interpreted, and then acted in the world around them. The men's narratives drew us into the complexities and layers of their lives, and as readers we saw how they were made and remade. We watched as those transformations gradually unfolded, and the men told us why they felt, thought, and acted in the ways that they did. Through their decisions and actions they actively participated in constructing their own unique personal histories. They did not, however, make and remake the social and cultural conditions that gave rise to those histories.

The claim that race and gender relations play critical roles in shaping life chances—where choices, options, and opportunities are restricted—rests upon a contested terrain, particularly in the current political climate. Some may argue that the men's narratives are "old school" and outdated, for, after all, they are of the postwar and baby boomer generation. In asserting such a claim, they may point to the ever-menacing argument that continues to gain popular momentum. It posits that race and gender are no longer significant impediments or barriers that inhibit individual needs and aspirations. In other words, as a nation we have moved beyond the importance of race and gender in shaping life chances; we have moved to a more inclusive and equitable society. From this particular view of the world we now live in what many would consider to be a post-race and post-gender America, where past structural arrangements reinforced by the presence of hegemonic power, control, and dominance are no longer relevant considerations, especially for individual achievements.

Sometimes this argument is presented in the political guise of conservative thought that readily points a finger at personal inadequacies and the opposition it poses to mainstream norms and values. Sometimes this argument appears at the liberal end of the political spectrum in the academic wrapping of postmodernist thought, where racial and gender identities are deconstructed to the point that allows only the relevance of personal style. Lingering somewhere in the middle of this current debate, is the widely held view of the rugged individual and the "can-do" spirit that triumphs against all odds, that penetrates American popular culture. What, then, becomes important to the narrative, regardless of presentation or positioning, is the debate over agency. Individual thoughts and actions are placed on trial: critics posit the assertion that the good, bad, ugly, and even messy things that happen in peoples' lives are somehow owing to either the presence or absence of character, values, hard work, and self-determination; they discount entirely social and cultural conditions that constrain choices, options, and opportunities based on rigidly defined race and gender relations.

With that line of reasoning, some may want to argue that if restrictive race and gender relations still fuel the fires of inequality and injustice, then the United States would have never elected Barack Obama as president, the first African American man to hold what is arguably the most powerful executive position in the world. Presumably the choices, options, and opportunities available to President Obama are now seen as available to all. What then is essential for human achievement and flourishing in a post-race and post-gender view of society is the ability to earn one's way in life through merit. With all things equal, then talent, competence, and achievement should indeed be rewarded through merit. However, race and gender relations continue to create an uneven playing field that not only devalue abilities but also inhibit human flourishing generally, but especially for many African American males.

To fully embrace the post-race and post-gender narrative the vast majority of black men, particular young black men, would somehow have to suspend how they look upon and deny their reality in the world. Instead, they would necessarily engage a fictitious narrative: one that poses enormous challenges to their reality, especially in light of the increasingly high drop-out, unemployment, incarceration, and suicide rates. To embrace such a narrative would require many to actively participate in a work of pure fiction. In so doing, as Roxanna Harlow aptly notes, black men can watch President Obama with a sense of pride, but then many will also gaze upon "their poor, segregated schools and neighborhoods, and the lack of economic opportunity and resources, and the racial profiling, and the lead paint, and the community disorder, and wonder what they are doing wrong" (Harlow, 2008, p. 6). As in the past, we, like the men whose narratives form the basis of this book, are again experiencing a gradual shift in race and gender relations in America that will surely impact our lives. Only time, however, will reveal the full meaning of that change. We do not know the precise nature or the full extent of the transformation that is occurring: unknown are the depth of the tensions, dilemmas, and contradictions that lay before us, and the role that race and gender relations will play, especially when accompanied by violence.

But certainly what is known, based on our well-documented human history, is that if change occurs within the prevailing order of things then race, gender, and violence will continue to provide an effective lens through which to understand the tensions, dilemmas, and contradictions we face; history obligates us to challenge the efficacy of hegemonic power, control, and dominance. This is a huge individual and collective imperative if we, like the men of this book, are to see the "other" as ourselves. Only then, through our decisions and actions, can we reach a true state of human rights that respects the dignity and worth of all.

References

Abramsky, S. (2002). *Hard times blues: How politics built a prison nation*. New York: Dunne Books.

Adler, P., & Adler, P. (1993). Review of Power at play: Sports and the problem of masculinity. *Gender and Society*, 7(4), 625–626.

African American men: Moments in history from colonial times to present. Retrieved January 22, 2007, from http://www.washingtonpost.com/wp-rv/metro/interactives/blackmen.

Albert, M. Million man march. Retrieved July 2, 2007, from Zmagazine Web site: http://www.zmag/articles/dec95albert.htm.

Alexander, C. N., & Weil, H. G. (1969). Players, persons, and persons: Situational meaning and the prisoner's dilemma game. *American Sociological Association*, 32(2), 121–144.

Alkalimat, A., & Gills, D. (1989). *Harold Washington and the crisis of black power in Chicago*. Chicago: 21st Century Books.

American experience. Retrieved April 22, 2008, from http://www.pbs.org/wgbh/amex/presidents/34_eisenhower/tguide/eisenhower_timeline.html.

American experience: Eyes on the prize, Ronald Reagan. Retrieved October 25, 2008, from http://www.pbs.org/wgbh/amex/eyesontheprize/profiles/29_reagan.html.

American experience: Race for the super bomb: The Korean war. Retrieved April 22, 2008, http://www.pbs.org/wgbh/amex/bomb/peopleevents/pandeAMEX58.html.

American experience. Timeline: The murder of Emmett Till. Retrieved March 4, 2008, from http://www.pbs.org/wgbh/amex/till/timeline/index.html.

Anderson, C. (2003). *Eyes off the prize: The United Nations and the African American struggle for human rights, 1944–1955*. New York: Cambridge University Press.

Anderson, C. (2006). Transcripts of keynote address at the "Human Rights at Home" conference, convened by the Women's Foundation of California, San Francisco. Retrieved September 16, 2007, from http://www.jointaffinitygroups.org/downloads/CarolAnderson.

Anderson, E. (1976). *A place on the corner*. Chicago: University of Chicago Press.

Anderson, E. (1990). *Streetwise: Race, class, and change in an urban community*. Chicago: University of Chicago Press.

Anderson, E. (Ed.). (2008). *Against the wall: Poor, young, black, and male*. Philadelphia: University of Pennsylvania Press.

Arthur, J., & Shapiro, A. (Eds.). (1996). *Color, class, identity: The new politics of race*. Boulder, CO: Westview Press.

Asim, J. (Ed.). (2001). *Not guilty: Twelve black men speak out on law, justice, and life*. New York: Amistad.

Baldwin, C. (2008, January 27). Whatever happened to masculinity? Retrieved November 23, 2008, from http://www.renewamerica.us/columns/baldwin/060127.

Banks, S. L. (1982). Dr. Martin Luther King, Jr. remembered: The fractured dream. *The Journal of Negro History*, 67(3), 195–197. Retrieved October 11, 2008, from JSTOR database.

Bederman, G. (1995). *Manliness and civilization: A cultural history of gender and race in the United States, 1880–1917*. Chicago: University of Chicago Press.

Bell, C. C. (1987). Preventive strategies for dealing with violence among blacks. *Community Mental Health Journal*, 23, 217–228.

Belton, D. (Ed.). (1995). *Speak my name: Black men on masculinity and the American dream*. Boston: Beacon Press.

Berger, P., & Luckmann, T. (1966). *The social construction of reality: A treatise in the sociology of knowledge*. New York: Anchor Books.

Berry, M. F. (1994). *Black resistance, white law: A history of constitutional racism in America*. New York: Allen Lane Penguin Press.

Bird, S. R. (1996). Welcome to the men's club: Homosociality and the maintenance of hegemonic masculinity. *Gender and Society*, 10(2), 120–132.

Birmingham, D. (1998). *Kwame Nkrumah: Father of African nationalism*. Athens: Ohio University Press.

Blackmon, D. A. (2008). *Slavery by another name. The re-enslavement of black Americans from Civil War to World War II*. New York: Doubleday.

Black men's "stressful process": African American men quietly combat negative stereotypes about them. (2006, July 2). Retrieved January 21, 2007, from MSNBC website: http://www.msnbc.msn.com/id/13560066/page/3/.

Blumstein, A. (1982). On the racial disproportionality of United States' prison populations. *Journal of Criminal Law and Criminology*, 73, 1259–1281.

Blumstein, A. (1993). Racial disproportionality in the U.S. prison population revisited. *University of Colorado Law Review*, 64, 743–760.

Blyden, E. W. (1971). *Black spokesmen: Selected published writings of Edward Wilmont Blyden*. London: Cass.

Booker, C. B. (2000). *I will wear no chain!" A social history of African American males*. Westport, CT: Praeger.

Boskin, J. (1986). *Sambo: The rise and demise of an American jester*. New York: Oxford University Press.

Bourdieu, P. (2001). *Masculine domination*. Stanford, CA: Stanford University Press.

Bowker, L. (1998). *Masculinities and violence*. Thousand Oaks, CA: Sage Publication.

Boyd, H., & Allen, R. L. (1995). *Brotherman: The odyssey of black men in America*. New York: Ballantine Books.

Brandy, L. (2003). *From chivalry to terrorism: War and the changing nature of masculinity*. New York: Knopf.

Brown, M. K., Carnoy, M., Currie, E., Oppenheimer, D. B., Shultz, M. M., & Wellman, D. (2003). *Whitewashing race: The myth of a color blind society*. Berkeley: University of California Press.

Brown, S. (2003). *Fighting for us: Maulana Karenga, the US Organization, and black cultural nationalism*. New York: New York University Press.

Browne, J. Rooted in slavery: Prison labor exploitation. Retrieved August 21, 2008, from http://www.urbanhabitat.org/node/856.

Bryne, W. A. (1994). Slave crime in Savannah, Georgia. *Journal of Negro History*, 79(4), 33.

Burke, P. J., & Reitzes, D. C. (1981). The link between identity and role performance. *Social Psychology Quarterly*, 44, 83–92.

Canada, G. (1995). *Fist, stick, knife, gun: Personal history of violence in America*. Boston: Beacon Press.

Canada, G. (1998). *Reaching up for manhood: Transforming the lives of boys in America*. Boston: Beacon Press.

Carby, H. V. (1998). *Race men*. Cambridge, MA: Harvard University Press.

Carelton, D., & Stohl, M. (1985). The foreign policy of human rights: Rhetoric and reality from Jimmy Carter to Ronald Reagan. *Human Rights Quarterly*, 7(2), 205–229.

Carmichael, S., & Hamilton, C. V. (1967). *Black power: The politics of liberation in America*. New York: Vintage Books.

Carter, Jimmy. (1977). Human rights and foreign policy. Retrieved August 17, 2008, from http://usinfo.state.gov/infousa/government/overview/carter.html.

Cazenave, N. A. (1981). Black men in America: The quest for manhood. In T. P. McAdoo, (Ed.), *Black Families* (pp. 176–186). Beverly Hills, CA: Sage.

Centers for Disease Control. (1986). *Homicide surveillance: High-risk racial and ethnic groups—blacks and hispanics, 1970 to 1983*. Atlanta: Center for Disease Control.

Chiricos, T. G., & Delone, M. A. (1992). Labor surplus and punishment: A review and assessment of theory and evidence. *Social Problems*, 39, 421–446.

Christianson, S. (1981). Our black prisons. *Crime and delinquency*, 27, 364–375.

Clatterbaugh, K. (1990). *Contemporary perspectives on masculinity*. Boulder, CO: Westview Press.

Cleaver, E. (1968). *Soul on ice*. New York: McGraw-Hill.

Clegg, C. A. (1997). *An original man: The life and times of Elijah Muhammad*. New York: St. Martin's Press.

CNN, Minister Farrakhan challenges black men. Transcript from Minister Louis Farrakhan's remarks at the Million Man March (1995, October 17). Retrieved June 28, 2007, from http://www.cnn.com/US/9510/megamarch/10–16/transcript.

Cohen, R. (1982). Human rights diplomacy: The Carter administration and the southern cone. *Human Rights Quarterly*, 4(2), 212–242.

Collins, P. H. (2004). *Black sexual politics: African Americans, gender, and the new racism*. New York: Routledge.

Cole, D. (1999). *No Equal Justice: Race and class in the American criminal justice system*. New York: New Press.

Cole, D. (2004). The color of punishment. In C. A. Gallagher (Ed.), *Rethinking the color line: Readings in race and ethnicity* (pp. 234–243). Boston: McGraw Hill.

Comer, J. D. (1969). The dynamics of black and white violence." In H. Graham & T. Gurr (Eds.), *Violence in America: The complete official report of the national commission on causes and prevention of violence*. New York: Signet, 1969.

Connell, R. W. (2003). Masculinities, change and conflict in global society: Thinking about the future of men's studies. *Journal of Men's Studies*, 11(3), 249–266.

Connell, R. W., & Messerschmidt, J. W. (2005) Hegemonic masculinity: Rethinking the concept. *Gender & Society*, 19(6), 829–859.

Cook, B. W. (1999). *Eleanor Roosevelt: The defining years 1933–1938* (Vol. 2). New York: Penguin Books.

Crenshaw, K. (1994). Mapping the margins: Intersectionality, identity politics, and violence against women of color. In M. A. Fineman & R. Mykitiuk (Eds.), *The public nature of private violence: The discovery of domestic abuse* (pp. 93–118). New York: Routledge.

D'Angelo, R., & Douglas, H. (2008). *Taking sides: Clashing views in race and ethnicity* (6th ed.). Boston: McGraw Hill Publishers.

Dalton, H. L. (1999). Pull together as the community. In D. W. Carbado (Ed.), *Black men on race, gender, and sexuality*. New York: New York University Press.

Davis, A. (1971). *If they come in the morning: Voices of resistance*. New York: Third Press.

Davis, A. (1997). Race and criminalization: Black Americans and the punishment industry. Reprinted from the *House that race built: Original essays by Toni Morrison, Angela Y. Davis, Cornel West, and others on Black Americans and politics in American today. (Ed.) Wahneema Lubiano*. New York: Pantheon Books.

Davis, J. K. (1997). *Assault on the left: The FBI and the sixties antiwar movement*. Westport, CT: Praeger.

DeLauretis, R. 1984. *Alice doesn't*. Bloomington: Indiana University Press.

Dennis, R. E. (1980). *Social costs of black male homicide to families and communities*. In *Summary Proceedings of Symposium on Homicide among Black Males*. Washington, D.C.: U.S. Department of Health and Human Services Publication, no. HRS-D-MCX6I.

Demetriou, D. Z. (2001). Connell's concept of hegemonic masculinity: A critique. *Theory and Society*, 30(3), 337–361.

Derian, P. M. (1979). Human rights and American foreign policy. *Universal Human Rights*, 1(1), 3–9.

Dubbert, J. I. (1979). *A man's place: Masculinity in transition*. Englewood Cliffs, NJ: Prentice-Hall.

Du Bois, W.E.B. (1973). The education of black people: Ten critiques 1906–1960 (Herbert Apthoker, Ed.). New York: Monthly Review Press.

Du Bois, W.E.B. (1975). *Dusk of dawn*. Millwood, NY: Kraus-Thomason Organization Limited. (Original work published 1940).

Du Bois, W.E.B. (1976). *In battle for peace*. Millwood, NY: Kraus-Thomson Organization Limited.

Du Bois, W.E.B. (1989). *The souls of black folk*. New York: Bantam Company. (Original work published 1903).

Du Bois, W.E.B. (1992). *Black reconstruction in America: 1860–1880*. New York: Atheneum. (Original work published 1935).

Du Bois, W.E.B. (2005). The spawn of slavery: The convict-lease system in the South. In S. L. Gabbidon & H. T. Greene (Eds.), *Race, crime, and justice: A reader*. New York: Routledge.

Duneier, M. (1992). *Slim's table: Race, respectability, and masculinity*. Chicago: University of Chicago Press.

Cruse, H. (1967). *The crisis of the Negro intellectual: From its origins to the present*. New York: William Morrow & Company.

Eisen, G., & Wiggins, D. K. (1994). *Ethnicity and sport in North American history and culture*. Westport, CT: Greenwood.

Eisenstein, Z. R. (1984). The patriarchal relations of the Reagan State. *Journal of Women in Culture and Society*, 10 (2). Retrieved October 11, 2008, from JSTOR database.

Ek, A. A. (2002). *Criminal identities in the war on crime: Race and masculinity in contemporary American prison narratives* (Doctoral dissertation, University of California, Santa Barbara, 2002).

Elder, G. H. (1986). Military times and turning points in men's lives. *Developmental Psychology*, 22, 233–245.

Elder, G. H. (1987). War mobilization and the life course: A cohort of World War II veterans. *Sociological Forum*, 2, 449–472.

Elise, S. (2004). How whites play their race card: Drylongso stories reveal "The Game." *Sociological Perspectives*, 47(4), 409–438.

Elliot, J. M. (1993). The Willie Horton nobody knows. *The Nation (August)*.

Eitle, T. M. (2002). Special education or racial segregation: Understanding variation in the representation of black students in educable mentally handicapped programs. *The Sociological Quarterly*, 43(4), 573–605.

Entman, R. M., & Rojecki, A. (2000). *The black image in the white mind: media and race in America*. Chicago: University of Chicago Press.

Estes, S. (2005). *I am a man! Race, manhood, and the civil rights movement*. Chapel Hill: University of North Carolina Press.

Fanon, F. (1967). *Black skin, white masks*. New York: Grove Press.

Feagin. J. R. (2000). *Racist America*. New York: Routledge.

Ferrell, J., & Websdale, N. (1999). *Making trouble: Cultural constructions of crime, deviance and control*. New York: Aldine de Gruyter.

Filene, P. G. (1974). *Him/her/self: Sex roles in modern America*. Baltimore, MD: Johns Hopkins University Press.

Fleisher, M. S. (1998). *Dead end kids: Gang girls and the boys they know*. Madison: University of Wisconsin Press.

Foucault, M. (1977). *Discipline and punish: The birth of the prison*. New York: Random House.

Foucault, M. (1980). *Power/knowledge: Selected interviews and other writing, 1972–1977*. New York: Pantheon Books.

Franklin, B. The American prison in the culture wars. Retrieved on August 18, 2008, from http://andromeda.rutgers.edu/~hbf/priscult.html.

Franklin, H. B. (2000). From plantation to penitentiary to the prison-industrial complex: Literature of the American prison. Retrieved August 18, 2008, from http://www.andromeda.rutgers.edu/~hbf/MLABLACK.htm.

Franklin, R. M. (2007). *Crisis in the village: Restoring hope in African American communities*. Minneapolis, MN: Fortress Press.

Frazier, E. F. (1966). *The Negro Family in the United States*. Chicago: University of Chicago Press.

Frey, J. H., & Eitzen, D. S. (1991). Sport and society. *Annual Review of Sociology*, 17, 503–522.

Gabbidon, S. L., & Greene, T. L. (Eds.). (2005). *Race, crime, and justice: A reader*. New York: Routledge.

Gamson, W. A. (1961). A theory of coalition formation. *American Sociological Review*, 26(3), 373–382.

Garfield, G. (2005). *Knowing what we know: African American women's experiences of violence and violation*. New Brunswick, NJ: Rutgers University Press.

Garland, D. (2001). *Culture of control: Crime and social order in contemporary society*. Chicago: University of Chicago Press.

Garrod, A. (1999). *Souls looking back: Life stories of growing up black*. New York: Routledge.

Gary, L. E., Booker, Christopher B., & Fekade, A. (1993). *African American males: An analysis of contemporary values, attitudes and perceptions of manhood*. Washington, D.C.: Howard University School of Social Work.

Gates, H. L. (1997). *Thirteen ways of looking at a black man*. New York: Random House.

Geiger, J. (1999). Unmaking the male body: The politics of masculinity in the long dream. *African American Review*, 33(2), 197–207.

Gettleman, M. E. (Ed.). (1965). *Vietnam: History, documents, and opinions on a major world crisis*. Greenwich, CT: Fawcett Crest Publisher.

Gibbs, J. T. (1988). *Young, black, and male in America: An endangered species*. Dover, MA: Auburn House.

Gilmore, D. D. (1990). *Manhood in the making: Cultural concepts of masculinity*. New Haven, CT: Yale University Press.

Goff, S., & Sanders, R. (1982). *Brothers: Black soldiers in the Nam*. New York: Berkeley Books.

Goffman, E. (1959). *The presentation of self in everyday life*. Garden City, NJ: Doubleday Anchor.

Griffiths, I.L.L. (1984). *An atlas of African affairs*. London: Routledge.

Hare, B. R. (Ed.). (2002). *2001 race odyssey: African Americans and sociology*. New York: Syracuse University Press.

Harlow, R. (2008). Barack Obama and the (in)significance of his presidential campaign. *Journal of African American Studies*. Retrieved November 29, 2008, from JSTOR database.

Harris, L. C. (1999). My two mothers, America, and the million man march. In D. W. Carbado Ed.), *Black men on race, gender, and sexuality: A critical reader* (pp. 54–67). New York: New York University Press.

Hartsock, N. C. (1984). Masculinity, citizenship, and the making of war. *Political Science*, 17(2), 198–202. Retrieved March 12, 2008, from JSTOR database.

Harrell, W. J. (2004). The brothers' Vietnam war: Black power, manhood, and the military experience by Herman Graham, III. *African American Review*, 38(2), 345–348.

Harris, D. S., & Eitzen, D. S. (1978). The consequences of failure in sport. *Urban Life*, 7, 177–188.

Hayes, F. W. (1982). The political economy, Reaganomics and blacks. *Western Journal of Black Studies*, 6, 89–97.

Hayes, F. W. (1992). Governmental retreat and the politics of African American self-reliant development: Public discourse and social policy. *Journal of Black Studies*, 22(3), 331–348. Retrieved October 11, 2008, from JSTOR database.

Hayden, T. (2008). *Writings for a democratic society: The Tom Hayden reader*. San Francisco: City Lights Publishers.

Henry, M. (2004). He is a bad mother*$%@!#: Shaft and contemporary black masculinity. *African American Review*, 38(1), 119–126.

Higate, P. R. (2003). *Military masculinities: Identity and the state*. London: Praeger.

Hill, R. A. (1987). *Marcus Garvey and the Universal Negro Improvement Association Papers* (Vol. 1). Berkeley: University of California Press.

Hilliard, D. (1993). *The autobiography of David Hilliard and the story of the Black Panther Party*. Boston: Little Brown.

History: Million man march. An historical perspective. Retrieved June 28, 2007, from http://www.millionsmoremovement.com/history.htm.

Holli, M. F., & Green, P. M. (1984). *The making of the mayor, Chicago, 1983*. Grand Rapids, MI: Eerdman Publishing Co.

Holmes, S. A., & Morin, R. (2006). Poll reveals a contradictory portrait shaded with promise and doubt, June 4. Retrieved January 22, 2007, from Washington Post Web site: http://www.washingtonpost.com/wp-dyn/content/article/2006/06/03.

Honneth, A. (1995). *The fragmented world of the social: Essays in social and political philosophy*. New York: State University of New York Press.

hooks, b. (1985). *Killing rage: Ending racism*. New York: Holt.

hooks, b. (1992). *Black looks: Race and representation*. Boston: South End Press.

hooks, b. (2004a). *We real cool: Black men and masculinity*. New York: Routledge.

hooks, b. (2004b). *The will to change: Men, masculinity, and love*. New York: Atria Books.

Hopkinson, N., & Moore, N. (2006). *Deconstructing Tyrone: A new look at black masculinity in hip hop generation*. San Francisco: Cleis Press.

Human Rights Watch. United States—Punishment and prejudice: Racial disparities in the war on drugs. Retrieved June 19, 2007, from http://www.hrw.org/reports/2000/usa.

Hutchinson, D. L. (1999). "Claiming" and "speaking" who we are: Black gays and lesbians, racial politics, and the million man march. In D. W. Carbado (Ed.), *Black men on race, gender, and sexuality* (pp. 28–45). New York: New York University Press.

Hutchinson, E. O. (1990). *The mugging of Black America*. Chicago: African American Images.

I am a man. Retrieved May 12, 2007, from Wayne State University Web site: http://www.reuther.wayne.edu/man/4Macing.htm.

International covenant on civil and political rights. Retrieved August 15, 2008, from http://en.wikipedia.org/wiki/International_Covenant_on_Civil_and_Political_Rights.

Irons, P. (2002). *Jim Crow's children: The broken promises of the Brown decision*. New York: Viking.

Irwin, J. J., & Austin, J. (1997). *It's about time: America's imprisonment binge* (2nd ed). Belmont, CA: Wadsworth.

Jackson, J. S. (Ed). (1988). *The black American elderly: Research on physical and psychosocial health*. New York: Springer Publishing Company.

Jackson, J. S., Chatters, L. M., & Taylor, R. J. (Eds.). (1993). *Aging in black America*. Newbury Park, CA: Sage Publication

Jackson, K. L. (1997). Differences in the background and criminal justice characteristics of young black, white, and Hispanic male federal prison inmates. *Journal of Black Studies*, 27(4), 494–509.

Jacobs, D., & Helms, R. E. (1996). Toward a political model of incarceration: A time-series examination of multiple explanations for prison admission rates. *American Journal of Sociology*, 102, 323–357.

James, J. (1997). *Transcending the talented tenth: Black leaders and American intellectuals*. New York: Routledge.

Jansen, S. C., & Sabo, D. (1994). The sport-war metaphor: Hegemonic masculinity, the Persian-Gulf war, and the new world order. *Sociology of Sport Journal*, 11(1), 1–17.

Jefferson, T. (2002). Subordinating hegemonic masculinity. *Theoretical Criminology*, 6(1), 63–88.

Jeffords, S. (1989). *The remasculinization of America: Gender and the Vietnam war*. Bloomington: Indiana University Press.

Joe, S., & Kaplan, M. S. (2001). Suicide among African American men. *Suicide and Life-Threatening Behavior*, 31, 106–121.

Joe, S., & Kaplan, M. S. (2002). Firearm-related suicide among young African-American males. *Psychiatric Services*, 53, 332–334.

Joe, S., & Niedermeier, D. M. (2008). Social work research on African Americans and suicidal behavior: A systematic 25-year review. *Health and Social Work*, 33(11), 249–257.

Johnson, A. G. (2006). *Privilege, power, and difference*. Boston: McGraw Hill.

Johnson, C. (2004). *The sorrows of empire: Militarism, secrecy, and the end of the republic*. New York: Henry Holt.

Jones, D. J. (Ed.). (1994). *African American males: A critical link in the African American family*. New Brunswick, NJ: Transaction Publishers.

Kail, F. M. (1973). *What Washington said: Administrative rhetoric and the Vietnam war: 1949–1969*. New York: Harper and Row Publishers.

Kaiser Family Foundation, the Henry J. (2007). Race, ethnicity, & health care fact sheet. From Key facts: Race, ethnicity & medical care. Washington, D.C.: The Henry J. Kaiser Family Foundation.

Karp, D. (1974). Review of Black Players. *Contemporary Sociology*, 3(3), 266–268.

Kennedy, R. (1995). The justice system and black America: After the cheers. *The New Republic*, October 23.

Kennedy, R. (1997). *Race, crime, and the law*. New York: Pantheon Books.

Kimmel, M. (1996). *Manhood in America: A cultural history*. New York: Free Press.

Kimmel, M. S., Hearn, J., & Connell, R. W. (2005). *Handbook of studies on men & masculinities*. Thousand Oaks, CA: Sage.

Kimmel, P. R., & Havens, J. W. (1966). Game theory versus mutual identification: Two criteria for assessing marital relationships. *Journal of Marriage and the Family*, 28(4), 460–465.

King, M. L. (1967). *Where do we go from here: Chaos or community?* The Martin Luther King, Jr. Research and Education Institute at Stanford University. Retrieved March 18, 2007, from http://mlk-kpp01.stanford.edu/index.php/kingpapers/article/where _do_we_go_from_here_1.

Kleppner, P. (1985). *Chicago divided: The making of a black mayor*. DeKalb: Northern Illinois University Press.

Kunjufu, J. (2005). *Keeping black boys out of special education*. Chicago: African American Images.

Kwame Nkrumah's vision of Africa. (2000, September 14). Retrieved April 25, 2008, from http://www.bbc.co.uk/worldservice/people/highlights/00914_nkrumah.shtml.

Langan, P. (1985). Racism on trial: New evidence to explain the racial composition of prisons in the United States. *The Journal of Criminal Law and Criminology*, 76, 666–683.

Lanning, M. L. (1997). *The African-American soldier: From Crispus Attucks to Colin Powell*. Secaucus, NJ: Carol Publishing Group.

Lemelle, A. J. (1995). *Black male deviance*. Westport, CT: Praeger Publishers.

Levine, D. K. Economic and game theory. What is game theory? Retrieved July 4, 2008, from http://www.levine.sscnet.ucla.edu/general/whatis.htm.

Lochner, L., & Moretti, E. (2004). The effect of education on crime: Evidence from prison inmates, arrests, and self-reports. *American Economic Review*, 94, 155–189.

Lotke, E. (1998). Hobbling a generation: Young African American men in D.C.'s criminal justice system. *Crime & Delinquency*, 44(3), 353–367.

Lusane, C. (1991). *Pipe dream blues: Racism and the war on drugs*. Boston: South End Press.

Lipsitz, G. (2002). The possessive investment in whiteness. In P. S. Rothenberg (Ed.), *White privilege* (pp. 61–84). New York: Worth Publishers.

Madhubuti, H. R. (1990). *Black men obsolete, single, dangerous? African American families in transition : Essays in discovery, solution and hope*. Chicago: Third World Press.

Mahoney, M. R. (1994). Victimization or oppression? Women's lives, violence, and agency. In M. A. Fineman & R. Mykitiuk (Eds.), *The public nature of private violence: The discovery of domestic abuse* (pp. 59–92). New York: Routledge.

Majors, R., & Billson, J. M. (1992). *Cool pose: The dilemmas of black manhood in America*. New York: Lexington Books.

Majors, R. G., & Gordon, J. U. (Eds.). (1994). *The American black male: His present status and his future.* Chicago: Nelson-Hall.

Mangeu, X. (2008, June 16). Harold Washington: A mainstream radical against the machine. Retrieved November 10, 2008 from http://www.swans.com/library/art14/mangcu01.html.

Mangum, G. L., & Seninger, S. (1978). Coming of age in the ghetto: A dilemma of youth employment: A report to the Ford Foundation. Baltimore, MD: Johns Hopkins University Press.

Marable, M. (1985). *Black American politics.* London: Verso.

Marable, M. (1986). *W.E.B. Du Bois: Black radical democrat.* Boston: Twayne Publishers.

Marriott, D. (2000). *On black men.* New York: Columbia University Press.

Marshall, G. B. (2007). *Race, law, and American society: 1607 to present.* New York: Routledge.

Marxist history: USA: Black Panther Party: SNCC. The basis of black power. Retrieved May 12, 2007, from http://www.marxists.org/history/usa/workers/black-panthers.

Marxist history: USA: Black Panther Party: SNCC. The ten-point program. Retrieved May 12, 2008, from http://www.marxists.org/history/usa/workers/black-panthers.

Marxist history: USA: Black Panther Party: SNCC. Guerrilla War in the U.S.A Retrieved May 12, 2008, from http://www.marxists.org/history/usa/workers/black-panthers.

Massey, D. & Denton, N. (1993). American apartheid: Segregation and the making of the underclass. Cambridge, MA: Harvard University Press.

Mauer, M. (1999). *Race to incarcerate.* New York: New Press.

Mauer, M., & Chesney-Lind, M. (2002). *The collateral consequences of mass imprisonment.* New York: Free Press.

McElrath, J. African American protest at the 1968 Olympic games. Retrieved May 12, 2007, from http://afroamhistory.about.com/od/athletes/a/196801ympics.htm.

McIntyre, C.C.L. (1993). *Criminalizing a race: Free blacks during slavery.* New York: Kayode.

Mendieta, E. (2003). Identities: Postcolonial and global. In L. M. Alcoff & E. Mendieta (Eds.), *Identities: Race, class, gender, and nationality* (pp. 407–416). Oxford, England: Blackwell Publishing, 2003.

Messerschmidt, J. W. (2000). *Nine lives: Adolescent masculinities, the body, and violence.* Boulder, CO: Westview.

Messerschmidt, J. W. (1997). *Crime as structured action: Gender, race, class, and crime in the making.* Thousand Oaks, CA: Sage Publications.

Messner, M. A. (1989). Masculinities and athletic careers. *Gender and Society,* 3(1), 71–88.

Messner, M. A. (1990). "When bodies are weapons: Masculinity and violence in sport." *International Review of the Sociology of Sport,* 25, 203–217.

Messner, M. A. (1992). *Power at play: Sports and the problem of masculinity.* Boston: Beacon.

Miller, A. (1989). *Harold Washington: The mayor, the man.* Santa Monica, Calif.: Bonus Books.

Miller, J. (1996). *Search and destroy: African American males in the criminal justice system.* New York: Cambridge University Press.

Modern History Sourcebook: All-African People's Conference: Resolution and Imperialism and Colonialism, Accra, December 5–13, 1958. Retrieved April 22, 2008, from Fordham University Web site: http://www.fordham.edu/halsal/mod/1958-aapc-res1.html.

Modern history sourcebook: United Nations: Declaration on granting independence to colonial countries and peoples, 1960. Retrieved April 22, 2008, from Fordham University http://www.fordhman.edu/halsall/mod/1960-un-colonialism.html.

Morin, S. F., & Garfinkle, E. M. (1978). Male homophobia. *Journal of Social Issues*, 34(1), 29–47.

Morris, A. D. (1984). *The origins of the civil rights movement: Black communities organizing for change.* New York: Free Press.

Morrison, H. R., & Epps, B. D. (2002). Warehousing or rehabilitation? Public schooling in the juvenile justice system. *Journal of Negro Education*, 71(3), 218–232.

Morrison, T. (1992). *Playing in the dark: Whiteness and the literary imagination.* Cambridge, MA: Harvard University Press.

Murphy, F. The MMM pledge. Retrieved July 2, 2007, from http://www.afro.com/history/million/pledge.html.

Mutua, A. D. (Ed.). (2006). *Progressive black masculinities.* New York: Routledge.

Neal, M. A. (2005). *New black man: Rethinking black masculinity.* New York: Routledge.

Newburn, T., & Stanko, E. A. (Eds.). (1994). *Just boys doing business: Men, masculinities, and crime.* New York: Routledge.

Nkrumah, K. (1970). *Consciencism: Philosophy and the ideology for decolonization.* New York: Monthly Review Press.

Nkrumah, K. (2006). *Africa must unite.* London: Panaf Books.

Obama, B. (1995). *Dreams from my father: A story of race and inheritance.* New York: Three Rivers Press.

Office of the High Commissioner for Human Rights. International Covenant on Civil and Political Rights. Retrieved August 15, 2008, from http://www.unhchr.ch/html/menu3/b/a_ccpr.htm.

Oliver, M., & Shaprio, T. (1997). Black wealth/white wealth. New York: Routledge.

Oliver, P. E. (2001). Racial disparities in imprisonment: Some basic information. *Focus*, 21(3): 28–31.

Oliver, W. (1994). *The violent social world of black men.* San Francisco: Jossey-Bass Publishers.

O'Reilly, K. (1989). *Racial matters: The F.B.I.'s secret file on black America, 1960–1972.* New York: Free Press.

Orfield, G., Losen, D., Wald, J., & Swanson, C. (2004). *Losing our future: How minority youth are being left behind by the graduation rate crisis.* Cambridge, MA: The Civil Rights Project at Harvard University. Contributors: Advocates for Children of New York, The Civil Society Institute.

Pager, D. (2003). The mark of a criminal record. *American Journal of Sociology*, 108(5), 937–975.

Paul Laurence Dunbar website, the collection, selected poems by Paul Laurence Dunbar. In the morning. Retrieved September 23, 2007, from http://www.dunbarsite.org.

Payne, J. W. (2007, March 13). For black men, disparities mean shorter lives. Retrieved June 19, 2007, from Washington Post Web site: http://washingtonpost.com/wp-dyn/content/article/2007/03/09/AR2007030901949.

Pettit, B., & Western, B. (2004). Mass imprisonment and the life course: Race and class inequality in U.S. incarceration. *American Sociological Review*, 69(2), 151–169.

Pharr, R. R. (1996). It's raining men. *Transition Review*, 6(1), issue 69, 36–37.

Pieterse, J. N. (1992). *White on black: Images of Africa and blacks in western popular culture.* New Haven, CT: Yale University Press.

Pinar, W. (2001). *The gender of racial politics and violence in America: Lynching, prison rape, and the crisis of masculinity.* New York: P. Lang.

Pollack, W. (1998). Real boys: Rescuing our sons from the myths of boyhood. New York: Random House.

Powell, K. (2003). *Who's gonna take the weight?: Manhood, race, and power in America.* New York: Three Rivers Press.

Powell, K. (Ed.). (2008). *The Black male handbook: A blueprint for life.* New York: Atria Books.

Powers, T. (1973). *The war at home: Vietnam and the American people, 1964–1968.* New York: Grossman Publishers.

President Barack Obama's Inaugural Address. (2009, January 20). United States Capitol, Washington, D.C. Retrieved from The White House Web site: http://whitehouse .gob/blog/inaugural-address/.

President Bush's eulogy at funeral service for President Reagan. (2004, June 11). National Cathedral, Washington, D.C. Retrieved from The White House Web site: http://www.whitehouse.gob/nes/releases/2004/06/20040611–2.html.

Preston, M. B. (1993). The election of Harold Washington: Black voting patterns in the 1983 Chicago mayoral race. American Political Science Association, 16(3), 486–488. Retrieved October 11, 2008, from JSTOR database.

Quinney, R. (1980). *Class, state & crime* (2nd ed.). New York: Longman.

Race + Child Welfare Project, The. (2004). *Basic facts on disproportionate representation of African Americans in the foster care system.* Washington, D. C.: Center for the Study of Social Policy.

Randolph, A. P. (1941). "The Call to March." *The Black Worker.* Retrieved September 16, 2007, from http://www.bsos.umd.edu/aasp/chateauvert/mowm.htm.

Reiland, R. (2004, June 15). Reaganomics and the poor. Retrieved November 10, 2008, from http://archive.newsmax.com/archives/articles/2004/6/15/101327.shtml.

Remarkable 1968 Mexico City Olympic Games, The. Retrieved May 12, 2007, from http://umsis.miami.edu/~jgawron/olympics.html.

Richardson, J. B. (2003). Contextualizing juvenile re-entry for young African American males: From prison yard to schoolyard. *General Psychiatry, 59,* 1133–1143.

Rivlin, G. (1992). *Fire on the prairie: Chicago's Harold Washington and the politics of race.* New York: Henry Holt and Company.

Roberts, J. W. Work, education, and public safety: A brief history of federal prison industry. UNICOR Federal Prison Industries, Inc. Retrieved August 21, 2008, http://www.unicor.gov/about/organization/history/overview_of_fpi.cfm.

Roediger, D. R. (1991). *The wages of whiteness: Race and the making of the American working class.* London: Verso.

Rome, D. (2004). *Black demons: The media's depiction of the African American male criminal stereotype.* Westport, CT: Praeger.

Rosenbaum, D. E. (1981, June 2). Blacks would feel extra impact from cuts proposed by President. Retrieved November 27, 2008, from New York Times Web site: http://partners.nytimes.com/library/national/race/060281race-ra.html.

Ross, M. B. (2004). *Manning the race: Reforming black men in the Jim Crow era.* New York: New York University Press.

Rudman, W. J. (1986). The sport mystique in black culture. *Sociology of Sport Journal, 3,* 305–319.

Russell, K. K. (1998). *The color of crime: Racial hoaxes, white fear, black protectionism, police harassment, and other macroaggressions.* New York: New York University Press.

Rustin, B., & Houser, G. (1971). *Down the line: The collected writings of Bayard Rustin.* Chicago: Quadrangle Books.

Sabo, D. (1985). Sport, patriarchy, and male identity: New questions about men and sport. *Arena Review,* 9, 1–30.

Sampson, R. J., & J. H. Laub. (1993). Structural variations in juvenile court processing: Inequality, the underclass, and social control. *Law & Society Review,* 27(2), 285–311.

Scott, L. D., & Davis, L. E. (2006). Young, black, and male in foster care: Relationship of negative social contextual experiences to factors relevant to mental health service delivery. *Journal of Adolescence,* 29(5), 721–736.

Sampson, R. J., & Laub, J. H. (1993). *Crime in the making: Pathways and turning points through life.* Cambridge, MA: Harvard University Press.

Schneider, M. L. (1979) Human rights policy under the Carter administration. *Law and Contemporary Problems,* 43(2), 261–267.

Shame in our own house: How segregation and racism have fed U.S. resistance to international human-rights treaties. Retrieved on February 9, 2008, from http://goliath .ecnext.com/coms2/gi_0199–2329210/Shame-in-our-own-house.html.

Silver, B. B. (1978). Social structure and games: A cross-cultural analysis of the structural correlates of game complexity. *The Pacific Sociological Review,* 21(1), 85–102.

Spierenburg, P. (Ed.). (1998). *Men and violence: Gender, honor, and rituals in modern Europe and America.* Columbus: Ohio State University Press.

Staples, R. (1982). *Black masculinity: The black male's role in American society.* San Francisco: Black Scholar Press.

Stouffer. S. A., et al. (1949). *The American soldier: Adjustment during army life.* Princeton, NJ: Princeton University Press.

Stoyanov, S. S. (2005). Moralism as realism: Jimmy Carter's human rights. Midwest Political Science Association, Palmer House Hilton. Chicago, Illinois. Retrieved on August 15, 2008, from http://www.allacademic.com/meta/p85057_index.html.

St. Pierre, M. A. (1991). Reaganomics and its implications for African-American family life. *Journal of Black Studies,* 21(3), 325–340. Retrieved October 11, 2008, from JSTOR database.

Staples, R. (1982). *Black masculinity.* San Francisco: Black Scholar Press.

Strauss, A. L. (1987). *Qualitative analysis for social scientists.* Cambridge, England: Cambridge University Press.

Summer, M. A. (2004). *Manliness and its discontents: The black middle class and the transformation of masculinity, 1900–1930.* Chapel Hill: University of North Carolina Press.

Terry, W. (1984). *Bloods: An oral history of the Vietnam war by black veterans.* New York: Ballantine Books.

Towards a united Africa!! Retrieved on April 22, 2008, from http://www.uneca.org/ adfiii/riefforts/hist.htm.

Uggen, C. (2002). Growing older, having a job, and giving up crime. *American Sociological Review,* 65, 529–546.

Uggen, C., & Manza, J. (2002). Democratic contraction? Political consequences of felon disenfranchisement in the United States. *American Sociological Review,* 67, 777–803.

United States Senate: Joint Economic Committee. (2007). The crisis of black male joblessness: Economic fact sheet. Washington, D.C.: G-01 Dirksen Senate Office building Joint Economic Committee. See http://jec.senate.gov/archive/documents/ Reports/blackmalejoblessness.pdf

U.S: Prison numbers hit new high. Blacks hardest hit by incarceration policy. Retrieved August 13, 2008, http://hrw.org/english/docs/2008/06/06/usdom19035_txt.htm.

Wacquant, Loïc. (2000). The new "peculiar institution": On the prison as surrogate ghetto. *Theoretical Criminology*, 4, 377–389.

War, M. (1998). Life-course transitions and desistance from crime. *Criminology*, 36, 183–216.

Warner, D. F., & Hayward, M. D. (2006). Early-life origins of the race gap in men's mortality. *Journal of Health and Social Behavior*, 47(3), 209–226.

Wars for Vietnam: 1945 to 1953, the. Retrieved April 22, 2008, from http://vietnam .vassar.edu/overview.html.

Wendland, J. (2008, February 25). Harold Washington: The people's Mayor. Retrieved November 10, 2008, from http://www.politicalaffairs.net/article/articleview/6528.

Western, B. (2006). *Punishment and inequality in America*. New York: Russell Sage.

Whyte, A., & Baker, J. (2000). Prison labor on the rise in U.S. World Socialist Web site Retrieved August 21, 2008, from http://www.wsws.org/articles/2000/may2000/prism08_prn.shtml.

Williams, W. A., McCormick, T., Gardner, L., & LaFeber. W. (1975). *America in Vietnam: A documentary history*. New York: Anchor Books.

Wilson, W. J. (1987). *The truly disadvantaged: The inner city, the underclass, and public policy*. Chicago: University of Chicago Press.

Winter, C. What do prisoners make for Victoria's Secret? Retrieved August 21, 2008, from http://www.motherjoines.com/news/feature/2008/07/slammed-lingerie-and -bullwhip.html.

Wright, R. (1994). *Black boy*. New York: Harper.

Young, A. A. (2004). *The minds of marginalized black men*. Princeton, NJ: Princeton University Press.

Yoruba religion and myth. Retrieved July 28, 2008, from http://postcolonicalweb.org/nigeria/yorubarel.html.

Yoruba religion. The orisha of the crossroads. Retrieved July 28, 2008, from http://members.aol.com/ishorst/love/Yoruba.html.

Index

ABOUT THE AUTHOR

GAIL GARFIELD is the author of *Knowing What We Know: African American Women's Experiences of Violence and Violation*. For more than twenty years she has been an educator, researcher, and activist on issues of violence against women. She holds a Ph.D. in sociology and is an associate professor at John Jay College of Criminal Justice, City University of New York.

Breinigsville, PA USA
04 March 2010
233638BV00001B/2/P